Unfinished Business!

*The Ultimate Guide for 8(a) Contractors Working
with the Federal Government*

by

Glenn L. Chatman

DORRANCE
PUBLISHING CO
EST. 1920
PITTSBURGH, PENNSYLVANIA 15238

Dorrance Publishing Co
585 Alpha Drive
Suite 103
Pittsburgh, PA 15238
Visit our website at *www.dorrancebookstore.com*

ISBN: 978-1-6442-6161-3
eISBN: 978-1-6442-6253-5

Dedication

First and foremost, I want to take this opportunity to acknowledge a host of individuals responsible for giving me the desire and strength to write this book. I grew up in a very small town named Lovejoy (Brooklyn), Illinois (St. Louis Metropolitan Area/north of East St. Louis), during the fifties, sixties, and early seventies, which was a 100% African American community. During my early child and teenage years, I learned the true meaning of struggle, survival, and why the 'family' structure is the ultimate answer to most of the world's problems. This personal belief may be debatable, but I'm sure the foundation of the family entity shapes, molds, leads, and has guided all our greatest leaders throughout the history of mankind. In retrospect, the family structure shapes all mankind past, present and future generations.

Life has its twists and turns. Some of the experiences are good, as well as bad. It is the internal fortitude that determines the ultimate effect on one's ability to quit, give up, or keep up the fight until the job is complete! Throughout everyone's life, you will get knocked down, but the real question is whether you will get back up. At the end of the day, as the old spiritual states: "Job well done!"

Things changed from my early days in Lovejoy where there was discipline, order, and a sense of community togetherness. The norm today is of violence, destruction, and a total disregard for human existence. I believed that then, and even today, if we can work together as a unified group, then we all shall have a better life and enjoy the American dream.

To all the teachers, friends, and residents of Lovejoy, a heartfelt thank you for the support, leadership, and direction that was so important growing up in an area that truly knew the meaning of togetherness and unification. My foundation (life) was laid from living in this little community, which gave me courage and internal fortitude to push even harder toward my end goal. Helping others was part of my beliefs and was part of the humanitarian demeanor, which quickly shaped my burning desire to assist others.

Whether it meant shoveling coal for my Uncle Jesse or staying next door with my neighbor as a youngster (due to her fear of being alone) was the beginning process of knowing the value of assisting others.

From a professional basis, Mrs. Karen Fountain (co-worker) provided necessary directional support in reaching my goal of doing more for the small business community. It must be noted this individual could have retired several years ago (prior to my retirement) but chose to stay the course until I reached retirement age. This is a true testament of working together and defining the real meaning of how two individuals came together to obtain a common goal. Her dedication over the years displays why all successful people or organizations need a "Karen Fountain" on their team. Again, I personally want to thank you for all you have done for me over the years. Again, job well done!

From a personal standpoint, a special thanks to my mother and father who provided me with the unconditional love and direction every individual need going forward experiencing life's up and downs. Although I lost my father at an early age, I had my brother (Bubba), who provided me the love, protection and direction that was so needed growing up in an environment that had many dangers lurking around each corner within the community. To my wife and kids who gave me the love, support, and fortitude I needed to endure the perils of life's ups and downs. I wholeheartedly can say that behind every great man is a great woman, and I thank you (Pam) for always being there for me during my own personal trials and tribulations.

Table of Contents

Preface

This publication contains solely the assumptions, opinions, and viewpoint of the author. This document is intended to provide insight, guidance, direction and increase the awareness of socio-economic small business contractors who desire to work with the federal government. Those socio-economic small businesses hereinafter are referred to those small businesses who are certified by the Small Business Administration (SBA) to participate in the 8(a) Business Development Program.

All of the information, documents, graphs, and data, are developed and written by the author with no intent on providing any views other than that of the author.

The contents of this book are oriented for 8(a) firms who have a desire to work with the federal government. The information is geared for those firms who are in the construction arena; however, it can be beneficial to any business entity regardless of size standard and area of business concentration.

The reason for writing this book entitled Unfinished Business is to leave the small business community a lifelong guide exploring a few hidden facts of working within the framework of the federal government. As a former government employee, I had a vision and a goal of witnessing great achievements of those firms who were willing to work hard, and within the confines of the legal system designed for the small business community to become successful. Despite my efforts, I fell short of fully reaching my objective, which was disturbing and quite disappointing. Therefore, I can safely say any of us may fall short of reaching our goals whether it is a job, idea, or process. At the end of my career, I concluded further work needed to be done in some capacity; thereby, the birth of *Unfinished Business!* was created. There are many views from the federal government, contractors, and those of the author on the correct course of action to take pertaining to business.

There is much work required by the government and contractor to ensure equality and balance is achieved by those who award contracts and those who perform the functions identified within each contract. In a society who rewards those who commit fraud and deception, is there justice for those who are committed to challenging work? This question, if not addressed, will lead to a situation that in some cases I refer to as "Code Red." By definition, this phrase is used to indicate a difficult or dangerous situation that has deteriorated drastically as to constitute an emergency! In most cases, Code Red is related to those who are in the hospital or in a dangerous life or death crisis. This is certainly not the case, but the relationship (to me) between the government and most 8(a) contractors is alarming and appears to be strained.

Therefore, the facts of this issue will be presented to you (the reader) and thereby your determination of guilty or not guilty shall fall within your own conviction.

There are facts that are never discovered by small businesses until major errors are made in the business world. This book is designed and written to provide information and direction to small businesses and newly developed firms in the Federal Business Development (BD) Program with the objective of working with the federal government. Specially, I'm referring to those socioeconomic firms classified as 8(a) companies and certified by the SBA. Hereinafter, any reference made to small business is directed toward 8(a) contractors certified and/or potentially certified newly formed small businesses. However, this book is beneficial to any small business entity starting out in the business community who may not meet the qualifications to be an 8(a) contractor.

Most of the hidden facts that 8(a) firms overlook relative to understanding the problems and issues are contained within the contents of this book. Well, not exactly everything, but certainly a wealth of data and information that will point you in a positive direction. At the end of the day, if I can reach one individual (of those who read this book) and provide you with something, anything, that changes your business from a positive perspective, then my goal and objective would have been reached. So, I want you (the reader) to close your eyes; pretend you are in my office; and the discussion has begun between you and me.

The following is the test. The answers to the test. However, I cannot take the test for you.

This book was written to provide a better understanding of various methods and processes that most small businesses and firms who are in the beginning stages of the 8(a) Business Development Program overlook. Throughout many years of experience in the private and public sector, the basic underlining guiding principles necessary to provide 8(a) contractors an opportunity to increase their level of success is non-existent. Most small companies in business struggle due to the lack of information and guidance. What are the reasons why most newly formed businesses struggle to survive in the business world? Are there similarities in the type of mistakes that are made or is there a lack of available knowledge and information necessary to (at least) give these smaller firms a level playing field? I have discovered there are major patterns that are followed by most firms struggling to survive and ultimately end up going out of business.

For the remainder of this reading, we shall take a closer look at these issues and develop counter ways of providing direction, understanding and a method of disseminating information that has not been provided to small businesses. This will provide any business increased opportunities for becoming a successful business entity. The centerpiece of any successful person, business, and/or organization is the understanding and utilization of "information." One of my favorite statements I used in presentations and working with small businesses is a simple but highly powerful statement is: Information is knowledge…knowledge is power… power to make a better-informed decision. This is a true statement when you analyze the contributing factors of failure small businesses encounter. It's not that these small business owners and participating employees aren't smart, brilliant individuals, but they have failed to develop a path and strategic plan that leads to success. In many cases, time, our most valuable resource, is wasted by many businesses. What does this mean? To put in simplistic terms, use your time in a positive manner through strategic planning, increased internal communication within the organization, and most of all, being prepared in the critical phases of business acumen. Enough of this small talk; let's all get together and take a journey "beneath the surface and explore the hidden facts of small business contracting" oriented toward certified 8(a) firms who desire to work with the federal government.

Everything that we do is centered around information and the manner that we process this data. Time, our most valuable asset, is wasted due to the misutilization of information!

As a final disclaimer, the information, data, and facts included within this book were based on my personal beliefs (as the author). Many of the underlying problems, issues and concerns discussed were based on contractors needs and desires of working with the federal government. The excerpts of contracting rules and regulations at the time of the compilation of this text may have changed, and thus may not be applicable to the governing bodies in the government sector. No reference is made, or is any attempt made to slander, or suggest that anything derogatory is oriented toward any person or organization. Any reference made to "federal government" is done based on the author's experience working in various offices, agencies and organizations within the federal government and not representative of views of the entire federal governmental system.

Introduction

In an environment where business is ever changing and challenges to survive in the marketplace are increasingly demanding, there has never been a need for a haven or a refuge for the small businessman. That was the mindset during the "early industrial revolution days." The pressures of economic strife have put enormous pressure on the small businessman just to survive in the business world. As a prior government employee with over forty years of experience in contracting/business arena, I have seen many contractors desperately trying to make it as a potential supplier to the federal government. I predetermined they didn't have the necessary tools to make the journey in the business world a successful venture. After many years of watching, evaluating, and most importantly listening to contractors (of all sizes), the various struggles of getting an opportunity to contribute to the business community has diminished to alarming proportions.

Don't get me wrong, there have been many successful small business entities in the past and will continue to be those companies in the future who really succeed. The real problem is related to those new small businesses that go through growing pains in the early days of being in business. I felt compelled to make a difference in some form or fashion. The question of how to assist those businesses was complex, undefined, and a mystery to me?

There are many resources available to assist small businesses in many ways, but it is obvious that something else had to be done. There are many books on how to be successful in the marketplace written by great writers and composers covering everything from "a" to "z," but why are firms not flourishing in greater numbers? It's a known fact (stated by past and current economic experts) small business is the economic backbone to a successful and strong economy. That was true in the early industrial revolutionary days and is still the underlying premise of today's business society. Nevertheless, my internal belief is, "Something greater must be provided to assist the everyday businessman/businesswoman in making those hard-core business decisions."

Those socio-economic contractors who have been certified by SBA to participate in the 8(a) Business Development Program for a period of nine years are in a highly favorable position. The 8(a) Business Development

Glenn L. Chatman

Program is designed to develop businesses owned and operated by socially and economically disadvantaged people, with the goal of being able to compete fairly in the American marketplace.

"To be eligible for the 8(a) Business Development Program, follow this eligibility checklist:

- be at least 51% owned and controlled by U.S. citizens who are economically and socially disadvantaged
- be owned by someone whose personal net worth is $250,000 or less
- be owned by someone whose average adjusted gross income for three years is $250,000 or less
- be owned by someone with $4 million or less in assets
- have all its principals demonstrate good character
- show potential for success, and be able to perform successfully on contracts
- be a small business
  - not already have participated in the 8(a) Business Development Program
  - have the owner manage day-to-day operations and also make long-term decisions"[1]

In addition, contents of this book can be beneficial to any person going into business (whether large or small) who does not understand the small hidden factors working with the federal government. For the final period of sixteen years of my career, the accumulation of information, tools, and guidance mechanisms stated within this book resulted in remarkable success for those individuals who chose to follow the concepts and methods indicated in the following four business modules...Business Theory, Business Presentation, Business Preparation and Business Functionality. Millions of dollars were awarded to numerous 8(a) firms who were justly deserving through their arduous work and determination to succeed.

Kudos to those firms.

Four Pillars of any Business Organization

Business Theory:
"Understanding the theoretical aspects
of working with the federal government"

Business Presentation:
"How to sway your target audience
with the right business presentation"

Business Preparation:
"How to negotiate the right way through preparation"

Business Functionality:
"Working in the field…how to get that outstanding rating"

In the Beginning

In everyone's life there is a beginning or the start of something that really changes your life forever. Whether it is your first car, going to college, marriage, or the birth of your children; the impact of that moment is or can be life changing. In some cases, it can be negative or positive, but one thing is for certain you will never be the same individual.

In 2008, something happened in my life that changed me forever. I was mobilized as a member of the United States Navy and assigned to serve one year in support of Iraqi Enduring Freedom. In my civilian job, I was the Director of the Small Business Program responsible for working with the small business community and major advisor to our District Commander on all small business matters. In that capacity, one of my main job functions was to develop a contractor base of socioeconomically disadvantage contractors to perform various job functions for the agency. This was a very rewarding job since I played a strong role in giving 8(a) contractors opportunities in support of project requirements. As I have stated many times over, this was the best job that I ever had because of the ultimate feeling of locating, developing, and nurturing those small firms through the entire governmental process. The end goal was to ensure their success through being a viable contractor to the federal government.

Over the years, I was a Contract Specialist, Supervisory Contract Specialist, Procurement Analyst, Contract Negotiator, and so forth. Basically, I've held every position within the contracting arena, but my position (before retiring) as the Small Business Program Manager (SBPM) was the ultimate job! I was in my element…teaching contracting/business protocol and telling the story of my job to the public.

Nevertheless, I wasn't satisfied with the way I was performing my day to day job functions. I had a passion and a need to do more!

The question that had to be answered was how do I develop a process that is beneficial to both the government and to contractors? Is there a price to pay for those involved regardless of the work that is required? There must be a way to create a win/win situation for all…not for a select few. There are many factors that affect a contractor's ability to be successful. Some contractor's follow the rules while others have their own personal viewpoint of winning in the business environment. Is it okay to bend the rules but at what price are firms willing to pay? Keep this thought in mind, I'll address this statement in detail in another section of this reading. In order to resolve a problem, it sometimes requires thinking outside of the box. Could this be the solution to my own dilemma? To all small business owners remember this statement: If you always do what you always done…you always get what you always got. Following my own advice, I knew change had to occur and it started with me.

"Winning isn't everything, it's the only thing…
Only if it is played fairly and squarely and by the rules of the game!"
This was the backside of the original quotation regarding being a winner.

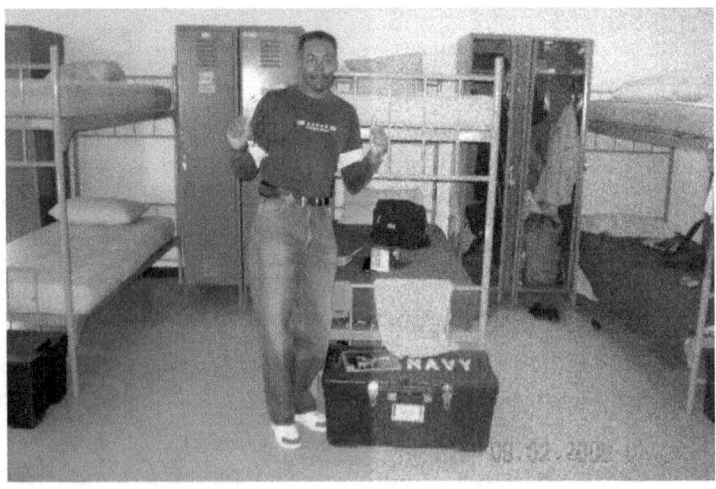

We had to be ready and prepared.

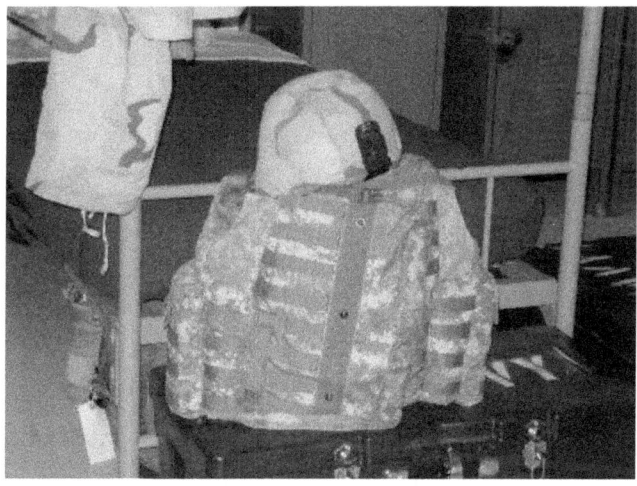

Equipment that was worn by soldiers in Iraq.
Full gear weighed approximately 90 lbs.

This was home during basic training.

Let's get back to memory lane and discuss why I felt something had to be done!

Regardless of the process, it had to be a plan that would make a difference to the small business community in determining whether they would be successful or end up in failure. I gave this thought a lot of attention back during 2008. It was now March of that same year and I was sitting on top of a sand dune. I wasn't concerned about my own fate at that time, all I knew being in the United States military I had been called to duty to defend my country. My thoughts and prayers were for my family and friends back home even though I was in harm's way. Sometimes when you are in a situation that is not favorable, you must stay focused and find something positive even during a situation such as going to war.

When talking to various contractors and participating in presentations, I often use the analogy of a glass half full of water. If an individual asked me for a glass of water and I only filled the container midpoint what would you say or think? Is the glass half full or half empty? I was alarmed, many individuals would state, "Why would you give me a glass half full of water?" However, the glass is half full rather than being half empty. This remark was and should be of concern. The glass is ALWAYS half full! Even in the mist of danger such as war, I had to remain positive and self-assuring that everything would be okay. As a small business owner, when things aren't going the way you feel it should, you must find something that is positive to get you through the rough times.

Believe it or not while in Iraq, I began that night to think about my job as Small Business Program Manager and felt that I wasn't making a difference to any contractor's success, but I contributed mightily to their failures. How could I feel I was a contributing factor to any contractor's failure in the business community? That's when I really felt within my heart, I would change my way of interacting with small businesses when I returned to my civilian job.

In many situations, how one views uncertainty dictates the degree of difficulty of being successful or being on the losing end. All anyone wants in business is an opportunity to participate as a viable contractor. This was my dilemma and problem that must be resolved. I was determined to make a difference. I was determined to show small businesses that someone really cared for them and about them. I was determined to provide some sort of guidance, direction, leadership, and be a major factor in the way the federal government viewed 8(a) contractors. Therefore, I wanted to develop a solid plan that could be used long after I had retired from the federal sector. As I constantly reiterate to firms, always have a Plan of Action (POA) and thus I decided to practice what I preached, which was to develop a winning plan for success for the small business owner. I now knew which direction I wanted to go in, and I could see clearly the pot of gold at the end of the rainbow for any small business owner who wanted to work hard and achieve success. This is something I was taught as a youngster: "Anything worth having is worth working hard to achieve your goal."

My newly developed plan was still disjointed and needed direction. There were several guiding principles I would use upon my return to my civilian job:

Personal Guiding Principles

1. Allow as much time needed for the contractor when a meeting was conducted/scheduled. My job is to ensure every question, concern, and issue they have is addressed to their satisfaction. If they took the time to meet with me, then I should have the courtesy to allow as much time as needed. Even if the meeting took all day allow the contractor to come back to the office any time. (By the way, one contractor held the record of meeting for four and a half hours in my office… a record which still stands.)

2. Always tell the contractor the truth about what is needed to be a successful contractor to the federal government. (As a disclaimer indicate to them…Do not take anything I say, personally nor negatively). Be honest and inform them of your true feeling of what is needed and required of them to be successful.

3. Develop a winning plan of action for them to follow to increase their level of opportunity to work for the federal government. This was the beginning of my desire to teach the contractor the methodology of working with the federal government from the art of how and why acquisition strategy was developed through the subliminal facts of negotiations and performance in the field. To me, this was the best way to develop and teach any contractor. Provide them the tools to be successful, even if it took several meetings.

February 9, 2008: This is the Barracks which was home during temporary training. There were over 300 military personnel stationed for a two-week period for training.

My job wasn't hard because I've spent many years listening to horror stories relative to failures of small businesses. The die was casted, and I was ready to lead the way.

The Plan

Now that I had so diabolically figured out the answers to my own concerns with helping 8(a) firms, what road blocks are still in my way of accomplishing my goal? One common link of being successful is based on those around you and whether they share and believe in the same vision and goal as you. This can be a hard obstacle to overcome regardless if you are in the private or public sector. Working together and sharing beliefs, experiences, and ultimately fighting for the same outcome is a major difference maker.

Within the federal government, the Chief of Contracting determines acquisition strategy (approves) and the Contracting Officers (KO) have varying degrees of Delegation of Authority/Power in obligating, awarding, and entering into a binding contract on behalf of the United States Government. These are the key players and the individuals whose final acquisition determination, and approval in the solicitation and award of government contracts, is inexplicable viable to the survival of 8(a) firms doing business with the federal government. Without the support of these individuals, the amount of business opportunities for any small business or 8(a) firms are limited.

Understanding and knowing the importance of developing a strong interrelationship within this small circle of individuals must be high on your priority list. In every federal agency, there are other key personnel who assist in the decision and determination of acquisition strategy for project requirements.

There is the SBPM whose major job function is participating in strategy sessions and working with other Project/Product Delivery Team (PDT) members in determining acquisition strategy (in-depth analysis of acquisition strategy determination discussed later). The role of the SBPM within the federal government is similar in many ways, but at the same time, can be succinctly different. It's highly important to understand the importance in developing a relationship that is built on trust, understanding, commitment, and most importantly honesty. You must remember the SBPM is there to assist and guide you through this maze of functions that is required and needed by you as a potential contractor. Throughout the federal government, these are the individuals whose level of involvement within each organization varies depending on the mentality of the SBPM relative to ensuring their job functions are done properly. Let me put it this way, in all organizations the SBPM is a strong staunch supporter of the small business program. However, their level of input in making critical small business decisions in support of meeting, or exceeding their organizational small business goals, varies. There are those SBPM who are less forceful in performing their job functions. This doesn't mean they care any less in the success of the small business community but have a different approach.

With these emotional thoughts from within, I could start the wheels in motion and develop a smooth course of action that current and future 8(a) firms could refer to within a drop of a pin. The relationship you (internally and externally) develop strengthens the level of understanding, beliefs, and consummates efforts toward reaching a common goal and objective. My end goal was clear: provide greater opportunities for 8(a) firms and eliminate the negativity that haunted these small business entities.

Image is everything relative to what people see, think, and believe about one's abilities, or lack thereof. In essence, every contractor needs the support of the SBPM who has the internal knowledge of the functionality of the federal government. Remember, you are only as good (at doing anything) as the perception of the people or individuals who you wish to develop a business relationship. You are only as good as others perceive you to be! Therefore, the image you portray is the image others see and remember.

How important do you think it is to win the support of the SBPM as well as the Chief of Contracting? Remember these two individuals are your key contacts in the federal governmental system. Over the years, my counterparts (referring to SBPM) may appear to perform and have the same functions, which is true. But there is an internal strength that some of these individuals have that some others may not. Most of the SBPM follow standard protocol when performing their job duties while others go the extra nine yards in developing a high-level relationship with you – the contractor.

Let's have our first test question of the day…What do you think this book is all about? The answer is quite simple…TEACHING! I know you have heard this phrase before: I can give you a fish and feed you for a day or I can teach you how to fish and you can feed yourself for a lifetime. I will continue to believe and preach knowledge is something that anyone or any organization can't take from you, therefore value this treasure forever. I'm not going to assume whether my counterparts (at that time) are providing the needed teaching of the principles of government contracting and processes or whether they are providing you with information that is readily available through your own reading habits. Don't underestimate the power of teaching the right information. I hear contractors as well as other government organizations/representatives talk about the need to understand functional aspects of the government process. These are examples of what I'm referring to as "functional aspects of the government process" (not in any order):

(a) Are you familiar with and understand how government projects are listed in the Federal Business Opportunities (FedBizOpps) system?
(b) Have you met or set up an appointment with SBA, Association of Procurement Technical Assistance Center (APTAC) or any of the other federal assisting organizations?
(c) Do you have an annual forecast that is available?
(d) Are you attending the annual small business conference?
(e) Are you attending this workshop or that workshop?
(f) May I come into your office and provide you with an overview of my organization?

The above information clearly provides you with varying degree of functions you have encountered in developing your relationship within the government sector. These are clear examples of functional processes that one can either touch, feel, see, and/or specifically follow. This is not the scientific approach relative to teaching and mental development of understanding various processes needed going forward in establishing your relationship with the federal government. I'm indicating that mental preparation of what, when, why, and how you are approaching government organizations is much more important than working with government organizations. You cannot go from point a to z in business without understanding and developing a strong strategic POA prior to the start of this long and arduous journey. Your mental thought processes of understanding a business is critically as important as starting a business based on functional demands and requirements. This may appear to be confusing to you, but the best way to do anything is based on mental preparation and understanding. Let's share some of the functional processes the SBPM are required to do on an internal basis (exhibit #1).

Small Business Program Manager Job Functions (abstract)
MISSION
1. The SBPM (referred to as Small Business Specialist) reports directly to the District Engineering (DE) Commander or the deputy (second in command), to promote maximum support in maintaining an efficient and effective Small Business Program.
2. The Small Business Specialist is instrumental in drafting, coordinating, and maintaining a small business strategy that supports all projects related to the organizational goals and mission relative to opportunities in support of large and small business organizations. Develop an ensure an acquisition strategy forecast is maintained on a current and on-going basis.
3. The Small Business Specialist advise and assist contracting, program managers, and all internal personnel on all matters relative to small business opportunities.
4. Conduct training to contracting, program managers, and internal offices as needed and on a continuous basis. Trainings includes internal organizational personnel and to other government personnel as needed. This training may be formal or informal to other requiring activities and program offices.
5. Provide maximum opportunities to small businesses, ensuring that mandated program goals are obtained utilizing various strategic processes developed that are efficient and effective.
6. The Small Business Specialist recommend to appointing authority the organizational small and disadvantaged business program goals including to monitorization of activities performance against assigned goals and recommended corrective action.
7. Reviews all contract actions exceeding Simplified Acquisition Threshold by assigning Control Number(s) on Small Business Coordination Record (DD Form 2579) ensuring accountability and providing historical reference correlating to current and future contract documents.
8. Review contract modifications that increase the scope of the contract that has a significant impact on small business subcontracting plans.
9. Ensure all copies of Small Business Coordination Records (DD Form 2579) are coordinated with SBA and Procurement Center Representative (PCR) in a timely and efficient manner. (PCR reviews and concur or non-concur with proposed acquisition strategy)

10. The Small Business Specialist must conduct annual reviews with appropriate internal and external personnel to ensure compliance with all applicable regulatory guidance.

OUTREACH

1. The Small Business Specialist must maintain an outreach program including participation in Government-industry conferences. This includes participation in local, regional and state conferences, workshops and other small business-related programs. These functions are to ensure that a qualified group of small businesses (SB), socio-economical businesses including historically underutilized business zone (HUBZone) small businesses, woman-owned small businesses (WOSB), small disadvantaged small businesses (SDB), and service-disabled veteran-owned small businesses (SDVOSB) are available in support of agency's requirements.

2. Ensure that contractors (large/small) are aware of the role and functions of SBA and other organizations who perform support in terms of training, guidance, and opportunities available for small business entities.

3. Perform internal small business outreach seminars and workshops on an annual basis to ensure that agency opportunities are known to interested and available small business contractors in support of organizations contract opportunities.

TRAINING

1. The Small Business Specialist must develop and implement training/education programs for internal and external personnel whose duties and functions affect the activity/office of Small Business Programs.

2. Ensure that annual training is completed on a continuous basis in courses in support of continuing education to maintain certification as a Small Business Specialist in the federal government. Training includes various small business courses to maintain a high level of expertise required to perform day to day duties.

OTHER DUTIES AS ASSIGNED

(The above is a _small_ abstract of the many duties and functions required of the small business specialist)

Glenn L. Chatman

Exhibit #1

"OFFICE OF SMALL BUSINESS PROGRAMS (OSBP) TOOLKIT

1.0 MISSION

1.1 Has the Associate Director developed command policy, signed by each newly assigned

HCA/commander or the deputy (second in command), to encourage maximum support of the Small

Business Programs?

1.2 Does the small business specialist assist in drafting the small business strategy in support of

each acquisition strategy; assist in the requirements process to maximize small business

opportunities; identify potential products or services suitable for award to small or small

disadvantaged businesses; and conduct informal training for contracting officers, specialists, requiring activities, and

program offices?

1.3 Do small business specialist advise and assist contracting, program managers, and

requirements personnel on all matters that affect small businesses and labor surplus area small

business concerns?

1.4 Do small business specialists ensure that financial assistance, available under existing

regulations, is offered and assist small businesses in obtaining payments under their contracts,

late payments, interest penalties, or information on contract payment provisions?

1.5 Do small business specialists recommend to the appointing authority the activity's small and

disadvantaged business program goals, including goal assignments to subordinate contracting

offices; monitor the activity's performance against these goals; and recommend action to correct

reporting errors/deficiencies?

1.6 To ensure maximum participation by Small Businesses, does the Associate Director advise and

 assist program managers and other related officials early in the acquisition planning, and throughout

the follow-on process, in the development of strategies and market research?

1.7 "Continued"

14

OFFICE OF SMALL BUSINESS PROGRAMS (OSBP) TOOLKIT

2.4 Is the Director, Small Business Programs pre-briefed on all service acquisitions exceeding $250

million?

2.5 Does the small business specialist serving the contracting office number the Control Number on

the DD Form 2579 (Small Business Coordination Record) consecutively starting with fiscal year?

2.6 Does the small business specialist review and sign the DD Form 2579?

2.7 Are copies of DD Form 2579s distributed outside the Army, including SBA PCR coordination,

marked "For Official Use Only?"

2.8 Are alternate small business specialist in the 1102 job classification series and do not have other

duties that cause a conflict of interest?

2.9 Does the small business specialist review modifications that increase the scope of the contract,

or the order under a Federal Supply Schedule contract, at a minimum, does the small business

specialist check to see if these actions impact the small business subcontracting plan.

2.10 Does the small business specialist report directly and are responsible only to their appointing

authority?

2.11 Does the Associate Director/Assistant Director/Small Business Specialist conduct annual

reviews to ensure compliance with Federal Acquisition Regulation (FAR) 19, Defense FAR

Supplement (DFARS) 219 and Army Far Supplement (AFARS) 5119?

2.12 Does the Associate Director prepare, review, and/or coordinate the HCA/command position

Section 8(a), Small Business Set-Aside, and Certificate of Competency secretarial appeals before

33

forwarding to the Director OSBP, in addition to requirements to be reviewed by the Army System

Acquisition Review Council and Army Service Strategy Panel?

OFFICE OF SMALL BUSINESS PROGRAMES (OSBP) TOOLKIT

3.0 OUTREACH

3.1 Does the small business specialist maintain an outreach program (including participation in Government-industry conferences and regional interagency small business councils) designed to locate and develop information on the technical competence of small businesses, Veteran/service-disabled veteran-owned small businesses, HUB Zone small business, small disadvantaged businesses, and women-owned small businesses?

3.2 Does the Associate Direct/Assistant Director/Small Business Specialist conduct and/or represent the HCA/command at procurement and outreach conferences in accordance with Procedures, Guidance, and Information and Army Directive (Department of the Army Conferences) (including participation in Government-industry conferences and regional interagency small business councils) designed to locate and develop information on the technical competence of small businesses or to improve the efficiency or effectiveness of the Small Business Programs?

3.3 Are contractors made aware by the Small Business Specialist of their right to pursue relief through the SBA under the Small Business Regulatory Enforcement Fairness Act of 1996 on matters such as excessive regulatory compliance, improper procurement procedures resulting from and other impediments to small business?

4.0 TRAINING

4.1 Has the Associate Director/Assistant Director/Small Business Specialist developed and implemented educations and training programs for personnel whose duties and functions affect the activity/office Small Business Programs?

4.2 Have small business specialist competed Defense Acquisition University courses SBP 101 and SBP 102 within four months of appointment?"   34

Given the internal duties and functions of the SBPM, all contractors should be mindful of the available time this individual has, given all the duties they perform. Every second or every hour of every day is critical. If you recall, the first guiding principle of my new way of working with contractors was to… allow as much time as possible until you (the contractors) are totally satisfied with the discussions that took place. This is my own internal way of working with contractors and not necessarily the way of my counterparts. As you can see, the SBPM is a busy individual, but the true determining factor centers around whether enough time is spent teaching and mentoring small business contractors. Somewhere during my career, there was mentioning of something I call the 85/15 Principle. Reference was specifically made to the amount of time the SBPM spent with contractors relative to time spent performing functions identified above. I was probably in less than 0.05 percentile who hold heartily felt that 85% of my time must be spent with the contractor(s). I'm referring to the time spent teaching the underlying principles and sharpening the mental aspect of the ordinary contractor. This is not to demean anybody or anyone, but most contractors act before they think when it comes to working with the federal government. Most people within society follow this same way of thinking or shall I say the lack of thinking in exercising good judgement.

This is where critical mistakes are made and, in most cases, marks the beginning of the end for most small businesses. Thus, be respectful and mindful of the available time of the SBPM; however, I feel that the SBPM should spend more time with contractors in the way of teaching and training.

I personally believe the initial level of expectations of the capabilities of the 8(a) companies are blown out of proportion. Let's take a closer look of what I mean by the level of expectations as it relates to everyday life. Think back in time when you had your first child (for those who are fathers and mothers). As an infant, your expectations of that child were limited and quite guarded. You had to watch over that child from birth and well into some of your children's adult hood. The infant couldn't crawl, walk, nor run. The child was basically helpless (I'm not inferring that any contractor is helpless). As responsible adults, we continued to nurture that child until one day the little boy or girl began to crawl, talk, and basically started to develop their own individual personality.

However, you could not let go, there were still things that had to be taught by you and learned by that child. As time passed, you spent more and more time with that child and continued to teach the correct way of being a responsible individual. Then one day, the child was no longer a child but a young adult. Still you couldn't walk away because your job as a parent was not over. You continued to guide, direct and mentor as a parent.

Before you knew it, graduation day from high school, on to college, marriage, children of their own, and you look back in time and you began to smile. No one knew why you were smiling, but internally, you knew because it was all the challenging work you put into the development and success of that child.

The same correlation can be made with the time (quality) spent with the 8(a) contractors, and believe me, it's more than 15% of your work day. This is the missing element in the lives of 8(a) contractors. All that is wanted by them is an opportunity, but much more, they are reaching out to the SBPM, SBA, and to anyone who's willing to provide them with an understanding and framework of working with the federal government. I have seen the look in their eyes. I've heard it in the way they speak. I've seen it in the way they do presentations and repeatedly the same mistakes are constantly made. I had a responsibility to do more and you as a SBPM have a responsibility to do more. If you intersect the parallel of raising a child and take a similar approach in assisting contractors, the results of your efforts are incomprehensible. Do not misinterpret that raising a child is a far greater challenge than teaching a contractor, but the concept of time spent is strikingly similar. At the end of the day, you have provided and contributed immensely toward the overall success of that company. Without a doubt, it took a lot of arduous work on both sides, but as a result, you have contributed to the success of that company and provided the federal government another contractor who is responsible, dedicated, and has the knowhow of being a successful contractor. The role of the SBPM is the heartbeat and lifeline of the 8(a) contractors and make no mistake about it.

Keys to 8(a) Contractors working with the Federal Government

There are many ideals, methodologies and best practices working with the federal government. Some of the concepts are proven guides to be used, but for the most part, there are no clear methods that can be consistently utilized, or at least that was the perception. I agree there are no straight path answers to many of the questions of being a successful government contractor, but there are sure ways of developing basic principles that increase opportunities for success.

In all the dialogue, discussions, meetings, telephone conversations, and other ways of two-way communication exchange, I concluded there are four basic building blocks that are key essential ingredients to successful government contracting and working with the federal government. Those four areas are (1) Business Theory, (2) Business Presentation, (3) Business Preparation, and Business Functionality (exhibit #2). In retrospect, when I first had the burning notion of reaching out to help the 8(a) community, I needed to develop a strategy that would cover the basic areas of concern starting from the very first time a contractor would call for an appointment and until the last "punch list" item was completed. So, if there was a definitive process that would redirect any contractor's effort in a positive manner thereby redirecting energy, time, and money...how would that process be developed?

Over the years, I noticed contractors were too busy with the urgency of need to obtain that first contract or expose the fact they are an 8(a) contractor and is now ready to go to work for the federal government. It doesn't work that way!

**BUILDING BLOCKS – KEYS TO GOVERNMENT CONTRACTING
(EXHIBIT 2)**

4 Building Blocks of Business Processes

Business Theory

Business Preparation

Business Functionality

Business Presentation

Well, not so fast! There are several misconceptions most 8(a) firms have once their certification has been received. Here are examples of the most overused misconceptions:

- (1) I'm 8(a) certified…Where's my government contract?
- (2) I'm 8(a)…I don't have to market my skills and capabilities because of my new certification – or I can now market my skills because I'm 8(a) certified.
- (3) I'm 8(a)…I'm now eligible, qualified, and capable of performing work for the federal government.

There are many more, but the above are the most widely internally expressed views of young developing firms. Therefore, how can the four building blocks that was developed increase and reduce some of the unknowns to the 8(a) firms? Let's take a closer look at these processes. [For a matter of reference, these principles/concepts are not found in any other guide, book, or pamphlets. These are views of the author relative to unfolding and discovering the 'hidden facts of small businesses working with the federal government']

Before we engage in full discussion of these concepts, there is a need to provide an overview of each process and its relevancy of being a successful 8(a) contractor:

A NOTE ABOUT THE FOUR MODULES

Every contractor must know and have a theological perspective of business. In simple terms this means, how do you know (as a business owner) where you are going if you do not understand where you came from and do not have a clear picture of where you want to go in the future? The Business Theory Module is designed to help the 8(a) firm develop a strategic plan and basis for building a solid firm from an internal perspective prior to making or coordinating that very first meeting with the federal government. This area is similar to developing or writing a term paper in college. There is a basic formula of gathering ideas, prioritization of those ideas and providing a clear strategy of executing those ideas.

Although the Business Presentation Module may not appear to be as important in the overall scheme of things, it is highly important to the 8(a) contractors as any of the other three modules. As stated throughout my involvement with minority and/or disadvantaged firms: Your first impression is your best impression is your last impression. This is a powerful statement in determining the degree of success at any business level whether your target market is the private or public sector. This statement holds truth and merit in everyday life. In many cases, you never know who is watching you regardless of the reason or situation. For the most part, you don't get a second chance to change that first image. It must not be forgotten or overlooked, there is a small margin for error and most mistakes are made during the first meeting between the 8(a) firm and the federal government, which negates all opportunities toward becoming a long-term contractor to that select market. [All four business process modules are interrelated and interdependent upon one another. Therefore, understanding each area separately and subsequently merging each process together provides a better understanding of creating a more effective and efficient business].

The Business Preparation Module is a tool developed to provide guidance, direction, knowledge and explore hidden aspects of government solicitations, proposal preparation and negotiation practices used throughout the federal sector. These are areas many 8(a) firms clearly overlook due to a lack of understanding or knowledge relative to the importance of working with the federal government. This area provides in-depth insight of what the 8(a) firm needs to know during the acquisition phase in-route to contract award. Before you obtain a government contract (either through direct award or competitive basis), there is a stigma that 8(a) firm prices are too high, don't self-perform and doesn't have the necessary skills/tools to be successful. This is not an internal belief of mine but a statement of fact relative to 8(a) contractors. This reverberates back to the negative image regarding first impressions toward 8(a) contractors.

The Business Functionality Module is the easiest area to understand but perhaps the most difficult and critical of all the modules regarding implementation of those practices. This section is oriented toward understanding and using various tools necessary toward performance and meeting the terms and conditions of the contract. This area is simply designated toward "working/performance in the field." This area covers administration of paperwork and performance by the prime contractor, working with their subcontractors and ultimately working with field government personnel. There are various functions and processes that will be covered in several modules due to the overlapping affect that each has on the entire business process effort. As an example, bonds will be covered in the Business Presentation Module but also in the Business Functionality Module.

The format for understanding the functions and processes of the underlying factors of government contracting will follow in the below manner (exhibit #3):

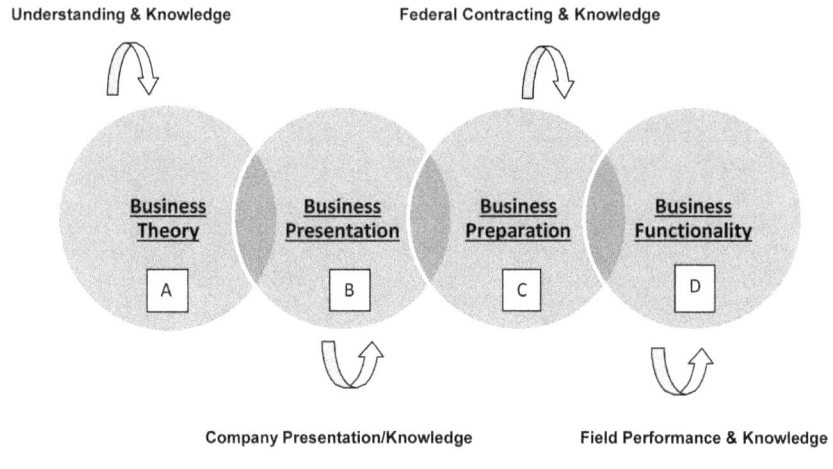

Exhibit #3

IT'S TIME

There has been a lot of information exchanged thus far; however, it is time to look beneath the surface and get into the intrepid waters of the unknown. The scenario is based on your first meeting with the government and you as an 8(a) firm is eager to start that relationship with the federal government. So, close your eyes, and concentrate deeply and experience the smooth transition of learning the facts of working with the federal government and gaining that knowledge, insight, and power of information not found anywhere before now! Always remember that "information is knowledge; knowledge is power; power to make a better-informed decision!" However, there is an underlying consequence: "For with much wisdom comes much sorrow; the more knowledge, the more grief" [2] (I will continue to interject this fact throughout this book.) The more information (fact/fiction) obtained relative to any situation, can never be taken away, however distorted or misrepresented. That's why you must always say what you mean and mean what you say when it comes to your capability, which invariably affects your reputation. Again, and I want to reiterate, you do not get a second chance to make a first impression!

CHAPTER 1
BUSINESS THEORY (Module #1)

The ideology behind Business Theory is to develop a group of functions that would strengthen your firm prior to contacting anyone in the business environment. As stated earlier, many business owners are too busy trying to figure out ways to obtain contracts and business opportunities rather than developing a course of action and a strategic plan to reduce the many road blocks that are in front of them. One of the keys is to develop a vision and a process to integrate this mind-set throughout your business organization. I'm not referring to the normal vision statement most organizations have implemented. Most business owners have developed a mission statement, goals/objectives, vision statements, etc. after the fact. These are great tools to use, but are these really words without meaning? No, they are very instrumental and help to shape and mold that organization. I'm referring to the development of a vision within your mindset from the beginning prior to starting your business. Look at the major difference between the above statements. In one sense, the development of these tools was reactive (after the fact) in comparison to the second statement, which was proactive (prior to). This is a wonderful place to interject an internal theoretical assumption regarding information and knowledge. In order to develop a course of action one must think outside of the box prior to finalizing any path forward. This relates to having a keen sense of imagination which invariably leads to processing information thus making a sound decision (hopefully). So, is it safe to say that imagination is the forefront of knowledge or is more important than knowledge? Remember the importance of information is the basis for developing knowledge resulting in the power toward making any decision whether a good or unwise decision. Therefore, is this a correct assumption that imagination is superior to knowledge? This is quite perplexing but a highly interesting viewpoint. In my analysis of this statement, the word knowledge can be looked upon as an "absolute" or based on prior experience that can be factual or fictional depending on the contents of the knowledge obtained. In comparison, the word imagination correlates to "creativity" that leads someone or an individual who has a thought, dream, or even a vision, on how something can be changed, shaped, and developed. Imagination can have a huge impact on the future success of any business. This leads me to believe that imagination is first in the thought process prior to developing any form of knowledge or determination of reality or fiction. Therefore, your level of imagination and degree of creativity prior to the development of any company is paramount in the infinite stages of the startup of any business. I have asked the question why would you start this type of business or better yet why would you go into business? Most of the responses I received were astonishing because many of the owners did not have a real concrete answer that made any sense. The top three responses were:

(1) I don't really know.
(2) I thought that I could make a go of it.
(3) I needed a change because what I was doing wasn't working.

The point of this matter is where was the mindset and thought processes of that individual prior to deciding to attempt to go into business? This concept is similar to writing a term paper in college. Develop an outline, prioritize the information, and complete the paper utilizing the format that was developed.

Let's further expound on this process called Business Theory prior to analyzing the actual contents of this theoretical approach. As an 8(a) contractor, you are required to be in business two years (along with other factors) prior to applying to SBA for approval to become a certified contractor in the 8(a) Business Development Program.[3] The two-year waiting period can be waived by SBA if you can show or prove you have related experience in the business environment. In some cases, I have known SBA to grant a waiver because of prior experiences and other related requirements. If you feel you are in this situation, it doesn't hurt to request a waiver based on prior experience. It doesn't cost anything to pursue this avenue. But stop and wait a minute! Are you ready to travel this path? This is where increasing your knowledge base on the various areas of understanding the elements of Business Theory is priceless! (Note: See SBA's homepage for complete details on the 8(a) certification waiver on the two-year rule.)

Earlier in the reading, I referred to how "information is knowledge; knowledge is power; power to make a better-informed decision." The true meaning of this statement starts right here with why this module is so important. There was a saying my parents and fore-parents used all the time and it's similar to this: If I knew then what I know now, then where would I be? In simple terms, one must understand all four modules (starting with Business Theory) prior to becoming certified in the 8(a) Business Development Program and/or even prior to starting a business. This is the process of being proactive and acquiring information and knowledge needed in the preliminary stages of starting a business. Let assume you don't obtain a waiver from SBA and you must be in business for the two-year period before you can apply to SBA for 8(a) certification. The bottom line is quite simple, if you know these four business process modules prior to obtaining 8(a) certifications (two years later) how much further down the road are you relative to expanding your knowledge base of government contracting or shall I say working with the federal government? The light bulbs should be coming brighter and brighter in your understanding of what is conveyed to you as a small business owner with the hopes of becoming 8(a) certified. This is a period of learning, understanding and fully preparing yourself for the day you are 8(a) certified by SBA. A little bit of effort now is worth a lifetime of success and reward later.

Let's go a little deeper into this process of Business Theory as it relates to building a solid foundation and platform going forward. I want you to remember these two statements: (1) In order to be a prime contractor, you must think and act as a prime contractor; and (2) In order to work within the federal sector, you must understand the federal sector (conducive to federal, state, local (city/county). Although I'm referring to "Business Theory" at this point, each of the four modules are interrelated but contain specific aspects of functionality as it relates to each separate area. Again, the same topic will be covered in various modules. Now that this is somewhat clear, let's role play two different scenarios indicating how important it is to be prepared in understanding the underlying principles of business.

The scenario is based on asking you (8(a) contractor/construction) several basic questions any potential contractor who (1) has done basic research prior to making a phone call to the government's point of contact for small business and/or (2) a potential contractor who is totally unprepared and who does not understand the basic principles of the government process as discussed herein. The following basic questions are asked to you the 8(a) contractor.

Questions:

(1) Bonding is one of the biggest issues regarding construction contracting especially for small businesses and 8(a) firms. Are there ways to offset this major problem/concern for a small business? (Answer: indemnification – Business Theory section)

(2) What is the greatest difference between Private Sector contracting and Public Sector contracting? (Answer: Profit driven verses Fair and Reasonable – Business Preparation section)

(3) What is the mission of my organization? (Answer: Business Theory section)

(4) When working for the federal government as a contractor, what are the four major elements that are contained in your proposal? In simplistic terms, what is the composition of your rate structure? (Answer: Direct, Overhead (home/field), Profit and Bond cost – Business Preparation section)

(5) What is Lowest Price Technical Acceptable (LPTA) procurement process? How does it differ from Best Value and Invitation for Bid (IFB) acquisition process? (Answer: Business Preparation section)

The above are sample questions a government representative could ask you any time during the meeting. Earlier, I stated if the federal government is your target market, you must understand federal contracting/process and the basic needs of your target market. This premise holds true regardless of your target market. The contractor (#2) who has not done his homework has no understanding of the basic four underlying principles of government contracting as an 8(a) firm and is not prepared to answer the questions appropriately. Conversely, the 8(a) contractor (#1) who has properly done his/her homework and understands the four basic business modules will answer the questions fluently and concisely. When I used the phrase "doing your homework," I'm referring to knowing and understanding the basic needs of your target market, which can either be Public Sector or Private Sector related. The bottom line is this: prior to contacting your potential target market ensure you have gathered as much information on the background and needs of your target market and fully/completely understand the basic business process modules (Business Theory, Business Presentation, Business Preparation and Business Functionality). Don't underestimate the real meaning of doing your homework and gathering as much information as you can prior to setting up an appointment. No one will know the answers to all questions asked, but it does indicate you have prepared yourself as much as possible.

This type of preparation process resembles going on your first job interview. If your interview is on Monday, you wouldn't wait until Sunday or the morning thereof to research your potential employer. The same concept is directly related to doing basic research prior to attending any meeting. The contractor (#2) in the above scenario who is unprepared shows a sign of "weakness" or better yet, not ready from a business standpoint to be a solid contractor to the federal government (or to your potential target market). Remember, you are trying to make a favorable impression and any sign of lack of preparation greatly reduces your success rate for future consideration as a potential contract supplier. Do not make this mistake! This snafu is 99% uncorrectable from an image standpoint. There will be more discussion later when the other modules are specifically reviewed. The contractor who is prepared displays an elevated level of confidence, soundly prepared, strength and fully ready to show that they can meet the needs of their target market.

The message in this scenario is perhaps the most significant of anything that is said in the remainder of this book. There are many trials, tribulations, and pitfalls an 8(a) contractor encounter. Those underlying areas will be covered periodically throughout the remainder of this book. There is a thin line between success verses an unsuccessful 8(a) firm. Image is by far the most important aspect affecting the level of success achieved by the 8(a) firm. Throughout the years, approximately 99% of all contractors I met, came into my office in a manner that indicated a lack of preparation and knowledge of the needs of my organization. In the earlier sections, I talked about developing a POA for 8(a) contractors, but first and foremost, I had to change my own approach prior to developing a winning strategy. One cannot be held accountable for things not known but for things known every attempt must be made to ensure full advantage is taken to increase the level of success going forward as a business entity. Beware as you proceed in the business world, there are individuals who are watching and analyzing everything done and said by you the 8(a) contractor.

Within certain areas of the federal government, the basic belief regarding the image of 8(a) contractors is less than favorable. Why is this true? What happened during the early development of the 8(a) Business Development Program (as established by SBA until today's 21st century)? Is it fair to stereotype this group of contractors? Who's at fault and who is to blame? The answer to the last question is easy…everyone is! If you haven't already heard it, you are going to hear it again and again and continuously within this reading:

- ❖ 8(a) firms do not perform (they are a pass-through) [definition of pass-through is a contractor who does not perform any of the major part of the construction effort or any effort regarding a government contract]
- ❖ 8(a) contractor's bid/proposal is too high
- ❖ 8(a) contractors have little skills and have little to no equipment needed to perform the job
- ❖ 8(a) contractors (by their standards) can perform any and every job that is presented to them (jack of all trades and masters of none)
- ❖ 8(a) contractors are not prepared and don't understand government contracting
- ❖ 8(a) contractors are only in it for the money and have little desire or initiative to develop long term goals for survival in the business world
- ❖ 8(a) contractors are a prime example of fraud, waste, and abuse of government funds when it comes to performing government contracts

There are many adjectives used to describe the deficiencies of 8(a) contractors. The above statements are *perceptions* on the ineptness of 8(a) contractors. Regardless whether these are perceptions are reality, this is the viewpoint of most individuals who work with 8(a) contractors. For clarification purposes, not all government personnel feel this way, but it is the basic reality of their internal viewpoint.

To the Author, how can something be factual and at the same time be the object of the above statements, which are based on perception?

There are a portion of Contracting Personnel, Construction Representatives, SBPM, Project Managers, Engineering, and other internal officials, feel these are true statements when it comes to 8(a) contractors. I will stake my entire reputation on this conclusion and (watch this) the majority of all 8(a) firms fail in one or more of the perception categories identified above. Both parties are guilty of false representation and perception. You (8(a) contractor) must ask yourself are these facts or these assumptions made on behalf of a segment of government personnel…true? Let me share a little secret with you… if the answer to any of the elements above are true, then you as an 8(a) contractor has failed and is guilty as charged. Wait a minute, if any government representative believes that anyone of the above perceptions are true, then they have failed, too! As you see, both parties play a key role in the overall success, failure, perception, and determining the faith or longevity of any contractor, as well as the success of any government's small business program.

The root of the problem regarding the 8(a) contractor is now exposed. For many years, the perception of 8(a) contractors has haunted them beyond comprehension. The reality of this is few individuals from either side (Government/Contractor) was willing to openly identify, discuss, and find solutions that would create a win-win situation for both groups for the long term. In many closed-door meetings, these concerns are discussed on a continuous basis. There are many harsh disagreements on why an 8(a) contractor should be considered for a project (negotiated/competitive). It's okay if on a competitive basis an 8(a) firm wins an award, but is this truly the objective of the program itself?

This mindset closely resembles race relations within the modern-day world; marriage between the sexes; issues within the Church; problems within various organizations, regardless of the type of business. We know there are problems, but we are reluctant to try to find a solution that is long term or at least develop a solution that is widely accepted within the business environment. There are many individuals fighting for 8(a) contractors but haven't reached a level of success that is necessary going forward into the future.

The below graph (exhibit #4) includes many interrelated thought processes on why the theoretical understanding of business is so important during the pilot stages prior of starting a business. Based on the discussions thus far within this module, you should have an understanding regarding the importance of mental preparation and why the element of think before you act is paramount in business as well as everyday life experiences.

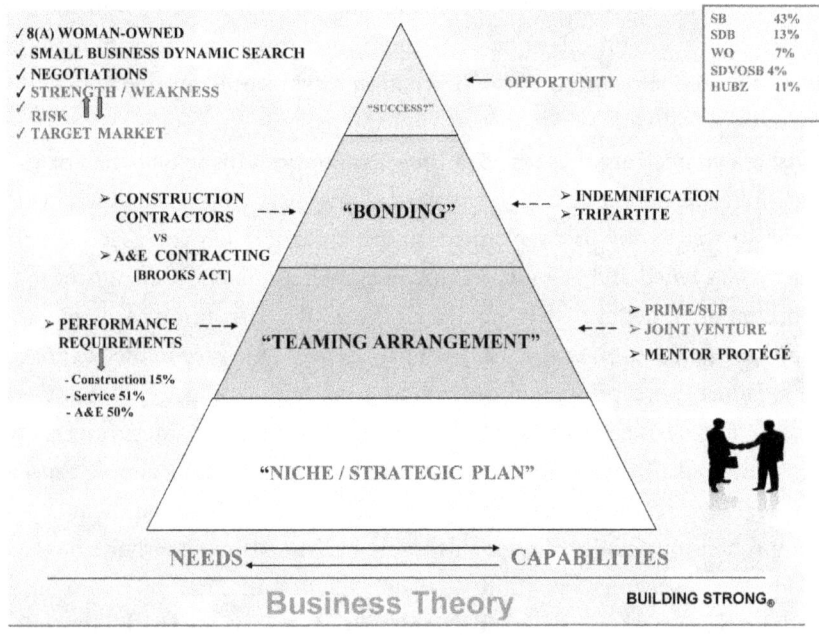

Exhibit #4

The Business Theory module is designed to increase the thought processes of the business owner from an internal intellectual standpoint. This analogy is continuously mentioned in the sports world, business sector, social environment, and in all walks of life. As an example, many of our sports figures have been referred to as being mentally tough in the world of golf, basketball, football, hockey, and so forth. Those individuals who are at the top of their profession are considered to have this internal tough trait.

This characteristic is one which separates them from the good, average, or below average athlete. What exactly does this mean? Are some of us mentally stronger than others? Are some of us more mentally prepared than others? The answer is a resounding and overwhelming yes! From a theoretical perspective, one must be able to take advantage of every opportunity that exists, and this means doing, or going the extra mile from a knowledge base level. This, too, goes back to the basis of gathering information and processing this data resulting in strengthening you and everyone within your organization. Following this mindset, a solid foundation has been laid and you are ready to build your company from a mental viewpoint. At this level, you're strategizing and developing a clear path forward.

Perhaps the most essential element in our lives (but the most overlooked) is the element of something called "time." A brief definition of time as stated in the Webster's Dictionary is: "The system of those sequential relationships that any event has to any other, as past, present, or future…"[4] Thinking back when I was a kid, it appeared to me Christmas would never come, or it couldn't come soon enough. What about the time when school was ending that year and summer was approaching? The time away from school seamed to last forever. As other responsibilities and burdens of life are thrown upon us, the element of time seamed to speed up and pass us by. My own analogy of the mystical characteristics of time is simple but realistic. As a youngster, we didn't have any place to go (theoretically, other than to play), therefore we did not pay attention to time, but as an adult, everything we do, say, or need centers around this thing call "time." As a result, time is moving at the speed of light! As a business owner, time or time management is your most important asset you never pay attention to.

TIME

Your most important asset is Time. Time is a relative term, but it is something you can never retract or take back. It is imperative you spend the majority of your time in the most productive manner possible. In the 8(a) Business Development Program, the firm has nine (9) years to develop, grow and ultimately (with a lot of luck) remain in the business environment as a viable small business. Eventually, losing the small business status, and ultimately becoming a large business (if this is your long-term goal). Again, you must be in business two (2) years as an established small business prior to applying for 8(a) certification; however, this directive can be waived by SBA depending on the past and historical strength of your business entity. This option is available but seldom enforced. So, understanding time is the most important and critical asset...don't waste any time that doesn't increase your opportunity for success. In other words, do not waste time but redirect your efforts in a positive manner. (Notice: everything discussed is based on the positive and not relative to anything negative). The two-year waiting period should be used understanding the direction and path for growth and success (which is the sole purpose of this book). Most firms don't take advantage of this phase or time frame that is available. Rather than waiting on your 8(a) certification to materialize, use the two-year period to polish and develop your internal and external skills while still working in the business path you had chosen. I am not recommending stop doing what is successful to you thus far (e.g., the bills must be paid). However, grasp as much information as possible. This will put your firm in a position of strength rather than weakness. If you over exert yourself with an overabundance of tasks, functions, goals, processes, etc., you will quickly become frustrated and lose focus on the objective at hand. Over the years, I've met countless of young entrepreneurs who were so wrapped up in day to day functions they failed to consider proper utilization of those individuals within their own organization. This is a common mistake most small business owners overlook.

Stop: Each CEO, President, or owner of a company should ask himself/herself a series of questions: Have I overburdened myself with issues, problems, and concerns? Have I properly utilized the skillsets of those employed by me? Do I rely too much on my own judgement and not trust my employees? It is truly understandable that one unwise decision by you (the business owner) can result in a major set-back to the growth and/or sustainment as an organization in the business world.

The sub-functions of understanding the theoretical aspect of business are predicated on proper utilization of this element. To direct your efforts properly, take the necessary time to completely understand how to integrate and administer this key ingredient to your advantage. Before this element is discussed any further, let's momentarily table this topic for later. Now that we understand what is labeled Business Theory, let's completely analyze some individual sub components in this area as indicated in exhibit #4.

1. Needs and Capabilities

Before we completely dissect this module, I want to set the tone for this area. Have you ever known a mountain climber to reach the apex of the mountain without starting at the bottom unless he jumped from an airplane or helicopter? Can a house be built without laying the foundation? Can you graduate from high school without starting at kindergarten or pre-school? Can you be the number one player in any sport without first defeating several opponents along the way toward becoming the champion? The answer is no...We must start at some point before our quest can be conquered. This is the same logical process that must be taken within this module. This area was developed to identify which road or path anyone must take to reach their goal.

The first area of concern (with any firm or contractor) is understanding the relationship between the Needs of the federal government and your firms Capabilities.

It is imperative that you have done your research prior to contacting your Target Market (e.g., federal government). Using the example of your first job interview, what would be the first thing done prior to showing up on Monday morning for the interview session? You would research the company and gather as much information as possible, so you could intelligently discuss the needs of your potential employer with the person (or personnel panel) doing the interview. Somewhere during the interview process the question may be presented to you regarding your 'knowledge' of the potential employer and 'why' you feel you have the skillset that is desired. By answering these questions properly displays a sense of confidence and most importantly preparation. This is the same mental preparation needed when contacting any organization to set up that first business meeting. Everything discussed in this Business Theory module is based on the relationship between Needs and Capabilities as the foundation. It's similar to building a brand-new home. Without a solid foundation, the structure of the home is weak and unstable thus resulting in the home collapsing. This is the same concept of building a successful business working with the federal government.

Time and time again (no pun intended), firms do not relate Needs and Capabilities and the level of importance of this relationship. As an example, would you contact an organization regarding Design/Build opportunities relative to Military Construction when in fact the District or organization may not have such a function as a part of their mission statement? Would you, as a business owner in the Janitorial field, contact an organization who is a tenant in a GSA building seeking a Janitorial contract (opportunities)? This is one of my favorite examples of a contractor not doing his homework…contact and set up an appointment for Information Technology (IT) services/opportunities with the agency when indeed all IT functions have been outsourced to a private contractor several years ago. These are prime examples of how companies waste that crucial element called "time." This, too, could have been avoided by doing a little fact-finding and homework directed toward understanding the needs of your target market.

Prior to discussing your capabilities with the Point of Contact (POC) of your target market, you must completely understand what your capabilities are but, more importantly, how you are going to explain your strengths during the initial meeting. In many situations, contractors came into the office with a host of skills and abilities. This is what I call a contractor who is a "Jack of all trades but a master of none". There must be a clear correlation between your capabilities and the needs of your target market.

The intended meaning of the word "needs" of your target market is specifically referring to a whole host of functions that are either skillsets; job and functions; support to external community involvement; types of work performed within the organization; etc. As an 8(a) contractor, your ability to function at the prime contract level for most government entities are limited. This is not to degrade the abilities of an 8(a) contractor, but the pure fact of the matter is no business (large or small) can 100% self-perform all job functions required to build a road, dirt berm, culvert, or whatever the project may be. As a safeguard, there must be a direct correlation between your capabilities and organizational needs of your target market. More discussion to come in the Business Presentation module regarding key ways to discuss your capabilities and needs of the organization, you have targeted as a potential customer. In simple terms, if your company performs a variety of Civil Construction functions such as building roads, dirt berms, culverts, clearing/grubbing, etc., tailor your presentation specifically on those areas that the federal government need. If you can perform vertical type construction projects, but the government organization doesn't have a need for a company who can perform that type of function, obviously do not talk about your capabilities in performing vertical construction.

Another example is companies who have design/build capabilities. For those laymen design/build is having the internal organizational capabilities to design a project (plans/specifications) and have organizational capabilities to build the project you designed. Why would you spend 50% (or anytime) discussing your design/build capabilities when that organization does not have a design/build mission?

Since much of my experience is predominantly working in the federal government, let's observe specifically the correlation between understanding how important it is to an 8(a) firm to completely digest this process…Needs verses Capabilities. These are some of the direct Needs of the federal government (keeping in mind depending on what area of the government needs may vary):

Needs:

(1) Federal Mandated Small Business Goals
(2) Socioeconomic Firms to meet Small Business Goals
(3) Civil and HTRW Contractors (Hazardous, Toxic, Radioactive & Waste) Mission (not Military Mission)
(4) Center of Expertise (Photogrammetric & Mapping; Dam Safety & Monitorization; Curation)
(5) Environmental Mission
(6) Operation & Maintenance (Rivers/Tributary related mission)

The above are basic subliminal examples of major needs of an organization within the Army. During my federal career, basic organizational needs were categorized in three major areas relative to mission/needs, which were Civil, Hazardous Toxic Radioactive Waste (HTRW), and Military Construction (MILCON). Some organizational mission may include all three areas or some combination of the three areas. On the surface and depending on the area and mission of that organization within the federal market targeted, it appears the above areas don't have a significant impact on the approach one takes, while trying to understand the importance of organizational needs. Seldom, if ever, does an 8(a) firm get a second opportunity to correct one's perception as a business organization. If nothing else register this concept within your thought processes…put this premise in the back of your mind and refer to it daily!

Let's further put into narrative some of the needs of the federal government. Most federal organizations have mandated goals for Small Business (SB), Small Disadvantaged Small Business (SDB), Woman-owned Small Business (WOSB), Historically Underutilized Business Zone (HUBZone), and Service

---

Glenn L. Chatman

Disabled Veteran Owned Small Business (SDVOSB). This means for every dollar obligated to any business entity a portion (percentage) of every dollar must be awarded to one of the small businesses within that category (to be discussed in detailed later). To meet these mandated goal requirements, there is a specific need for socioeconomic small businesses certified in those categories. In addition, the SBPM must maintain an adequate small business contractor base to fulfill these needs. It's imperative to understand the organizational structural needs of your target organization. The basic definition of the above small business categories is:

"Small Business (SB):
The SBA recognizes a small business in terms of the average number of employees over the past twelve months, or average annual receipts over the past three years. In addition, SBA defines a U.S. small business as a concern that:

- Is organized for profit
- Has a place of business in the U.S.
- Operates primarily within the U.S. or makes a significant contribution to the U.S. economy through payment of taxes or use of American products, material, or labor
- Is independently owned and operated
- Is not dominant in its field on a material basis"[5]

"Small Disadvantaged Business (SDB):
(1) The firm must be 51% or more owned and controlled by one or more disadvantaged persons
(2) The disadvantaged person or persons must be socially disadvantaged
(3) The firm must be small, according to SBA's size standards"[6]

"Woman-Owned Small Business (WOSB):
(1) Be a small business
(2) Be at least 51% owned and controlled by women who are U.S. citizens
(3) Have women manage day-to-day operations and also make long-term decisions requirements set forth in the final rule." [7]

"HUBZone Small Business (HUBZone):
   (1) Be a small business by SBA standards
   (2) Be at least 51% owned and controlled by U.S. citizens, a Community Development Corporation, an agricultural cooperative, a Native Hawaiian organization, or an Indian tribe
   (3) Its principal office must be located within a HUBZone
   (4) At least 35% of its employees must live in a HUBZone" [8]

"Service-Disabled Veteran-Owned Small Business (SDVOSB):
   (1) Be a small business
   (2) Be at least 51% owned and controlled by one or more service-disabled veterans
   (3) Have one or more service-disabled veterans manage day-to-day operations and also make long-term decisions
   (4) Eligible veterans must have a service-connected disability" [9]

So, what approach do you take? Keep your research simple but thorough. All federal organizations have a home (web) page. This is the first area to obtain a lucid understanding of the entire organization. Gather as much information and knowledge regarding your target organization as possible. One must ensure all members of your company are well-informed about the mission and needs of that organization. The federal government (SBPM of your target organization) should have a qualified list of socioeconomic contractors who are certified in a variation of those small business categories as identified above. A description of the functions performed (division/departments/offices) are contained on the home page providing an overview of their mission and functions. It is imperative to understand the needs of the federal government come in a variety of ways (e.g., goods and services). There are mandated small business goals enforced by the federal government in support of meeting small business goal requirements.

This approach should be used every time prior to setting up a meeting. Identify the key personnel such as SBPM and Chief of Contracting. These are the two individuals who have access to the program forecast and have a complete knowledge of current and future projects. These are the main contact personnel, but your strategy when setting up the first meeting is not to discuss project opportunities. What on earth do I mean? Isn't this the sole purpose for meeting with your target market? As a potential contractor to the federal government, doing your homework and knowing the functions of the organization are highly important. One should have an awareness of the type of product, goods or services needed; various mandated program requirements (goals) that must be followed...and so forth and so on.

Another approach helpful to you as a contractor is to list your capabilities (in a broad sense) and list the needs of the federal government (or state, city, local, county government) prior to setting up the meeting. This is a simple but effective exercise:

(1) Take a sheet of paper and in one column title it 'My Capabilities.' List the basic qualities, functions, skills, and/or projects you have the capability of performing.
(2) Make a second column and title it 'Government Needs.' List the different type of projects that are common to that organization.
(3) Cross match those areas, items, projects, skills of those that are similar or identical.

There should be a lot of areas that are a match between what you can perform and the requirements of your target market. A common mistake made by the majority of contractors is talking about their capabilities to perform any and everything under the sun. They can perform construction, supply/services, personal services, IT functions, and on and on and on. If you take this approach, there's a strong possibility you will never obtain a sole source contract of any magnitude.

This is when you use a different marketing strategy, which I call the <u>reverse psychological marketing approach</u>. Upon entering the room, conversation is based on your "capabilities" and how you can meet and support the "needs" of your target market. I must reiterate, never start a conversation or integrate the idea to the federal government representative, at this point, wanting to discuss project opportunities. This approach indicates a sign of strength from the standpoint you are prepared and know specifically the areas where you can best help the federal government. In most instances, the contractor rattles on and on about wrong areas to the government representatives. At least follow this tactic on your initial visit. You already know the District or agency doesn't do or have a Military function; you know they (federal government) build berms, levees, pump stations, relief wells, roads, and various environmental/civil project efforts. During your discussion, the integration of this information is included thereby exemplifying the knowledge you have accumulated based on prior research efforts. This is one of the most damaging mistakes most contractors make.

Let's ensure this concept is clearly understood:

"WRONG APPROACH - WRONG APPROACH

(1) Normally, contractors come to the office inquiring about project opportunities and how they are "jack of all trades" and a "master of none." In essence, wanting to discuss projects regardless whether they have the skills, knowledge and most importantly the 'right' capability to meet the federal government needs:

RIGHT APPROACH - RIGHT APPROACH

(2) Clearly start and continue the conversation focusing on your "capabilities" as a prime contractor to meet a specific target area within the federal government's litany of project requirements. Thus, slowly integrating your knowledge relative to the strengths of your organization through continuous discussion."

By taking this approach, you have passed the first test of getting the attention of the small business representative or whomever you are meeting with. This shows you are confident, knowledgeable, and somewhat prepared (if given an opportunity) to meet the needs of the government. This entire process is very integrated and convoluted with bomb shells that can preclude you from getting that desired opportunity of becoming a contractor to the federal government. The process of acquiring information, knowledge and facts are critical, but not knowing the art of presenting this data can be detrimental to the success of reaching the top of the pyramid. Many individuals can understand, absorb, and perform if given an opportunity, but in many cases, do not have the communication skills to what I call "Telling Your Story". The art of this process is based on verbally and clearly explaining your company's capabilities to your target audience. If you don't master this tactic, your level and degree of success is extremely limited.

This is a small but highly important strategy that is overlooked and probably not considered from the offset. How many meetings have you arranged that followed this failed approach? Approximately 99% of all contractors whom I have met followed this approach and were not aware of the mistake.

Principle #1:
Know the needs of your target market (e.g., federal government) through due diligence by researching and fact finding the requirements and mission of that organization.

Principle #2:
Understand your capabilities and know prior to the meeting how you are going to discuss and present your strengths to meet the needs of your target market.

Principle #3:
Never discuss project or agency requirements on the initial meeting and most importantly let your strengths or your capabilities compliment the needs of your customer.

Principle #4:
Finally, understanding the needs of your target market in relations to understanding your own capabilities is the backbone of the Business Theory module.

2. Strategic Plan

Since the underlying foundation of Business Theory have been established, let's look at the next critical area, which is developing your "Strategic Plan" and incorporating your "Niche" (or vice versa). Let's dissect what is meant by developing a Strategic Plan as it relates to an 8(a) firm. In simple terms, we understand a plan is a mechanism (including) various processes or ways can be used either short or long term to accomplish a goal or an objective. The basic definition of strategy (or strategic) is: "a plan or method for achieving a specific goal."[10] Therefore, when you combined both words together (strategic plan) from a mental perspective is a sense of direction can be developed for the short term and can be used as a basis for long term planning, development, and growth.

Most successful organizations develop a three - or five-year strategic plan and modify that concept as they proceed in the business environment as it relates to financial, managerial, and corporate expansion. This is a great approach under normal circumstances. All businesses should develop a short/long term course of action as it relates to growth and development. However, a new business must take a different mental viewpoint when developing their strategic plan relative to their company strengths. Let's discuss these two processes in the right context and in order of importance and relevancy.

In developing this process called Strategic Plan and Niche: (a) develop your Plan from the standpoint of "survival" in the short term rather than from the perspective of growth and development for further sustainment and (b) your Niche should be concentrated on specific opportunities identified in the business environment as it pertains to your target market and internal business capabilities. Growth and prosperity will come, but it's irrelevant if you take a failed approach early in business resulting in going out of business. This is not rocket science and hard to understand, but new companies must take a different mental approach toward doing business with the federal government or anywhere in the private or public sector. Another way of developing a strategy is understanding the very day you receive your 8(a) certifications is the same day you start preparation of exiting the program. You must start this strategy and planning process well in advance prior to applying for the 8(a) Business Development Program.

You must remember the discussion within the section on Needs and Capabilities. The interrelationship in developing your Strategic Plan and Niche are systematically connected with each other and with everything discussed henceforth. A company should be organized and developed from the "Outside In" rather than from the "Inside Out." This is a very strange statement and to most people it is not a logical approach. I'm sure we have heard (at one point in time or another) don't underestimate the power of critical thinking. (exhibit #5) In developing any type of plan of action, whether it is short or long term, you go through a wide process of analyzing and dissecting many things. The objective is to develop a course of action that will guide your company on a successful path. **This is certainly the right way of thinking, but there is a Catch 22 with this methodology. Most CEOs and/or owners of any company go into business based on their own internal strengths. If you went to school and majored in Engineering, chances are you are going to start a business related to one of the disciplines in Engineering: e.g., Electrical, Structural, Architectural, or whatever the area may be. If you have a burning desire to become an interior decorator because this has been your lifelong dream, then you start some sort of decorating or design business. The point is most people start a business based on their own internal skills and abilities. Historically, most individuals start businesses in an area that are fully within their comfort zone.

THE POWER OF CRITICAL THINKING

INSIDE OUT APPROACH: (1) DEVELOP FIRM BASED ON INTERNAL SKILL SET
(2) SURROUND YOURSELF WITH SIMILAR SKILL SET AS OWNER
(3) SEEK OPPORTUNITIES BASED ON MARKETING
COMPANY CAPABILITIES TO THE VARIOUS UNDEFINED
TARGET MARKET
(4) RELY ON FINDING THE RIGHT MARKET AT THE RIGHT TIME

OUTSIDE IN APPROACH: (1) IDENTIFY NEEDS OF THE BUSINESS WORLD
(SUCCESS/NEEDS OF CURRENT BUSINESSES)
(2) IDENTIFY TARGET MARKET (PUBLIC OR PRIVATE)
(3) DEVELOP SKILLSET OF PERSONNEL NEEDED TO MEET
NEEDS OF TARGET MARKET)
(4) MARKETING COMPANY BASED ON A SPECIFIC
IDENTIFIED TARGET MARGET

Outside in - Approach Advantages: (1) An enormous amount of time saved by
knowing your Target Market
(2) Higher percent of success rate of obtaining
an opportunity (right market / right capabilities)
(3) More time to develop correct market strategy

Exhibit #5

Whoa, your niche is thereby born! Therefore, going into the business world, you now have a niche and strategic plan that meets your own internal needs, wants, and desires. This concept is defined as developing a company from the "Inside Out." Henceforth your company is developed from the standpoint the skillset of your company may not be in demand at that time. Most businesses are created not based on market demand or the demand of your potential customer base. Please, do not misunderstand the true meaning of what is being conveyed. This concept may be the correct way to start a business, but I'm confident that there will be many trials and tribulations encountered. I want you to think about an alternative approach to this method. [STOP: Go back and re-read starting at the sentence…**"This is certaintly] There is a different approach!

Let's look at the other approach, which is building a company from the Outside In concept. Let's assume you are in the early development stages wanting to start a business and you and two of your other partners are having a meeting to discuss an appropriate course of action to pursue. You are the owner of the potential new company and your educational background is PhD in Psychology from Harvard (you are a minority in ethnicity and female). One of your other partners have a degree from Georgia Tech in Engineering (Electrical /owned an electrical company for five years) and your second partner has twenty years of experience in Management and has a PhD in Management from UCLA (worked at a major Food Chain in management). You open the floor up for discussion and the first topic is what type of business should we start? Before anyone speaks, you, the potential head honcho, states, "Let's start a company based on the demand of the business market." The other two individuals look at you as if you have lost your mind. Let's fast forward the rewind button and you have determined (based on doing your homework relative to business needs within the market) there is a need to start a woman-owned construction company. You (through due diligence) determined the federal government had mandated woman-owned goals, had a major shortage of woman-owned construction firms, and potentially have great opportunities through the 8(a) Business Development Program. Look at the skillset of those three individuals. The potential owner is a psychologist; one is an engineer and the other one worked in management at a food chain. The teaching point is they wanted to start a company that had a prominent level of success rather than starting a company based on their own internal strengths. The second scenario is not centered on specific strengths of individuals but is focused on what presented them the best opportunity of starting a successful business. They weren't concerned about each other strengths but looked at external opportunities.

Therefore, during the initial stages of developing your strategic plan and niche take a sound look at both approaches. Most owners take the Inside Out approach, but in times whereby businesses are closing, I would rather build a company based on external needs and integrating proper personnel to proceed forward. In most cases thinking outside of the box can have short/long term gains. You must overcome the fear of the unknown because of doing something different. Most inventors who have come up with the unthinkable are successful because of deviating from the norm or standard practices of what society has classified as being politically correct.

In the above paragraphs, discussion covered the traditional processes of what a strategic plan should include. The normal areas that any business entity would cover are depicted in the first three years, five years or even a longer period. However, you must realize as an 8(a)-firm new to the business world, your margin of error is minimal. In essence, the day you are in business or have received your 8(a)-program certification (nine-year period) is the same day you start preparation to exit the program. This may seem to be a confused state of mind or way of thinking, but you must realize time (as discussed earlier) is one of the most important elements to any business owner. Although the best laid plans often go astray, its' much better to have some sense of direction rather not to have any plan at all. The foundation of this module is certainly the relationship between capabilities and needs, but everything is a part of the strategic plan that has been developed. There is nothing set in concrete that cannot be modified. This entire process is a continuous living document meaning changes and modifications to your strategic plan is part of the process. Don't be afraid to change your plan along the way. In many instances, outside pressures such as upturns or downturns in the economy can have a tremendous effect on your ability to operate your business in the same manner you have been accustomed. Remember that success is always based on some sort of failure or setback that occurred somewhere along the way prior to obtaining a certain level of success. There's no one who have not witnessed failure in life. Failure is not negative but indicates (somewhere along your journey) you have tried to reach or obtain a goal. Nothing beats a failure but a try!

3. Niche

As an 8(a) contractor, a clear understanding of your Niche is mandatory. Niche is an activity or function for which a person or thing is best fitted...or a specialized market. Since the organic definition of Niche is revealed, what or how does this relate to you in the business world? In real terms, why are some businesses successful? Is it because they are much smarter than their competitor and the rest of the marketplace, or have they found a key process or function that separates them from others? As an example, this individual (who represented this company) wore a white suit and had a white beard, and the company did one thing and only one thing…who was this person? To me, this advertising strategy wasn't concerned about the competition but focused on having the best product on the market. The success of this organization ultimately resulted in the development of a "secret" receipt which was different from competition. Various locations for this product were superbly established and strategically located for traveling from point A to point B. Another example was used by another fast food organization. There are many places throughout our country where the basic hamburger, fries and soft drink can be purchased. One of the most unique developments occurred within this organization, which set them apart (from my viewpoint) from the competition: providing a basic meal with a toy inside! Most parents that I know wondered why this organization was so successful. The answer was simple: Focus on the children and develop something that would lure children to this establishment. There were numerous times when my family and I were traveling, and we could not pass this organization. The kids would hollow and scream until we pulled into that fast food place. Personally, the advent of the fast food sandwich with the toy as a part of the meal was a brilliant strategy among many. The rest of this story is history!

Most entrepreneurs who start a business immediately lose sight of the right course of action prior to completing the initial paperwork to start a company. One thing to remember is every large business was once a small business and a small business was only a "thought" someone had in the back of their mind. If you have a desire to get into some sort of services, supply, environmental, architectural/engineering, or construction business arena, have a clear understanding of your company's mission, goals, and objectives. There is a direct correlation between your Niche, Strategic Plan, Capabilities and Needs of your target market. Everything discussed has a direct relationship that affects the success of your organization.

Before we proceed forward, let's go back into the past and discuss an essential element during the early development stages of your business. This is a wonderful time to briefly discuss the time prior to starting your own business. Earlier there was discussion of how a large business ultimately evolved from the thought processes of an individual who wanted to start a business. At this point you are trying to determine a name for your organization, as well as what type of business to start. This is the infant stages of the foundation of any business. But this is a critical time whereby the name of your company selected will (not may) have a significant impact on the direction that you choose later. Let's use a common name like Johnson. You as an owner decide on the name John J. Johnson Woodworking Company (fictious name) for your business. What's wrong with the selected name? There are two issues. First the name John J. Johnson Woodworking Company indicates you are a business of one. The name is individualized and second you have categorized your company as solely being in the woodworking business. There's nothing wrong with being in the woodworking business, but what if the market changes down the road and business opportunities are severely reduced in the woodworking arena? Later a decision by you (company owner) to get into the construction business but is stuck with a name at the end of your business called "woodworking." It not easy to change company names once they have been incorporated or registered within the system. The teaching point of this example is to be careful of the name selected for your company. Things constantly change in the business environment and you want to ensure you have the flexibility to get into other business areas and your company's name won't be a hinderance. A firm with a company name of John J. Johnson Woodworking is going to have a challenging time transitioning to construction with the objective of working in the federal market.

As a potential contractor to the federal sector (assuming that is your target market), a determination must be made to be a Prime contractor or a first, second, or third tier subcontractor to a Prime firm working for the federal government. For those who may not know, a Prime Contractor is the company who has a contractual agreement with the government to perform certain functions from a legal contractual standpoint. The agreement is strictly between you and the federal government. As an example, you decided your company is going get in the plumbing business and your objective is to be the best plumbing company in the area. In addition, the federal government is your target market. The first question of concern is whether your capabilities meet the needs of the federal government relative to plumbing opportunities and if so in what capacity? Are there any requirements I can bid on as a prime contractor or my services more suited to meet one of the line item requirements within a bid schedule (proposal)? There is a possibility a requirement could materialize for plumbing work as a small procurement action but highly unlikely. So basically, your key role as a potential contractor is limited and relegated to fulfilling a small part of a project requirement or in this case being a subcontractor to another company who is considered the Prime. This certainly doesn't mean your company can't survive but focus may shift toward the private sector for opportunities. Nevertheless, this is a critical decision a business owner must determine prior to starting your firm. This is a part of understanding the type of firm you want to establish in relation to your target market and whether you have the capability to act as a prime or subcontractor. Time and time again, many small business owners came into my office not knowing the difference between the organizational structure of the two types of companies and certainly didn't understand the role they would play as a potential contractor to the government. This is a major factor many 8(a) firms overlook when selecting or determining, which business direction to pursue. This is a critical function relative to starting a new business and focusing your attention in the right area. (Additional discussion will ensue later in "partnering," which will provide alternative methods of acting as prime or subcontractor for the federal government.)

The overall understanding of "Niche" should be clear at this point. In simplistic terms, you must determine your role either as a prime or subcontractor but clearly integrate this thought process early in the conceptual development of your business plan. If nothing else, you must be clear as to who you are and the type of company you have developed relative to your business specialty and at what level you can perform if the federal government is indeed your target market.

Principle #1:

Therefore, as a contractor determine and develop your "Niche" in a way your entire business organization understands the strengths and weaknesses of your company. As a business owner, determine your trademark for business regardless whether it is in construction, services, or supplies, and stay the course. Develop your strategic plan as if you are in "survival" mode, ensuring as a Prime contractor your capabilities meet the needs of your target market, and the strengths of your company are fully engrained within the mission and goals of your organization.

In addition, something as mundane as your company's name must not be overlooked. Most companies fail to understand that a company's business name should be reflective of your skills and abilities, and for the most part be in concert with the needs of your target market. As indicated earlier (and it's important to restate), if your company's name is John J. Johnson's Woodworking, LLC, how are you going to sell your overall company's image to the federal government if you wish to become a contractor in the construction arena. This may not seem important to you initially, but later down the road, your company's name can prohibit you from obtaining business opportunities. Therefore, be fully aware when determining the name of your business organization.

Principle #2:
Principle #2 incorporates the fundamentals of Principle #1. [Hint: You and your company are still in the business theory mental preparation mode.] A company's name should reflect who you are, and what type of business you represent. Do not pick a name that "pigeon holes" you into one line of work. Using the above name (Johnson's Woodworking), what do you think will happen if he decides to go into the construction business from the civil standpoint? He may have restructured the company's skillset to perform basic construction functions, and in reality, have become a sound contractor in the construction arena. Do you think he is going to have a challenging time selling his skills and abilities in construction, when in essence, his companies name is oriented toward performing woodworking functions? The first concern to the potential target audience, is how can a company who does woodworking build a road, dirt berm or construct a levee? Just be aware of the company name selected prior to completing your business documents. Your company name is practically impossible to change once your company has been incorporated as a business entity.

Thus far in our journey, beneath the surface of analyzing 8(a) firms doing business with the federal sector, we have explored the intricacies and interrelationship of the building blocks of laying a solid foundation. This specifically relates to understanding your firm's capabilities, needs of your target market, and developing your Niche incorporating these fundamentals into a strategic plan. So far, so good!

The next section of discussion is determining which alternative course of action is or should be used to ensure you as an 8(a) firm have the best possibility of getting an opportunity to work for the federal government. However, before proceeding forward, it is critical to understand the process called acquisition strategy determination. There are a couple of facts you must know regarding the thought processes relative to (1) "Acquisition Strategy" as determined by the government and (2) what I call "Acquisition Strategy Determination" or "Rules of Engagement (RoE)." Let's assume somehow you convinced the government to enter into a negotiated contract. It is imperative as an 8(a) contractor, to understand what determines the decision of the KO to proceed in the manner chosen for a project. To reiterate, the final decision on Acquisition Strategy rests with the Chief of Contracting, although recommendations can be made by various groups such as the Product Delivery Team, Small Business Review Committee (SBRC), or whatever group involved with reviewing and analyzing projects. There are many text book definitions that describe and define "Acquisition Strategy" and the elements and processes included. However, Acquisition Strategy is determining which solicitation process will be used for a particular project. For our purposes we'll define acquisition strategy as: the process used to determine whether a solicitation will be advertised as (a) unrestricted, (b) small business set-aside (small businesses only; HUBZone set-aside, or Service Disabled Veteran Owned Small Business or Woman-owned Small Business), (c) 8(a) negotiated (requirements under $4 million), and (d) 8(a) competitive (actions exceeding $4 million restricted to only 8(a) contractors). For information and understanding purposes, here is the basic definition as it relates to acquisition strategy and its sub elements: Unrestricted Solicitation: (1) full and open competition; anyone or any type of business can provide a bid or proposal regardless if they are a large or small business. (2) Small Business Set-aside: Only a small business (who meet all the small business size standards (and other related factors) as defined by SBA) can bid. A small business set-aside of a single action may be total or partial set-asides.[11]

These are the two major categories of Acquisition Strategy (unrestricted /small business set-asides), but what are the true elements that compose the decision to advertise a requirement as unrestricted or using one of the small business processes? I've concluded there are four distinct categories applicable in determining acquisition strategy. Those four project areas are based on (1) mission criticality, (2) project complexity, (3) project dollar value, and (4) available contractor base (see exhibit #6).

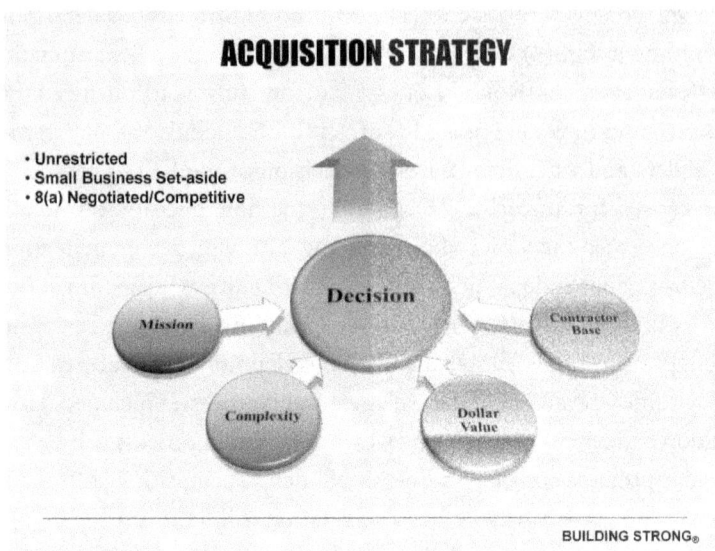

Exhibit #6

The underlying thought process in determining whether a project is advertised as unrestricted or small business set-aside is based on looking at each individual element, then reviewing collectively the impact these elements have on the entire project.

Let's examine each one of these four areas and analyze how collectively they affect the final decision relative to acquisition determination:

(1) Mission Critical: The first concern regarding acquisition strategy determination is the criticality of a project relative to mission accomplishment. The major question centers on what happens to a community, area, or location if this project is not completed as soon as possible? Are lives involved that could be in grave danger? Could there be great damage to property, as well as the environment? Can you use "Urgency of Need" or some other prescribed situations under the Federal Acquisition Regulation (FAR) that grants the KO the authority to use certain acquisition methods? What are the overall short and long-term implications to the surrounding area if the project is not completed in a timely manner? Does this effort have national implications to the sustainment of economic balance of trade? This should be the first and foremost topic of discussion between team members from the inception of the new effort. In analyzing the above questions, sound judgement must be used in un-

derstanding the criticality of the project. Mission critical as a project classification doesn't necessarily mean danger is now but could mean it's eminent, if appropriate action isn't taken within the near term. Thus, mission essentiality does not mean being in a position of ultimate danger but has an impact on making the right acquisition strategic decision.

As an example, there were large rock pinnacles (boulders) located in a major river (place unimportant) and as the river fell below a certain level, the boulders were exposed thereby impeding the flow of river traffic up and down the river basin. As we know, the economic movement of goods and services within our country centers around air, rail, road (trucks) and river transportation. If there are any interruptions of movement by any one of these major transportation arteries, a major catastrophic shutdown of the flow of goods and services could have a devastating impact on our entire nation. This could result in billions of lost dollars in revenue and cripple our nation from an economic standpoint. This situation would affect millions of people and have a major impact to the nation if this type of situation occurs even for a brief period. Therefore, can any business entity overlook or not consider the mission of projects that are interrelated to our local, state or nation best interest?

From my perspective this is the number one concern and factor that is discussed internally in the determination of acquisition strategy… "the mission of the project."

(2) Project Complexity: The next area of discussion is the degree of complexity of the basic project. The basic definition of complexity is: "composed of many interconnected parts; compound; composite…so complicated or intricate as to be hard to understand or deal with."[12] In using the above example of rock pinnacle removal, the type of work required on the river can certainly be considered difficult and hard to understand, as well as the level of effort needed for completion. One other essential element in understanding whether a project is simple, or complex is analyzing the degree of safety present in undertaking a project of this nature from a contractor's perspective. Is safety a major part of Project Complexity? Safety is always at the top of anyone's list, regardless, if the effort is as simple as going to bed at night; stepping into a bath tub; driving a car; or whatever the situation may be. Safety precautionary measures cannot be ignored, or not considered regardless of the situation. As a contractor, if a project has an element of complexity, you can be assured some sort of safety factor is included.

In determining Project Complexity, a complete review of the plans, specifications and drawings are dissected and discussed. Is there any way to put a number on the amount of known or unknown factors that compose the complexity of a project? Is there specialty equipment needed? Are there specialty skill levels required? Some experts may say you can measure the degree of complexity by using a simple scale of one (1) through ten (10), with the lower end of the spectrum 1 indicating less risk in comparison to 10 indicating substantial risk. This method appears to be an acceptable measuring tool; however, every precautionary step should be used to ensure safety is kept to a maximum level. This cannot always be done, so common sense and good sound judgment should be exercised when determining the complexity of a project.

(3) Project Dollar Value: In most cases, the dollar value of a project is interrelated and commensurate to the complexity of the project requirement. This premise is true, relative to most projects, but there are exceptions to this statement. Sometimes, the dollar value may be significantly under a million dollars but could require a unique tool or have an environmental impact that could compound the ability to complete a project under normal acquisition processes. This is not the norm, but an exception to the norm. Remember, each of these elements are viewed on an independent basis, but at the end of the analysis, are collectively grouped in determining acquisition strategy for a project.

Again, in our river example, the estimated dollar value of the effort was significant and well above normal dollar value of a standard project effort. For discussion purposes, let's assume the estimated dollar value for this phase of the effort was approximately $20 million. Under any circumstance, this is considered a major acquisition. As stated earlier, is the dollar value commensurate with the project effort?

Based on acquisition regulatory guidance, can you obtain phone quotes, or follow the simplified acquisition threshold guidelines? Are funds readily available in the prescribed amount to start, complete, or used various option methods due to lack of available funds? These considerations are a part of the overall scheme in determining acquisition strategies for a project. In this example, the project is mission critical, highly complex, and has a high dollar value.

(4) Contractor Availability: The final area considered in determining Acquisition Strategy is the availability of contractors who have the capability to perform the necessary tasks of the project. The key is whether there are contractors that possess the "skills and equipment" to perform the requirements

of the project. Therefore, is it safe to say there may be a select number of contractors with the necessary skills to perform the requirements of the job? There are numerous ways to make this determination as it applies to any new project. The teaching point is the contractor pool (local/nationwide) plays an important aspect in the final acquisition method used for each project.

It is important to note some areas within the country have a greater number of contractors than other areas. This is true when it comes to small business and/or 8(a) companies. Some locations have a greater number of HUBZone Companies, Woman-owned Small Businesses, or Service Disabled Veterans Owned Small Businesses. This can be the case when there are a small number of only certified small businesses who can meet the needs of the federal government small business goal requirements. This is important because of the additional costs any contractor will incur when performing or accepting jobs that are in another location. It's always cheaper to utilize local pool of contractors who are qualified and capable than utilizing contractors who are from other locations (to be discussed later).

It's now time to integrate the four factors associated in the decision making of determining acquisition strategy. The results of determining acquisition strategy of a project is to decide whether the effort will be advertised as "unrestricted"; e.g., open competition to all potential bidders or as a "small business" using one of the small business sub-categories.

The following guide can be used only as a template:

Unrestricted Project Characteristics	Small Business Set-aside Characteristics
Mission Critical	Non-Mission Critical *
Highly Complex	Not Complex *
High Dollar Value Effort	Low to Medium Dollar Value Effort
Limited Qualified Contractor Base	Available Qualified Contractor Base

(There may be instances whereby a project may be critical or non-critical depending on the magnitude of the effort. The distinction between the two must be viewed in a proper manner relative to the degree of mission essentiality and complexity.) *

For teaching purposes, using the above process, let's see how applying the four elements to a project and subsequently make the right determination relative to acquisition strategy:

Scenario #1:

The project is to remove rock pinnacles at various locations within the river basin. The project is mission essential and will have a tremendous economic effect on the entire nation due to the amount and variety of goods that are transported up and down the river from north to south with stops along the way at various ports. There aren't many contractors who can perform this job and potential contract value is significant. Local and state political interest has heightened and reached a level that they are now involved. The Project Manager has funding to cover the entire amount of the estimated cost of this effort.

> Acquisition Strategy Review: Project is mission critical, highly complex, high dollar value, and with limited contractors with required skillset. What is the acquisition strategy for this effort?
> Answer: Unrestricted

This example was very simple and followed specifically the elements that either make up one acquisition process or the other. However, it must be noted all projects aren't this clear relative to the four factors we discussed. There are projects that have some of the elements of an unrestricted requirement or one that could ultimately be classified as a small business set-aside. Therefore, the entire project team must be objective and look at the associated factors from the very onset of determining acquisition strategy. There are other factors involved, but I feel these are the four main elements. Let's do a few more scenarios before we move forward in our discussion.

Scenario #2:

The project consists of building a road, clearing, and grubbing, fence, tree planting, and trash removal. Dollar value to complete this effort is less than $1.5 million.

> Acquisition Strategy Review: This project is simple, not complex; low dollar value, not mission essential; and certainly, an abundance of small business contractors. What is the acquisition strategy?
> Answer: Small Business Set-aside (using 8(a) Business Development Program processes or one of the small business set-aside efforts)

Scenario #3:

The project consisted of building a dike, chevron, and bank stabilization alone mile marker 0 – 90 along the river. The estimated dollar value is $2.5 million. The Period of Performance (POP) is 365 days. Final plans and drawings are totally complete. There's a possibility of adding a second or third dike as a part of the procurement effort.

> Acquisition Strategy Review: This project is not highly complex; low to medium dollar cost, not mission critical, substantial risk with regards to safety and possible small businesses but many large business contractors with capability and expertise to perform this job.
> Answer: Unrestricted.

Although there are a combination of elements that dictate either an unrestricted or small business set-aside, the element of risk, location of the project, and 'possible' small business availability indicates this requirement serves the best interest to the government to be solicited as unrestricted.

The above scenarios are to provide a brief understanding on how acquisition strategy is determined. There are other integrated elements such as procurement history, results of "Sources Sought", as well as other acquisition processes that can be used by the review team to assist in making this type of acquisition decision. Just remember these four elements are basic guides and provide a simple tool in understanding how acquisition strategy can be determined. As a potential contractor to the federal government, it is imperative to understand what the term "unrestricted" and "small business set-aside" mean when reviewing a solicitation. [These four elements are based on the author's viewpoint.]

The second aspect referenced earlier in this section correlates to determining acquisition strategy referred to as Acquisition Strategy Determination or Rules of Engagement (RoE). There are basic rules within the FAR that has a direct effect on determining acquisition strategy for many projects that integrates the four basic elements previously discussed. Regardless of the type of project, there is definitive guidance included in the FAR that (in most cases) dictate acquisition strategy from a legal/contractual standpoint. There are a couple of areas to be aware when determining acquisition strategy utilizing the RoE concept.

There are two critical areas relative to RoE that fall under the auspices of the SBA program. Those two concepts/rules are: (1) projects previously approved by SBA to be in the 8(a) Business Development Program remain in the 8(a) Business Development Program and (2) in accordance with the Rule of Two. These two concepts or rules take precedence (in most cases) over the four areas previously discussed (mission critical, complexity, contractor base, and dollar value) in determining acquisition strategy. Let's briefly examine both rules:

(1) Projects in the 8(a) Business Development Program:

The underlying concept to understand when the determination has been made by the KO to offer a project to SBA for concurrence as 8(a) negotiated or competitive action, the project shall remain in the 8(a) Business Development Program. As an example, if a project (such as the construction of a road) was previously approved by the KO and SBA to be in the 8(a) Business Development Program, then any follow-on effort (similar in project scope) shall (or should) remain as a part of the 8(a)-program procured either as a negotiated or on a competitive basis.[13] This is under the assumption there is a qualified pool of 8(a) contractors available to perform this type of work. This has been a valuable process and has provided certified 8(a) contractors continuous opportunities going forward in the future. As a reminder, these contractors are certified to be in the 8(a) Business Development Program, but are they qualified to perform the work? I cannot over emphasize the importance of being a highly-qualified firm relative to any type of business you are in. It is the Chief of Contracting who has the final decision on acquisition strategy.

(2) Rule of Two:

In accordance with contract guidance in FAR states: "If there are two or more small businesses have performed these types of services in the past, the current project will be procured as a small business set-aside."[14] Again, you must remember sound judgement must be used when past data indicate there were two or more small businesses who had the capacity to perform a requirement. In basic federal contracting, every six months a "Sources Sought" is required regardless of previously determined acquisition strategy. "The Sources Sought may be seen on many contract opportunities posted on FedBizOpps, the place federal agencies advertise their upcoming contracts. A Sources Sought is not an actual bid or solicitation; instead, it's a solicitation of interest."[15] Just because there were two or more small businesses a year or two years ago, who could perform these services, current market conditions may have changed. Those small business firms may have gone out of business or could have been reclassified as a large business. The point of the matter, consideration must be given by the acquisition authorities to ensure proper channels are followed relative to projects in the 8(a) Business Development Program and utilization of the Rule of Two. Both processes are critical in determining proper acquisition strategy and one can see how the integration of analyzing a project from the standpoint of mission critical, contractor base, complexity and dollar value is considered in determining acquisition strategy.

Therefore, determining proper acquisition strategy provides small businesses ample opportunities to bid and compete for federal jobs. I know you may be thinking why is this important to you as a small business owner. As stated earlier, and I will continue to stress how valuable information is, the more information you acquire, the more knowledgeable you are regarding anything done in business and in life.

Since we understand Acquisition Strategy Determination and Rules of Engagement, let's review both processes and see when this decision is most critical. The below graph is a modified version of an "Acquisition Strategy Timeline."

PDT MTGS	S/SOUGHT	SYNOPSIS	RFP	AWARD
		ACQUISITION PROCESS		
				(modified)

Legend:

PDT MTGS – Product Delivery Team Meeting (group of team members from various branches/offices) within the organization lead by the Project Manager. Representatives may include personnel from Project Management, Contracting, Small Business, Construction, Engineering (to name a few).

S/SOUGHT – Sources Sought…advertised process by contracting done every six months on a reoccurring basis to determine a level of interest in the contracting community (in this example let's assume the sources sought is for this specific project). Sources Sought is a way of determining the level of interest in the business arena for a specific good or service.

SYNOPSIS – Contracting advertising a requirement on an open market as Unrestricted or Small Business Set-aside (using one or more of the socioeconomic programs)

RFP – Solicitation will be a Request for Proposal.

AWARD – Contracting Officer has completed the acquisition process up to the award process. (Note: this is only a modified example of the acquisition process timeline)

The question is: Where in the acquisition timeline is most important to the contractor (starting at PDT MTGS ending with contract AWARD)? Throughout years of asking this question to prospective contractor's many responses have been received and for assorted reasons. The critical point in any acquisition process is at the very beginning of the timeline. The PDT meetings is normally where or when the acquisition strategy is determined. Several meetings will occur during this early stage, but somewhere a group decision will be discussed and approved that will ultimately determine your opportunity of fulfilling the needs of the federal government. Oh, by the way, acquisition strategy has been known to be determined in hall ways, bathrooms, and even at the golf course! Again, the teaching point is to realize your fate as a potential contractor seeking an opportunity to work with the federal government is determined early in the acquisition process. It is critical and paramount the SBPM is present at these meetings and fighting for the project to be set aside in one of the small business categories. Therefore, any contractor must be proactive in marketing your capabilities to your target market. Take advantage of various Industry Days, Conferences, Business Meetings, Workshops, and other avenues, which allows an opportunity to communicate your qualifications, as well as your business objectives.

Let's take a break from the main discussion topics and digress a little to cover something very important to a small business owner. That area is understanding the definition and true meaning of "Target Market." Okay, we kind of touched bases earlier in the section call the "The Power of Critical Thinking" (exhibit #5), defining the Inside/Outside approach and the sub topic of Target Market. (Remember, throughout this book, I will constantly refer to previous topics and show how everything is interrelated in understanding the art of the hidden facts of working for the government). In many cases, most small businesses truly do not understand how to market themselves properly, because they choose the wrong area as their primary focal point.

My personal definition of Target Market is: identifying a potential business or segment of the federal government whose 20% of their workload meets or exceed 80% of what you do as a business organization. Wait a minute, this concept is not new, it's the old 80/20 principle! You know (as an example) 20% of the people own 80% of the wealth, or you can substitute this basic premise to any category you deem appropriate. The bottom line is simply 20% of something has 80% control or effect over something else. Well, it's not quite that simple. Anyway, you get the point. As a new contractor, this concept will have some type of effect on 80% of your organization in relation to your main product line. This will save you an unbelievable amount of time. As discussed earlier, time is something you can never get back, so make wise use of your time. Earlier in our readings we touched on ensuring our niche was in tuned with the needs of our target market, which provided a clear view of distinguishing the importance of the two concepts. However, it's imperative you fully understand these two important concepts because they are hidden within the process of identifying the proper area to target as a potential customer. Let's set the stage!

Scenario: You are an 8(a)-general construction contractor. Your company performs most services/functions within the civil construction arena; e.g., build roads, culverts, relief wells, and other services that fall into the construction area. You are certified as an 8(a), SDB, WOSB, HUBZone business entity. You've been in business for only three years and things are going somewhat smoothly. You have a small amount of heavy duty equipment on hand; bonding is low but strong enough, and you have teamed with a very solid small business as a subcontractor. Your primary place of business is in the same town as the federal organization who just happens to (you believe) be a suitable place to obtain contracting opportunities. So, what is your marketing approach toward this federal organization? Do you just call the POC (Small Business Program Manager/Contracting Office) at the organization and set up a meeting? No, here's hidden fact number one relative to Target Market...determine what type of goods/services the targeted federal organization need or provide. To make this determination, divide the organization into five categories and ensure that one of the sections include the type of work your organization perform at its highest level (in this case civil/construction). Better yet, ask the POC what are their five top functions that make up their entire organization and just make sure one is construction. For this example, the five-basic classification of functions are:

- o   Construction
- o   Architectural & Engineering (A&E)
- o   Dredging
- o   FUSRAP (environmental clean-up type services)
- o   Supplies/Services (support functions within the organization)

This information is vital in determining whether you have the right organization as a potential target market. Let's continue with the example. So, the Small Business person provides you with a breakdown of the amount of funds spent in each category. The data doesn't have to be exact because you are only trying to determine whether you are pursuing the right organization. Thus, the organization potentially could spend $25 million in A&E; $30 million Dredging; $45 million FUSRAP; $10 million Supplies/Services, and $50 million Construction. It's estimated the organization will spend/obligate approximately $160 million during the fiscal year (exhibit #7). Remember, information is knowledge and knowledge is power; power to make a better-informed decision. Graphically, the information is shown as:

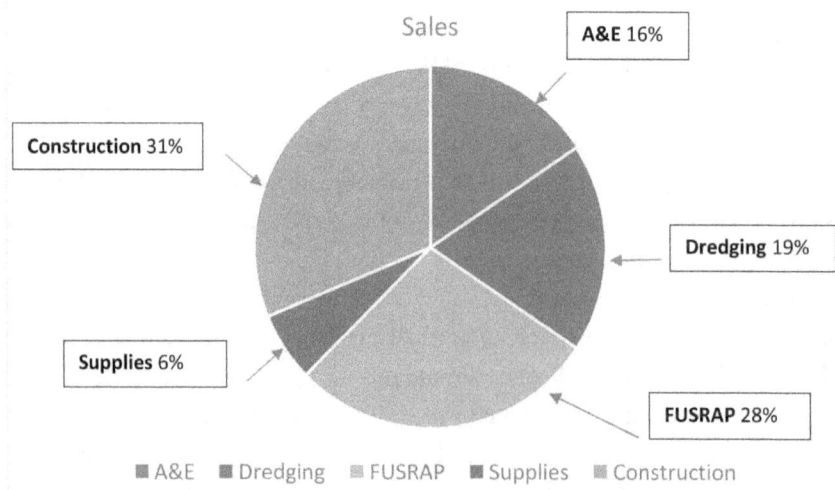

Organization Breakdown Exhibit #7

Estimated Total Dollar Obligation: $160M

Construction $50M	A&E $25M	Dredging $30M
FUSRAP $45M	Supplies/Services $10M	

The above chart indicates that construction is a major part of the needs of the organization. In percentage terms construction ($50M) is approximately 31% of the total projected obligated dollars for the entire year. This meet the 80/20 or 20/80 principle, but your analysis is not done. In construction, the federal government will obligate approximately 31% (exceeds 20% of the non-business line, which is other than construction) of the total amount of dollars for the entire year. The key issue is 80% of your entire business is directed toward construction efforts, which leaves 20% in another category. The relationship is simple: If any agency is exceeding 20% of your non-direct business line, this organization is a potential target market. Look at it in this manner, 80% of your business is in the construction arena and 31% (exceeding 20%) of your target market is directly in the construction arena. The question is: How much of the $50 million is geared toward small business and how much is set aside for the 8(a) Business Development Program (negotiated/competitive). This type of analysis will work in any area of business when determining a target market. In most cases, the small business owner has totally overlooked this type of analysis. This process is a straightforward way of saving a lot of time and effort from knocking on the wrong door. Remember, this information is available from any organization (exhibit #8) who is a potential targeted agency so make wise use of it! [Note: The total dollar obligations of an agency will have an impact of the percentages used in the 80/20% methodology.]

Another hidden fact that is overlooked is small business data that is available, but seldom used by small businesses. The federal government is your target market and the various departments (within the federal sector) have mandated small business goals. The goals and the process that the data is obtained may be different in some ways, but in every department, data is available through some acquisition data system. As an example, Department of Defense (DoD) uses a system call Federal Procurement Data System – Next Generation (FPDS-NG). "The FPDS-NG is a single source public users access to the spending patterns of the federal government's procurement data…FPDS-NG offers the public greater visibility and transparency into how the government is spending taxpayer money."[16] This is the procurement system that captures small business data in reportable categories that compare organization performance against assigned small business goals. The data is real-time information captured as contracts are awarded and posted within this system. For instructional purposes, data is tabulated on a continuous basis, however it is most useful at the end of the year because it provides a historical view of the organization's performance. As an example, the following is a sample graphic view of data captured at the end of Fiscal Year 16 for an organization:

Kentucky District
FY16

| | | | Area #1 Total |
| | | | Dollars Obligated |

Total US Business	Actions	Dollars	
US Business	1,304	$130,000,000	

Area #2   Area #3

Socio-Economic Category	Dollars	% Dollars	Goals	Variance
Small Business	90,000,000	69%	48%	21%
Small Disadvantaged Business	28,000,000	21%	16%	5%
8(a) Procedures	$19,000,000	15%		
Service Disabled Veteran S/B	$18,000,000	13%	7%	6%
Woman-Owned	$9,000,000	7%	8%	1%
HUB Zone	$4,000,000	3%	5%	2%

[sample data only] Exhibit #8

The fiscal year begins on 1 October (of that year) within the federal government.

The new fiscal year is now 1 October 2017, the information you want to review is data from fiscal year 2016. Let's assume the above data is from the Kentucky District year ending 2016.

Area #1: Total dollars awarded to LB $40 million and $90 million to SB.

Area #2: Percentage of dollars is the percentage of dollars awarded against each small business category relative to the total obligated dollars ($130 million) awarded during the year. The "Goal" category is assigned goals from Division/Headquarters to each District. Total dollars awarded in each category is measured against the assigned goals. Variance is the difference between actual dollars (percent) minus assigned goals.

Area #3: In review of the Variance category indicate this District supports small business (69% dollars awarded); having difficulty making WOSB and HUB-Zone SB goals; supports 8(a) Business Development Program by awarding 15%.

Question: Is this District a target market given the available data? The answer would be yes, due to the substantial number of dollars awarded in the small business category and the fact this organization did not meet/exceed their assigned goals in the WOSB and HUBZone categories. There could be reasons for the difficulty this District is having relative to meeting assigned goals. There may not be enough small businesses certified in either the 8(a) Business Development Program; HUBZone and/or classified as WOSB.

This type of data is available from various branches and segments of the federal government. If you have three or four organizations, you have identified as target markets utilization of this type of information is highly valuable. You can determine which organizations support small business, 8(a) Business Development Program, as well as indicators in areas exceeding small business goals. This chart indicates areas an organization may have difficulty locating certified and qualified socio-economic small businesses.

These are two subtle hidden facts that can really streamline your efforts to identify target markets. One process is a simple method of dissecting an organization to find if your capabilities are in line with the needs of the targeted organization, and second, is utilizing data readily available but is seldom used. The data contained in FPDS-NG is public information; all you have to do is ask for it from your small business POC. In either case, anytime you can save time, as well as money is a positive course of action to take.

4. Prime/Subcontractor Relationship

There are several methods that can be used by an 8(a) contractor toward obtaining the goal of getting an opportunity to work for the government. There is no clear-cut method or process that definitively ensures you and your company have chosen the right course of action, and even so, developed the right relationship with other contractor's in the business market. The question is: Which partnering relationship is going to provide the greatest opportunity to become a solid 8(a) firm that everyone is talking about?

Before we explore those potential avenues, let's revisit the needs of the government and the importance of an 8(a)-firm meeting those needs. The federal government is committed toward supporting small businesses in every way imaginable. There are guidelines and rules instituted within the system to ensure (where possible) priority is given to a small business.

Many organizations within the federal government have entered into basic agreements indicating small business set-asides would be the focus (when plausible) in obtaining goods and services. As an example (within the Army), mandated small business goals are assigned by higher Headquarters (HQ) and coordinated within each Division and District indicating a percent of every dollar obligated should be awarded to various small business categories. Therefore, an important underlying need of the federal government is to maintain a solid group of small businesses to assist in meeting assigned goals. (In normal circumstances, no one company or organization self performs 100% all work under contract. This is a key factor going further into discussion within this section.)

Specifically, let's clearly define the needs of the federal government stated earlier relative to small business goals. There are many Memorandum of Understandings (MOUs) with various agencies between the federal government and SBA. The extent and details of the agreement defines the level of support between that entity and the SBA. As an example, within the Army, there are six areas within a specific support agreement that is defined and paralleled to Federal Acquisition Regulation (FAR) Part 19 - 26, Socioeconomic Programs. These areas are Small Business (SB), Small Disadvantaged Business (SDB), Woman owned Small Business (WOSB), Service Disabled Veteran Owned Small Business (SDVOSB), Historically Underutilized Business Zone (HUBZone), Historically Black Colleges Universities, and other Minority Interests (HBCU/MI).

There are areas within the other MOU's that are important topics, but this section is focused on these six areas. Each Agency has assigned/approved goals assigned to each organization reflecting a percent of dollars allocated to each required small business category to meet or exceed the mandated SB goals. As an example, let's suppose a District has the following dollar percentages allocated to each category: SB (43%), SDB (18%), WOSB (5%), SDVOSB (3%) and HUBZone (10%). (HBCU/MI is a recommended area but not a mandated small business reportable goal.) For every dollar obligated, the minimum dollars awarded must meet/exceed the percent identified for each category based on total dollars obligated within that District or organization.

Let's take a closer look at various scenarios and define how this process works (small business goals process/exhibit #9):

Acquisition Process: Exhibit #9

Prior to a $3M contract award – Total Dollar Obligation $50 million

Goal:	SB (43%)	SDB (18%)	WO (5%)	Hub zone (10%)	SDVOSB (3%)
Target:	$21.5 M,	$9.0 M,	$2.5 M,	$5.0 M,	$1.5 M
Obligated:	$19.2 M,	$7.0 M,	$1.1 M,	$4.8 M,	$3.0 M
Percent:	38.4%,	14%,	2.2%,	9.6%,	6%

[Calculation example: Total District obligations equal $50 million multiplied by 43% (SB mandated goal; e.g., every dollar awarded must go to a small business entity ($21.5 million); 18% of $50 million equals $9 million awarded to SDB as a Target dollar amount and so forth for the remaining categories. Obligated dollars are total dollars currently obligated for each category. Percent of dollars obligated (SB – $19.2 million divided by $50 million equals 38.4% and so forth for the remaining categories). If your current percent of dollars executed (SB = 38.4%) is below the mandated goal amount (SB 43%), then for that area you are negative or "red" in terms of meeting your SB Goal requirements. Do the same for each business category. The difference between Target $ and Obligated $ shows the difference in dollars needed or exceeded relative to mandated goals.]

*Later a contract for $3 million was awarded. – Total Dollar Obligations increased to $53 million. * A contract was awarded to an 8(a) firm who happens to be certified as Women-owned and located in a HUBZone. In addition, the owner was hurt during the war and was certified as SDVOSB. The contract was a negotiated contract and was in the amount of $3 million. Remember, all 8(a) contracts under $4 million are negotiated contracts (or should be). The District's total dollar obligation total was $50 million.

After contract award the total District's dollar obligations goes up to $53 million. Each of the SB categories are increased by $3 million respectively… e.g., small business +3.0 million; SDB +3.0 million; 8(a) category +3.0 million; HUBZone +3.0 million; woman-owned +3.0 million and SDVOSB +3.0 million; Current Total Dollar Obligations $53 million

Goal:	SB (43%)	SDB (18%)	WO (5%)	Hub zone (10%)	SDVOSB (3%)
Target:	$22.7 M,	$9.5 M,	$2.6 M,	$5.3 M,	$1.5 M
Obligated:	$22.2 M,	$10.0 M,	$4.1 M,	$7.8 M,	$6.0 M
Percent:	42%,	18.8%,	7.7%,	14.7%,	11.3%

Results: The award of one contract in the amount of $3 million to a contractor with multiple certifications in various small business categories immediately has an impact on the federal agency's ability to meet/exceed its small business goal requirements.

It is obvious the federal government is the biggest supporter when it comes to providing opportunities to small and large businesses. We've scratched the surface when it comes to mandated small business goal requirements, but what is the best course of action for the 8(a) firm to take in support of this mega organization called federal government? It's a known fact, that no one business organization can 100% perform all the functions under one contract agreement. In most instances, something or some functions must be subcontracted to other businesses to accomplish the mission. As an 8(a) firm, there are two primary basic avenues available providing the greatest opportunity for success working for the federal government.

The first recommended process is to operate as a (1) "Prime" contractor, followed by (2) developing another partnering relationship called a "Joint Venture (JV)." Your long-term goal is to self-perform as much of the work as possible utilizing your own personnel and equipment. Do not exclude the fact you can always perform at the subcontract level, but your focus should be at the prime level. Before both avenues are explored, let's review some of the concerns or the overall perception of the capabilities of an 8(a) firm:

(a) 8(a) contractors don't perform their percentage of work as required as a Prime contractor. (Per regulatory guidance, construction prime contractors must perform 15% of the work; service contractor 50%)

(b) 8(a) contractors are a "pass through" …Once the contract is awarded and signed, the subcontractor basically performs all the work. The 8(a) firm doesn't show up at the job site or very little resulting in minimal performance – this is the biggest problem confronting 8(a) firms.

(c) 8(a) negotiated contracts are higher than competitive contract actions, so why utilize this process.

(d) Work provided by 8(a) firms are of less quality.

(e) 8(a) perceptions of receiving 8(a) certifications automatically mandates federal organizations to set-aside projects/requirements for them despite their lack of capabilities (certified but not qualified).

(f) 8(a) firms don't have the bonding capacity to meet contract requirements (construction contracts).

(g) 8(a) firms have little business acumen or lack thereof.

(h) 8(a) firms are only qualified to work in a restricted location or area.

(i) 8(a) firms are uneducated relative to federal rules, regulations, and guidelines.

These are some but highly important viewpoints of most 8(a) firms as a viable business entity. It is obvious the underlying concerns when it comes to performance by the 8(a)-prime contractor is less than desirable. This observation is based on many years of experience and participating in meetings both internal and external within various organizations. Is there any malice between those who make these types of remarks or is this reality? Regardless of anyone's personal viewpoint, this ideology relative to 8(a) contractors, must be addressed and changed. In the media and other forms of business networks, various small business organizations have been victimized (in one way or another) by this type of scrutiny. Is this fair? That's the million-dollar question. There are many instances when the 8(a), woman-owned, Veteran (including SD-VOSB) and/or any of the small business entities justly deserved this type of criticism. Any of the viewpoints (stated above) have a direct effect on performance and how they are viewed in the business environment. Yes, whether you want to hear it or not, many small business firms are not meeting the expectations required of them. Everyone involved is somewhat responsible for the perception of the 8(a) firm. Every time an 8(a) firm fails to perform in any magnitude directly affects the perception of the next firm who's trying to do the right thing. To all small businesses and especially 8(a) firms throughout the country, stop playing games with the system for personal capital gain!

Let's get back on track! To reiterate, there are two basic avenues (there are others) I feel are the best course of action to pursue as an 8(a) firm, which are performing as a Prime Contractor (working with a suitable subcontractor) and the second option is working together with another company under the parameters of the Joint Venture Agreement. Let's explore the parameters of the second alternative… "Joint Venture."

5. Joint Venture (JV)

Joint Venture Facts: "As required by regulation, to enter into a JV with any firm, the 8(a) firm (as a prime) must have a Mentor Protégé Agreement on file and approved by SBA, unless rules have changed. This program encourages private-sector relationships to be developed with the overall purpose of teaching, assisting and providing a sense of direction to the 8(a)-firm relative to participating and performing contract opportunities. Since it has been established that a Mentor Protégé Agreement must first be approved and in place before entering into a JV arrangement, are you now ready to reap the benefits of this program called "JV?"[17] [Same as Mentor Protégé program, the parameters and guidelines of JV program can be read by visiting the SBA's homepage; rules may have changed after book publication.]

Some of the benefits of entering into a JV agreement in support of government contracting are as follows:

(1) "The experience of the Mentor (in the JV arrangement) can be included as part of the 8(a) qualifications when consideration is given to a contract vehicle or acquisition proposal review.

(2) Up to three (3) contracts can be performed under the same JV arrangement (negotiated and/or competitive contract awards) within duration of two (2) years.

(3) Performance risk of the JV extremely low regarding failure and acting as the Prime contractor.

(4) Provides government entity another avenue to meet/exceed small business goal requirements."[18]

The above are four main reasons I concluded (there are others) JV agreements are beneficial to government organizations who have small business mandated goals or have an acquisition process that must be followed. Let's take a closer theoretical look at the above reasons and determine why they are important to you as an 8(a) firm.

Most 8(a) firms are completely uninformed when it comes to the importance of the qualification processes of the subcontractor as it relates to their overall performance capability as a prime contractor. The skills, qualifications, personnel, tools, machinery, experience, etc. of the mentor can be reviewed as part of the 8(a)-prime contractor's experience as long as the newly formed partnership is still majority owned/operated by the 8(a) firm (51% of the JV must be in the name of the 8(a) firm. A major benefit is to ensure credit can be given to the federal government on related small business goals).[19] This process, or business structure, has been proven to be successful in the business world and has in many cases been the only way an 8(a) firm would have an opportunity to compete for a project or obtain a negotiated contract. The JV agreement is a great way to benefit both entities for the short and long-term basis.

This is one of my own personal concerns when it comes to any JV arrangement of this nature. What is the overall intent of the other contractor working with the 8(a) firm under the JV guidance and direction? Many times, I've witnessed the company working with the 8(a) firm is not in this business relationship for the long run. Personally, I look at the JV arrangement from another perspective. If as a prime contractor (8a firm) cannot (at least) independently perform 15% of the work under a construction contract, the overall capability of that 8(a) firm is highly suspect. As required by the parameters of a 8(a) JV Member must perform 40% of the work performed by the JV (which includes work performed by non-8(a) member and any of its affiliates at any contracting tier)[20] I've seen situations when the 8(a) firm does not have the skillset in an area (such as in construction) and enter into a JV arrangement to perform a construction contract. I chose 15% as a target percentage because this is the required amount for an 8(a) firm to perform as a prime contractor on a negotiated contract. The JV agreement may require more in terms of work performed by the 8(a) firm and affiliate. This type of arrangement is very suspect. This is a concern that is (1) difficult to determine and (2) ultimately can hurt the reputation of the 8(a) firm, as well as other minority firms trying to do the right thing. So, 8(a) contractors please beware! The JV agreement is only to be used as a short-term learning process going forward into the future. There are review processes in place to determine the capability of the 8(a) contractors, however, in actuality their overall performance ability is highly suspect and questionable.

It must be understood there is a defined set of initiatives, goals, and objectives in the Mentor Protégé Agreement. Beware of the true intent of the Mentor! There are "warning signs" after the first job has been completed or even before there is a job at all. How does the 8(a) firm recognize there are concerns while working with another firm either under the JV arrangement or as a prime/subcontractor?

The following are factors that are clear "red flags" the 8(a) owners should be aware relative to the JV and Mentor/Protégé agreement based on the Mentors actions:

(1) Lack of Interaction: Once the agreement has been written and confirmed (even after the first job was done), there are many times when the Mentor shows a lack of interest in the dialogue occurring among the two entities.

- o Are you (as the 8(a) firm) always calling for a meeting to discuss internal process and functions defined in the agreement?
- o Are you (alone) finding project opportunities in the marketplace?
- o Is the partnering agreement followed in accordance to the milestones or timeline that was originally agreed upon?
- o Are meetings continuously rescheduled or delayed?

Hopefully, you can understand my point when it comes to interaction among both parties. These are areas the Mentor should be leading, directing, supervising, and coordinating on a continuous and smooth basis. Anything less than described above is unacceptable and is a clear warning sign that maybe your best interest is not being taken on a serious note. It must be totally understood from the 8(a)'s standpoint…you have something to bring to the table, which is the 8(a) certifications and its distinct advantages. Caution, the other party (Mentor) is fully aware of this golden opportunity. The certifications you have are only parts of your qualifications, but your ability to perform is just as important. Your goal is to become a full fledge self-performing organization with the objective of reaching your maximum potential. Don't misunderstand this statement, this situation happens more than you imagine and has a massive impact on your short/long term survival in the business world.

(2) Negative Comments are Indicators: This is a classic case of maybe it's time to move on and locate another partner. Whenever the following phrases are stated somewhere/anywhere in the conversation…Beware!

You shouldn't go for this effort (Why shouldn't we pursue this project? Remember, your qualifications are now based on the qualifications of both organizations.)

- a. You're not qualified (Same as above, if the Mentor is qualified, then you as an 8(a) firm is qualified.)
- b. Last minute withdrawal from bidding. This may happen in some cases when specifications have change or there may have been a

last-minute change in the magnitude of the basic effort; should be the exception rather than the rule.

c. All of a sudden, the Mentor can't be reached via telephone on a continuous basis. Lately it appears the Mentor is more difficult to contact. Phone calls are being returned several days, weeks later.

d. There are no bidding opportunities only those you seek out. There are subcontracting opportunities working with a large business*. Every large business must submit a subcontracting plan prior to contract award so you should be a part of this business opportunity. [*Any large business who wins a government contract must submit a subcontracting plan including various categories of socioeconomic business…later discussion.][21]

f. Available equipment and personnel assignments. Most minority firms don't have adequate equipment needed for construction purposes (or whatever the supplies/goods/services rendered) and certainly doesn't have the financial capability to obtain necessary related equipment.

(3) Detailed Teaming Agreement: This is another tough pill to swallow. There have been many 8(a) firms who entered into Teaming Agreements that were so tightly written the 8(a) firm was a total prisoner and under seized by the other partner. This process is what I called having every "i" dotted and every "t" crossed. Under these circumstances, the non-8(a) firm is ensuring all risk, liability, and concerns have been covered in the agreement. Do you know what they are really telling you, the 8(a) firm? They do not trust you in any capacity and they are only in it for the money. What ever happened to the "good old days" when there was a firm hand shake and a pat on the back was as good as any written contract? I'm certainly not indicating an agreement must be this loose, but it doesn't have to be 100% or 95% in favor of the other business. Realistically, there should be protective language in the agreement, but certainly any and everything you can think of shouldn't be covered in the agreement. Beware of this type of agreement and pay close attention to the wording of the language. In the past, I have agreed to review Teaming Agreements

for the 8(a) firms prior to final signature by both parties. As a safe-guard, it is always a good business practice to have an independent third-party review your agreement and look for those areas that are just too overbearing. If everything must be covered in this agreement...stop now and run! Get away from that contractor as fast and quickly as possible.

Just as there are clear warning signs, there are basic areas you want to ensure are covered. Before we proceed, it must be noted there are differences between JV, Mentor Protégé Program, and a Teaming Agreement. Brief discussions have been made relative to JV and Mentor Protégé Agreements (which are interconnected), but there is another safeguard contained in a good Teaming Agreement. It must be understood in a Contractor Teaming Arrangement means an arrangement in which:

(1) "Two or more companies form a partnership or joint venture act as a potential prime contractor; or

(2) A potential prime contractor agrees with one or more other companies to have them act as its subcontractors under a specified government contract or acquisition program."[22] You may say these requirements are similar in nature to the parameters of the JV and Mentor Protégé program and you are certainly correct. However, there are things you must be aware!

Just as discussed above, there are huge problems when it comes to detailed language in a Teaming Agreement, but there are (at a minimum) basic requirements (clauses) or areas that should be included. Here are top ten areas to include in a Teaming Agreement:

1. Designation of a Prime Contractor and a Subcontractor
2. Purpose and Scope of the Agreement
3. Incorporation by Reference of a Non-Disclosure Agreement
4. Protection/Allocation of Technical Data/Inventions/Patents
5. Division of Responsibilities between the Prime Contractor and the Subcontractor and Definition of the Relationship of the Parties
6. Duration of the Agreement and Termination Provisions
7. Limitation of Liability

8. No Assignment without Consent
9. Exclusivity/Non-Competition
10. Identify the Nature and Key Terms of the Expected Subcontract between Team Members

All ten areas are clearly essential elements that should be addressed. There is one section I feel separates itself from the other topics. Go ahead and take a guess at which one of the above areas you feel is most important. There is no right or wrong answer. The most significant segment of the Teaming Agreement is section 9, which is "Exclusivity/Non-Competition." All teaming agreements should address at a minimum those ten areas, but they do not have any substance if some terms of the agreement are only for the major subcontractor and not inclusive for both parties. By definition, a Mentor can have several Proteges , but a Protégé can only have one Mentor. In some cases, per regulation, a Protégé can have up to two Mentors during its business' lifetime.[23] I'm in complete disagreement with this type of working relationship between a Protégé and Mentor relative to the JV agreement. A true teaming agreement will be based on integrity, understanding, and loyalty to each other with one mission, and one goal resulting in one team. To me, this arrangement resembles a marriage. This way of thinking may not be in accordance with the definition of what a JV consist or Mentor/Mentee agreement, but the subliminal elements of the Teaming Agreement must be contained in the JV agreement. The Teaming Agreement is a subset of guidance contained in the JV agreement. Each of the various elements are interrelated in any of the three areas…JV Agreement, Mentor/Protégé Agreement, and a Teaming Agreement. Any contractor can form a Teaming Agreement regardless of their 8(a) or non 8(a) status. You must ensure that the basic language is predicated on a relationship that is exclusive between the 8(a) firm and the other contractor. As you can clearly see, the purpose of the JV agreement is an important way 8(a) contractors can increase opportunities within the federal government, but only if it is used properly and by the rules identified above.

6. Prime/Subcontractor Arrangement

Prime/Subcontractor Arrangement: As stated earlier within this book, if you want to be a prime contractor you must act and think as prime contractor. Your short and long-term goal should be as clear today as it was when you first decided to go into business. As a prime contractor, the decisions made are based on how well you have prepared yourself and your company for the long-term. It's understandable that it takes time to grow, but it doesn't preclude anyone from having higher goals and expectations.

You are a prime contractor!

CHAPTER 2
BUSINESS PRESENTATION (Module #2)

There's one thing that appears to be confusing in the analysis of the four key areas of the business modules: Business Theory, Business Preparation, Business Functionality, and Business Presentation, as discussed herein. Just as in any process, procedure, or function, what is the pecking order relative to the degree of importance as defined within each area? Is it important to consider there may be stepping stones in every sense of the word when you are trying to comprehend the pit falls of business processes? It's clear the processes of Business Preparation and Business Functionality are contiguous to each other as it relates to proposal preparation and performance in the field. Is it more important to understand the theoretical (theory) aspect of business or how do you (as a business owner) present your company to your potential target market? There are a lot of major and minor elements that are found in each area that are critical to the overall success of these two areas but also to the entire gamut of all four of the process modules. Personally, to decide the prioritization of learning and understanding Business Theory or Business Presentation is like picking the winner of the Kentucky Derby...it's too close to call!

Before we get into the perils of understanding Business Presentation, let's take a closer look at both areas (business theory/presentation) as to which area is first on the priority list of knowledge expansion and comprehension. Let's say, for discussion purposes, you have a full understanding of Business Presentation, but you are clueless (to a certain degree) on the various processes discussed earlier regarding Business Theory. This isn't good and by the way you have just blown a fantastic opportunity because you and your firm didn't understand the interlocking process of Business Theory as it relates to the very first meeting between you and your target market. What about the reverse actions of these two business modules...e.g., the initial interaction between your firm and target market is great! Everything done regarding the introductory or initial face to face meeting is going smoothly. Conversely, you are missing a vital point of in-depth knowledge behind the basic guidelines of the various facets of Business Presentation. It's important I touch based on these simple but sometimes complex modules due to the interrelationship one has on the other. Over the years, I witnessed firms make this mistake repeatedly. Either they were adequate in understanding in Business Theory and weak in Business Presentation, or vice versa. Notice I used the adjective "adequate" to measure an 8(a)-firm's knowledge understanding the underlying principles and concepts of business.

Approximately 99% of contractors I've met (in one form or another) were subpar in terms of knowledge and understanding business acumen. I'm specifically referring to understanding as it relates to federal government processes and related contracting knowledge. This is the norm which insinuates the knowledge level of business owners is substandard when it comes to government contracting. This is not negative, but how can you fault anyone for "not knowing" the things they don't know? Hopefully, the need to understand one concept verses the other (in one form or another) hasn't been over whelming, but the point of this matter is simple: Know them both prior to meeting any prospective business client. The bottom line is clear, don't go forward into the business world without knowing both modules to the greatest extent possible. If you as an 8(a) business owner are not versed in both areas, you have lost the war even before the battle has begun.

Military training continues in preparation for the unknown in Iraq

Training and preparation are the key to survival in war and peace time!

Regardless of the training and preparation,
there has to be time for relaxation!

Now that I've muddled the water with what is important, just remember understanding Business Theory has a slight advantage over Business Presentation, but at the end of the day, they are essential elements in understanding the finite details of being a successful businessman or woman. All four modules are critical to your degree of success, or possibility of failure, due to a lack of understanding.

Therefore, what is meant by Business Presentation and why is it an essential element in the overall business scheme for 8(a) firms to master? As stated earlier in the readings, "Your first impression is your best impression is your last impression." In simple terms, this means the very first time when you made an appointment to visit your client, which in this case could be DoD, state, city or county. Let me re-state the meaning and importance of doing your homework. As discussed earlier, prepare yourself and learn as much as you can about the organization you are going to visit.

Let's assume you have done your homework and your team is well-prepared about the needs of your target market. In other words, your knowledge base regarding Business Theory is between acceptable to outstanding. Each member has a clear understanding of going forward with your initial meeting.

The following are two important steps to implement relative to Business Presentation (These steps are not necessarily cut in stone and should be modified to meet your own basic strategy).

Step #1 – Presentation Format:

In forty years of experience in contracting and sixteen years directly as the Small Business Program Manager, nearly all small businesses have major flaws when it comes to doing a presentation to their target market. In this sense, I'm referring to a presentation that is done in hard copy, DVD presentation, and verbal. What is the major problem? It's a combination of things that invariably reduces the effectiveness of their presentation. In today's environment, social media has taken over. Whether it's a combination of Facebook, Tweets, Teleconference, and/or some form of video communication, the small business owner has not taken advantage of this process. All presentations are based on image. Was the presentation professional, well-organized, informative, or just another boring group of individuals with nothing to say? These questions must be in your mind regardless of your target market. It doesn't matter, you will get one shot at impressing your audience. Don't blow it and stay focused!

The correct terminology for this segment is referred to as Team Dynamics. The composition of Team Dynamics is a combination of group/team members and their roles; the type of company you are presenting such as Prime contractor only; combination of Prime and Subcontractor; Joint Venture; etc. Although we covered the basic definition and composition of these areas, they are a major part of critical elements in the Business Presentation Module. Other areas covered is the role of the Bonding Agent, Technology, Website development and utilization of References.

Let's lead off discussing the basic type of presentations that I've witnessed over the years that should be avoided:

Wrong Presentation Format
o   Individual Presentation (one person/an army of one). This is the least effective of any presentation I've seen. This person has all answers relative to his organization, as well as knowledge about

your organization. If you really want to have the door shut in your face, use this approach (this is under the assumption your company is a small organization).

   o   Group Presentation (one person/owner doing all the talking). This is a common way most companies follow. There may be two or three individuals within the group, but the only knowledgeable individual is the owner. This is an ineffective approach. Remember, you are trying to impress and the best way to do it is through strength in numbers.

   o   Group Presentation (subcontractor/individual on the subcontractor team is doing all the talking and answering many of the questions). This, too, can be the beginning of the end relative to an opportunity. This approach indicates the prime contractor (in this case 8(a) firm) has little knowledge of his own capabilities and subsequently is a pass-through (the subcontractor, perhaps, will perform all or most of the work). This is not a good image to portray.

The above scenarios address negative presentation formats from an organizational perspective, but there is the presentation itself. It's important to understand the dynamics of people relative to presentations, but let's examine the contents of the presentation and the way it is presented. This refers to a verbal presentation; presentation on paper; presentation via PowerPoint (slide/DVD); and PowerPoint (paper). Let's look at each one of the above:

   o   Verbal. A presentation that is 100% verbal can be successful and may have a positive effect on your target audience. However, in this case, the group must be knowledgeable of both their organization and their target audience. Each member of your group must have a clear understanding of what you're trying to accomplish during the presentation. Relying on a complete verbal process is a risky method to use. I can't totally rule against doing a verbal (only) presentation, but there are pitfalls...just beware!

   o   Presentation on Paper (qualification briefs). This is the most common type of presentations I've seen over the years in concert with the individual and/or group approach discussed earlier in this section. Personally, I know standard teaching techniques from various learning institutions used this approach as a way of communicating skills/abilities and experience of 8(a) contractors. In addition, the standard "elevator pitch" is a part of the presentation effort. This approach has value if it is not overstated and convoluted with information that is overbearing. You must be careful not to include everything done and everything you are proposing to do. One thing is for sure, the attention span of most individuals is low relative to reading a lot of information. To be honest, once you leave the office, most qualification briefs are put in the trash can. Some organizations retain this information in some sort of repository. Just ensure your qualification brief is succinct, direct, and have an equal balance of words and pictures. I won't get into the necessity for equal balance between words/pictures, but it can make an enormous difference on the overall effectiveness of your presentation.

o   PowerPoint Presentation (slide/DVD). This is my most preferred method of doing a business presentation. (Later, during the very end of this section, I will provide you with a sample presentation I found to be highly effective.) If possible, request some sort of media device to be used for the PowerPoint presentation. However, be very careful in the way your presentation is formatted relative to words and pictures. The main objective is to fully, clearly and with confidence, cover the primary areas showing your companies capabilities in relation to the needs of your target audience. Again, everything reverts to needs and capabilities. (As stated earlier, we shall cover a detailed presentation.)

Step #2 - Pre-presentation Meeting:

At a minimum (the day before), there should be a meeting to go over the agenda of your presentation, as well as define "HOW" the format will be followed. Discuss your presentation in full detail. There are several ways you may present your presentation. I intentionally wanted to talk about this area second in relation to the types of presentation format, so you can have an idea of the discussion that will occur the day before the actual meeting. It doesn't matter if you have this meeting one day, two days or three days prior to the actual meeting, but as long as the Pre-presentation Meeting is held.

We should (at this moment) understand the text book definition of Business Presentation. Let's explore the hidden facts of this section and the importance of underlying functions that generally results in a failed presentation. Let's pick the best parts of doing a presentation the correct way. For the remaining of this area discussed, let's assume the following Team Dynamics:

> Right Presentation Format:
> - (a) Going to do a group presentation with the owner of the company, project manager, key technical employee, and your bonding agent.
> - (b) Presentation format is the PowerPoint (DVD) method either using your computer or in a room with video capability. (If possible, I really prefer the room with video capability because it's more professional.)
> - (c) And, of course, the pre-presentation meeting was conducted.
> - (d) Presenting your company functioning as a Prime Contractor (only).
> - (e) All team members are briefed, well-informed, and prepared.
> - (f) The 8(a) firm is totally committed to self-performing with equipment, laborers, and operators.

The stage is now set utilizing the elements of Team Dynamics as related to Business Presentation. The following is an example of a presentation designed as a modified version for the Business Presentation Template (slide #1 through slide #17):

Sample Presentation

Slide #1

#1 Title: Is there anything peculiar about the title? Let's go back and have a refresher when it comes to company titles. The importance of your business title/name was discussed in the Business Theory Module. When a business is started, one of the important considerations is your company's name. The above title is clear, succinct and portrays a group of people with the same common goal. I could have easily used the name, GL Chatman Construction Company, Glenn Chatman Construction Company, etc. Be careful and ensure you have the correct name/title for your company.

#2 Picture: It is safe to add a picture and location of your business. Be careful not to show a picture of the target agency. You cannot show a picture of the federal agency, which may give the appearance of endorsing you from a legal standpoint. To be safe, always provide a copy of your presentation in advance to the organization you are presenting, as well as have your own legal staff review the information. In some cases, include in your email (cover letter) requesting permission to proceed with this type of presentation.

#3 Location/Date: Always add the location of the presentation and date. [Note: each slide is followed by a specific narrative explaining the contents of that slide.]

(Note: The words Who, What, How and Why are four areas that you must identify):

- Chatman Construction Company (who)
- Types of Equipment (what)
- Performance Work Plan (how)
- Efficiency/Effectiveness (why)

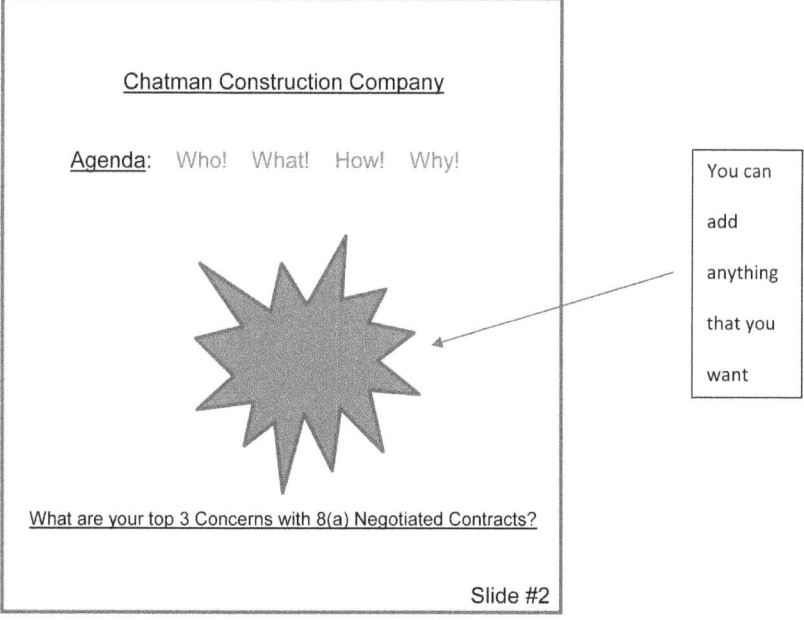

Slide #2 Discussion Notes:

Agenda: The question of Who, What, How, and Why is the best Agenda you can have. The reason is based on explaining to your target audience the meaning of each of these areas. Most presentations have an agenda based on specific functions rather than creating an agenda broad enough clearly emphasizing the type of company you have created. In any presentation format, provide a brief overview of each area of the agenda:

- Who: Provide the audience with information relative to your company's background and any specific data that will set you apart from other 8(a) firms. You may have added a federal section to your organization or information related to the timing of your 8(a) certifications.
- What: Provide basic information on the type of services and/or capabilities of your company from an overview perspective.
- How: This is the most crucial element of the Agenda. The "how" is relative to performance. You will explain how you are going to perform the work for your customer.
- Why: This part of the Agenda indicates why working with your 8(a) firm results in a win/win situation for both parties.

You must remember, only indicate those four areas as your talking points and make sure don't get "into" either of those areas in detail. A complete explanation will be provided within each slide that is related to that specific area.

What are the top three concerns with 8(a) Negotiated Contracts? This question must be asked to the audience during this point in your presentation. It's critical you ask this question now, rather than later. This allows you to cover the concerns of contracting and other agency personnel later during your presentation. This question is directed to the Chief of Contracting and if she or he is not available, it is asked to the most senior contracting person in the room. Don't get into discussions as to why these three areas are the most problematic; instead, make a note and write it down. As a result, 99% of all answers to this question is going to be:

- Performance or lack thereof by the 8(a) firm—8(a) firm does not perform
- Price—8(a) firm's prices are too high
- Location—do not have a bona-fide place of business (Again, bona-fide office is based on law; any 8(a) firm must have an official office located in the area where they are working.)

Performance and unreasonable prices are always two of the three areas, but I want to make sure that all individuals understand why location is also a major key working with 8(a) firms.

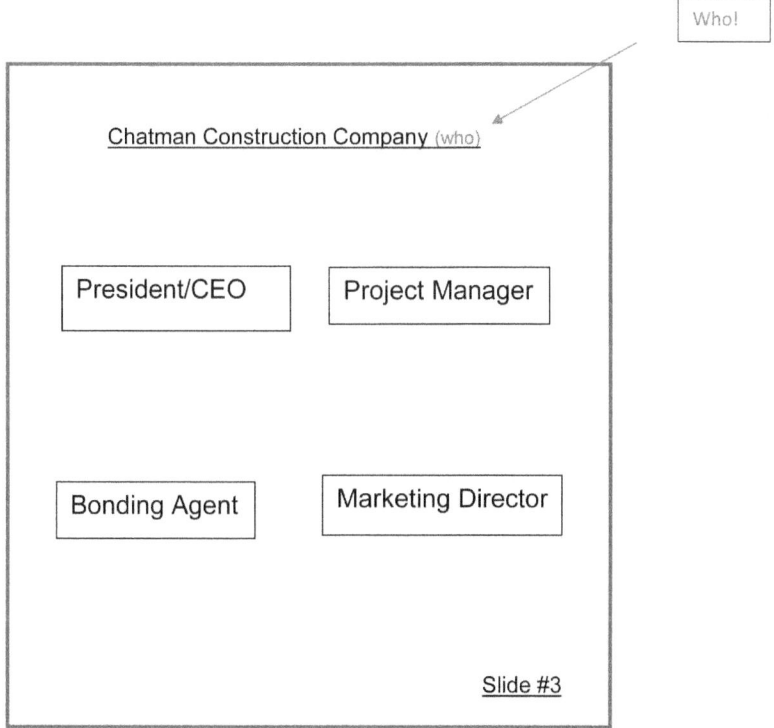

Who!

Chatman Construction Company (who)

President/CEO

Project Manager

Bonding Agent

Marketing Director

Slide #3

Show Pictures of the Four Individuals

Slide #3 Discussion Notes:
Within any presentation format, feel free to add no less than three but not to exceed five individuals as key personnel in your discussion. If you are proficient in PowerPoint, you want to add a phase-in transition element to each picture starting with the President/CEO of the company:

Title: Take a close look at the title on this slide. This is the beginning of the start of your Agenda outlined in slide #2. The title has in smaller caption – 'who' in parentheses.

At the end of the title is the start of following the Agenda. You can point this out to the audience, something to this effect: "This is who we are as a part of the Chatman Construction Company."

Remember, it is the little things in a presentation or speech that can result in major changes to your organization.

President/CEO: Start with the President of the company. It's imperative to get off to a good start! Provide information as to who you are; where you are located; and most importantly thanking (again) the organization for this opportunity. Be brief but succinct (each person tells his/her own story).

Project Manager: This individual should provide a brief background on his experience as a project manager and focus on how his crew is going to perform in the field. FLASH note: "How" you are going to perform was a part of the basic Agenda. Anywhere during the presentation (when you get a chance) reinforce the performance aspect of your company…take that opportunity!

Director of Marketing: This may or may not be one of your key personnel. If so, this person should stress why this agency is a major part of several target markets as potential clients. Let your Marketing person display his/her marketing skills!

Bonding Agent: If possible, always have or bring your Bonding Agent/ Representative with you to your presentation. Earlier you asked a critical question, which was: "What are the top three concerns with negotiating 8(a) contracts?" You received the top three answers, but I can assure you a close third answer behind Performance (first), Price (second), and Location (third) is bonding concerns. You can easily substitute Location with Bonding because both rank high in the priority list of major concerns. This is when, the Bonding Agent stresses his support for the 8(a) firm. This is when the Bonding Agent indicates the bonding capacity either on a single and aggregate levels. A smart and experience Agent will talk about the amount of "risk" or lack thereof associated in support of the 8(a) firm. The amount of risk is critical relative to the strength of your company's ability to bond any project.

This is another way of answering (up front) the question regarding bonding and the ability of the 8(a) firm to perform without issues and concerns.

The Bonding Agent is a critical part of your Team. As stated, "Don't leave home without him!" [Note: this is for construction requirements only.]

Appearance: Team appearance is an area most firms don't consider important.

Somewhere in the Business Theory Module, we discussed the importance of your first impression because you may not get a second opportunity to present yourself. I believe we can agree on this premise.

However, I recommend each team member dress for the occasion. If your company has a specific uniform, all members should be in that uniform. If not, wear business casual dress but stress that the gentlemen wear a jacket and females wear something professional and not revealing, or common business attire. Appearance is a critical part of acceptance as a professional, as well as indication of character, demeanor, and attitude.

This slide represents key team members and it allows each of them to present their roles, responsibilities and provide a comfort level to the target organization relative to their capabilities.

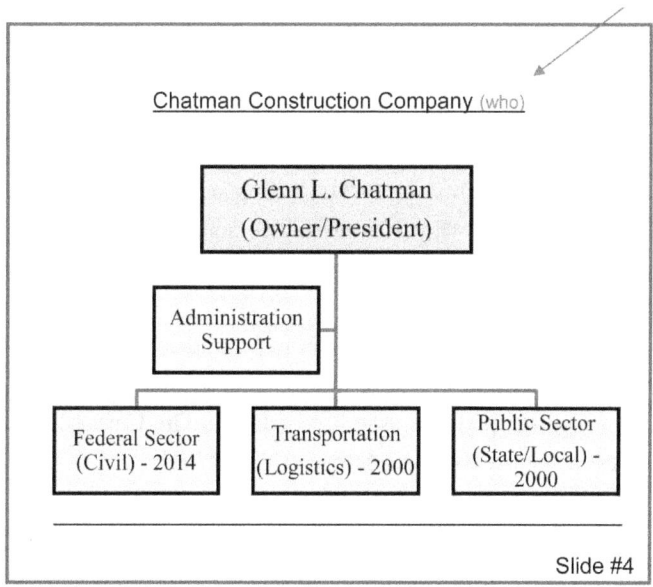

Slide #4 Discussion Notes:

Title: Still discussing "who" – Chatman Construction Company

Organizational Chart: This is another opportunity to display (organizationally) the structure of your company and the various entities that exist. In the above example, you can determine the company started a Federal Sector in 2014, which means they may be new to federal contracting but have been in existence as a company since 2000. So, beware! A company may have little experience when it comes to the federal market but may have utilized what was called the "The Power of Critical Thinking Approach" discussed in the Business Theory Module. This company probably hired personnel who knows the federal sector and have many years of experience and overall understands the federal government. Don't forget one important statement that was made earlier in this text…to work or be a part of federal sector opportunities you must understand the federal sector.

In this example, the owner surrounded himself with a Project Manager, Marketing Director, and other personnel who has many years of experience in federal government business functions and operations. The owner recognized the need to change. Therefore, he added an additional division to his business entity and elected to go outside his current structure to hire the right personnel in pursuit of government contracting opportunities. It's imperative as a business owner, to recognize the need for change, but make sure the right personnel are hired who have the knowledge, skills, and abilities to ensure you are now qualified, as well as certified to do business on the federal government level.

An organizational chart provides your target audience a clear picture of your business structure. Most importantly, it provides another chance to tie together those individuals who are your key personnel into the new roles they play in seeking government opportunities. [Your company is geared toward performance.]

Note: Before we go any further, you must understand each slide within this PowerPoint Presentation has a particular meaning and they are geared toward answering the question asked in slide #2. The Catch 22 is this: You asked the question of the top three issues in slide #2 relative to 8(a) negotiated concerns, but your presentation is already prepared in a manner to answer this question. You knew the answer to the initial question. This is referred to as the "Setup". Ask a question when you know the answer to the question prior to any response made or given. I used this approach many times when contractors came into my office.

This was a training tactic used to get the contractor to understand the importance of honesty, integrity, and don't try to have all answers to any question.

Anyone, can use this element of surprise whether it's business related or on a personal basis. In other words, don't talk too much about things that aren't relevant to the issue at hand!

Organizational Chart (Transportation/Logistics 2000): This is not a huge area of concern, but I must point out the importance of continuing to do what has gotten you through the rough and tough times. In the above chart, this owner has been in business since 2000 and I suspect was successful in the logistics business. There will come a time in business when things change, market change, and the overall dynamics of any business module require modification due to those factors. The smart owner slowly but surely integrates change in a manner that won't overwhelm the balance of his/her business foundation. There is a whole lot of truth to this premise that consistency and persistence pays off at a much greater rate and in a safe manner. Regardless of the change in your organization such as adding a new branch/division, always show some sort of chart that displays the structure of your company. Keep it as simple as possible but show the various components.

Slide #5 Discussion Notes:

Title: Still referring to "who" Chatman Construction Company, include the date of your certification:

HUBZone Building: This slide may not apply to you.

Your company may be 8(a), Woman-owned certified; 8(a) Woman-owned and HUBZone certified: or just Woman-owned certified. If you have forgotten the various socio-economical categories applicable to various small business areas, go back and review the section in Business Theory.

For teaching purposes, we shall assume this company is 8(a), small business, SDB, woman-owned and originally was not located in a HUBZone. Under these circumstances, this slide can be very impressive. We know the federal government has goals and one is certified under the HUBZone law; e.g., principle place of business must be in a HUBZone and 35% of employees must live in a HUBZone (along with other requirements). In the past there has been much concern whereby firms are stating they meet the law under HUBZone requirements relative to location and number of personnel, but in actuality after review reveals the organization does not meet the required standards.

In most cases, the HUBZone program has been affected over the years because of this behavior by various small business firms. Don't misinterpret what I'm saying, there are many firms who are doing the right thing. However, contrary to what have gone on in the past, what if a firm is truly trying to meet the HUBZone standards? What if the owner of Chatman Construction Company happened to buy a building in a HUBZone location and met all the required laws? I have known this to be a true situation, when the owner of a company did buy a building in a HUBZone location. The point is there are known small business owners who move or purchase a building in a HUB Zone location, and thereby becomes their Principle Place of Business. To be eligible for HUBZone certification and per regulation, an organization must:

- "be a small business (according to SBA standard)
- be owned and controlled at least 51% by U.S. citizens, or
- a Community Development Corporation, an agricultural cooperation, or an Indian tribe,
- be located within a "Historically Underutilized Business Zone and
- at least 35% of its employees must reside in a HUBZone" [24]

If your organization is fortunate to make this transition, this slide is highly important. This company has gone beyond the extra mile to take advantage of this type of move. In business, you must position your firm when any opportunity comes your way. In this case, the federal government may have a challenging time meeting and/or exceeding goal requirements in the HUBZone area. If this is the case, your organization has a big advantage over other small business firms who does not have this certification. I'm fully aware most small businesses cannot afford to take advantage of this situation. I cannot stress how important it is to pay close attention to changes and needs within the market.

The HUBZone certification provides this company contract opportunities under the 8(a) program and under the HUBZone set-aside program. It doesn't matter how this move is made as long as it becomes a major part of your presentation (if applicable). This indicates to your target audience you are a serious player and understands the small business process. This is the last part of the slide presentation discussing the "who" aspect of your company. If you want to add other slides, please do so but ensure the "who" is indicated in the slide title area.

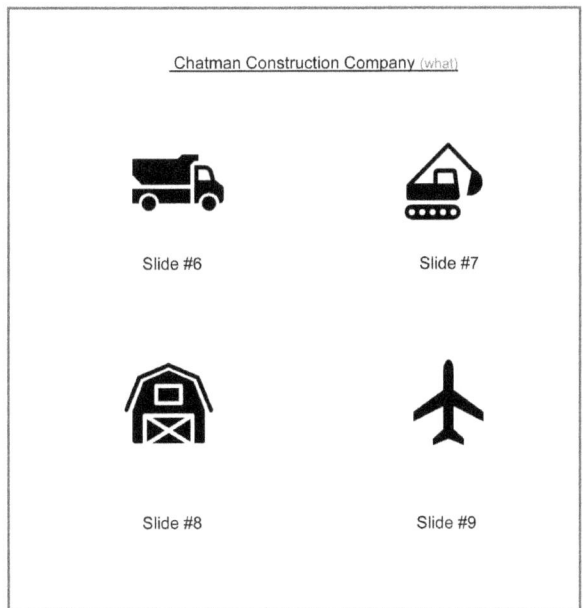

Slides #6 - #9 Discussion Notes:

Title: Now referring to "what" type of goods, services you are going to provide. In this section, provide several pictures of construction efforts you have done in the past (or the specific services that you are providing).

Slides: This is a perfect time to show any related projects you have completed either for the current organization, or any organization similar in nature. Here are points to remember:

- show pictures your company has performed similar work (work won on a competitive basis or on a negotiated basis)
- show pictures of equipment you own
- show laborers and operators who work for you (job site related)
- do not use the word "Construction Management or Construction Oversight" (this was discussed in the Business Theory Module. Stress clearly and succinctly your company self performs in all possible areas)

It is understandable most 8(a) firms don't have this capability…but this slide presentation is based on an 8(a) who is DOING IT THE RIGHT WAY! Most firms do not have the capital resources to take this course of action. Thus, the majority of 8(a) firms who are Partnering and/or have a JV arrangement have access to equipment and personnel resources. Go back and think about the area in Business Theory, which talked about Partnering, Teaming Arrangement, Prime/Subcontractors and forming a JV. If there is a true and honest relationship between both parties, then the ability to perform with your own equipment and personnel is doable. Things such as equipment can be purchased for $1; you must get creative!

So far in your presentation you have covered "who" your company is and "what" your company can do regarding meeting the needs of your target market. Specifically, in these slide(s)… "It's not what your target audience can do for you, but what you can do for your target audience."

If you know your target organization has requirements building slides, breaches, relief wells, roads, etc., show related efforts that are the same or similar in nature. Stay on track in your presentation.

Slide #10: This slide does not exist, and I didn't show it for a reason. Whatever slide is last in this section, show a real project that is potentially coming out either as a negotiated or competitive 8(a) effort. You want to show the direct correlation between your capabilities and upcoming project(s) that specifically fall within your company's abilities. This is the beginning of answering the initial question(s) asked: what are the three major concerns with 8(a) negotiated contracts? One of the answers to those questions was 'performance.'

You have planted the seed that you can perform; have performed in the past; and utilizing your own people and equipment. It must be conveyed at this point during the presentation. Go ahead and asked the question, "Do you have a project you think we can perform?" Come right out and ask the above question to the group. At this point in your presentation you have captured their attention. Go forward and do wonderful things in the remaining part of your presentation!

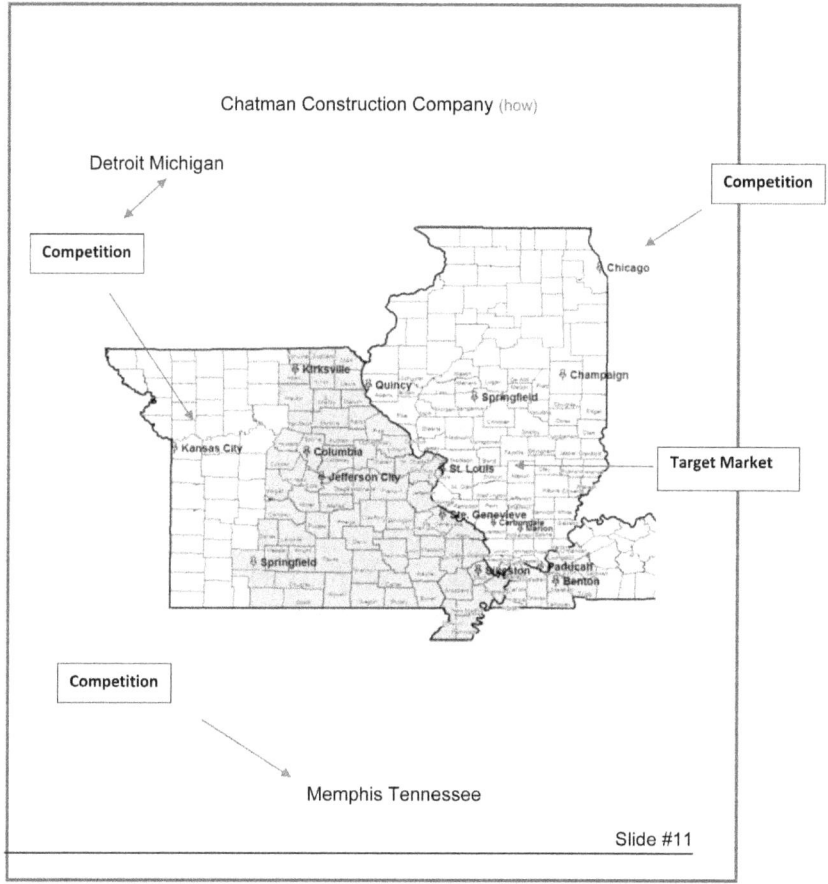

Slide #11 Discussion Notes:
Title: The most critical area of the four sections of your Agenda is the "how" segment. The basic definition of the word "how" refers to the way or manner or to what extent the services will be provided. We started with a basic question and in this section, you will clearly explain and cover the answer to perform-ance (or lack thereof), price, as well as location. This is the answer to the

"Setup" process that was talked about earlier in the discussion. An enormous amount time and conversation will be spent in this entire section.

Remember, the assumption is the company doing this presentation is based in the St. Louis metropolitan area. Always start with a company or organization (as your target market) within your own vicinity. There is an important question asked by yourself, as well as to representatives of your target market. That is, "how can a firm work for an organization in another location if indeed the firm is not working within the area where his company is located?" For example, if your company is in Chicago, start with marketing in Chicago; if your company is in St. Louis, start with marketing in St. Louis. We have talked about this earlier…don't forget this premise.

Target Market: The presenter starts discussion as to 'who' and 'why' those three areas (firms located 700, 400, 500 and 300 miles away) are identified as their target markets. The obvious answer is location. If performance is one of the major factors of concern for the federal government, thereby being co-located within the same town as one of your target market organization provides a big advantage. The other locations were identified for the same reason regarding location, but there are additional factors as to why those other locations are target markets. Again, no one can be everything to everyone. Only target areas where you can maintain self-performance at the highest level. (further discussion on targeting the above areas to come)

Competition: The map shows four locations of other 8(a) firms (e.g., your competitors).

Why would you, at this point, talk about the location of your competition? Let's take a closer look. The example indicates four locations where other 8(a) firms are doing business in the St. Louis area or have marketed this location at some point in time. As a result (let's assume) they were successful in convincing an agency they can meet the needs, and requirements of an 8(a)-firm relative to performance and other criteria required by law. This should sound familiar to many organizations working with the federal government. Time and time again, 8(a) firms all over the land are following this course of action and many firms are getting opportunities. This is the problem! I'll explain as we go further.

Therefore, on this slide these are areas that must be communicated to your target audience:

- Identify a target market (we know where we can perform that makes sense).
- Start in your own back yard (easier to go elsewhere if you have experience at home).
- Show example of locations of your competitors.
- Reiterate the need for performance and exploit how the competition can only utilize local contractors as subcontractors.
- Stress the ability of the ease of mobilization of equipment, laborers, and operators.

Most firms coming miles and miles away aren't concerned with performance but with oversight as construction managers. The principal factor with companies coming from other locations is the lack of performance relative to personnel and mobilization of equipment. The only salvation a company has is to call a local contractor who can perform the work and lease equipment.

The teaching points should be quite clear:

- You are a local contractor who has a bona-fide office with people and equipment ready for mobilization. This may be your Principal Place of Business.
- As a prime contractor self-performance is your whole objective.
- There's not a need to utilize other company's resources other than your own.
- Question to target audience:
  - how can a company located in another location mobilize laborers/equipment to meet performance requirements? (those firms who are 300, 400, 500, 700 miles away)
  - how can an outside company be competitive?
  - are those firms performing for organizations within their own jurisdiction – do they have contracts at firms within their own business location?

(Note: each of your slides are specifically answering those three areas of concern for the federal government – performance, price, and location)

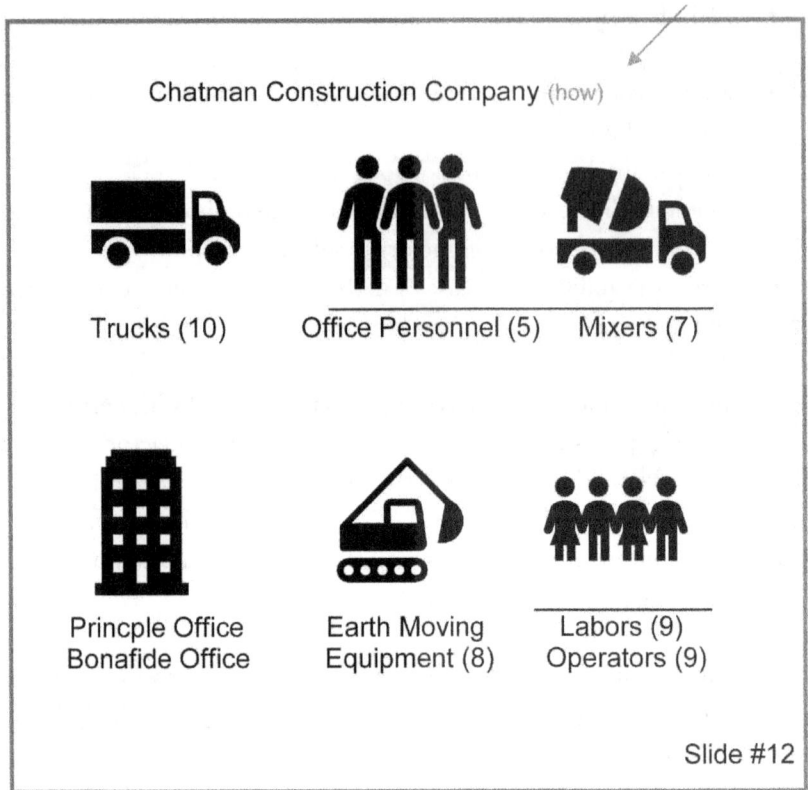

Slide #12 Discussion Notes:

Title: The key area of the four sections of your Agenda is the "how" segment – continued.

Slide #12 – Performance: This slide is totally integrated with information contained on slide #11. The Chatman Construction Company (recognizing a new division was needed) made the decision to add another section to their business line. The basic business structure was in place but needed to make minor changes as discussed earlier in this section. In this part of the presentation, clearly identify all personnel, equipment, operators, and laborers committed to self-performing. In addition, each of the pictures depicts your commitment (not only to performing) but where office locations are positioned. Clearly explain your ability to perform multiple jobs at various locations.

On slide #11, reference was made to competition or your competitors. Special emphasis should be stressed relative to the major difference between a firm who's committed to performance in relations to your competitors. The key is to discuss the correlation to other firms coming from other locations and how they normally would proceed with working in an area with little or no intention to perform. The following are points of concerns that should be noted:

- 8(a) Firms Coming from an outside location

    - Committed toward Construction Management.
    - After notification of potential negotiated contract, firm immediately contacts local small and/or large business to start a teaming agreement or operate as a prime/subcontractor.
    - Don't have a Performance Work Plan (PWP) indicating anticipated work breakdown structure.
    - Do not have any intention of mobilizing any equipment.
    - Will only assign a Quality Control person to either act as a Project Manager and/or Superintendent (in most cases).
    - Fact – the federal government performs Quality Assurance, which is the same function as the 8(a) firms assigned individual who functions on the basis as Construction Management.
    - Fact – Due to the lack of performance relies extensively on the subcontractor who increases the cost of the project based on their increased performance level.
    - 8(a) firm may perform approximately 8% of the contract effort, which doesn't include materials and supplies.
    - Fact – How can a firm located hundreds of miles from the job site perform or have any realistic intentions of performing?
    - 8(a) firm, based on law intends on opening a bona-fide place of business but instead may open a post office box or profess to rent a room.

- 8(a) Firm who is committed to Performance, Bona-Fide Office, Personnel and Equipment will:

- Provide a PWP clearly describing percent of work committed as a prime contractor and most importantly how the work will be performed.
- Depending on the nature of work will perform anywhere from 25% to 40% of all work.
- Depending on specialty work needed, will identify <u>teaming partner</u>, as well as type of functions performed. (special note: The 8(a) firm who has the right intentions will team with the same subcontractor when and only when (in this case working with the same subcontractor on multiple projects) needed. Most 8(a) firms will team with any and everyone who meets their needs depending on the type of work pursued).
- Will mobilize equipment, laborers, and operators needed to complete the job.
- This firm will not accept more or any type of work that may exceed their performance and bonding capability.
- Will immediately locate a Bona-Fide place of business with office personnel and necessary office arrangements to meet the bonafide office requirements.

There are more distinctive elements that separate the two types of 8(a) firms, which will be further explored in slides forthcoming. Hopefully, you can understand why it's important to target organizations within your own geographical area before moving elsewhere. This is a fantastic way to vet a potential 8(a) firm in determining capability. The final factor that will solidify those differences is found in looking at who is on the job site. Enough said at this point, but I can ensure you more to come.

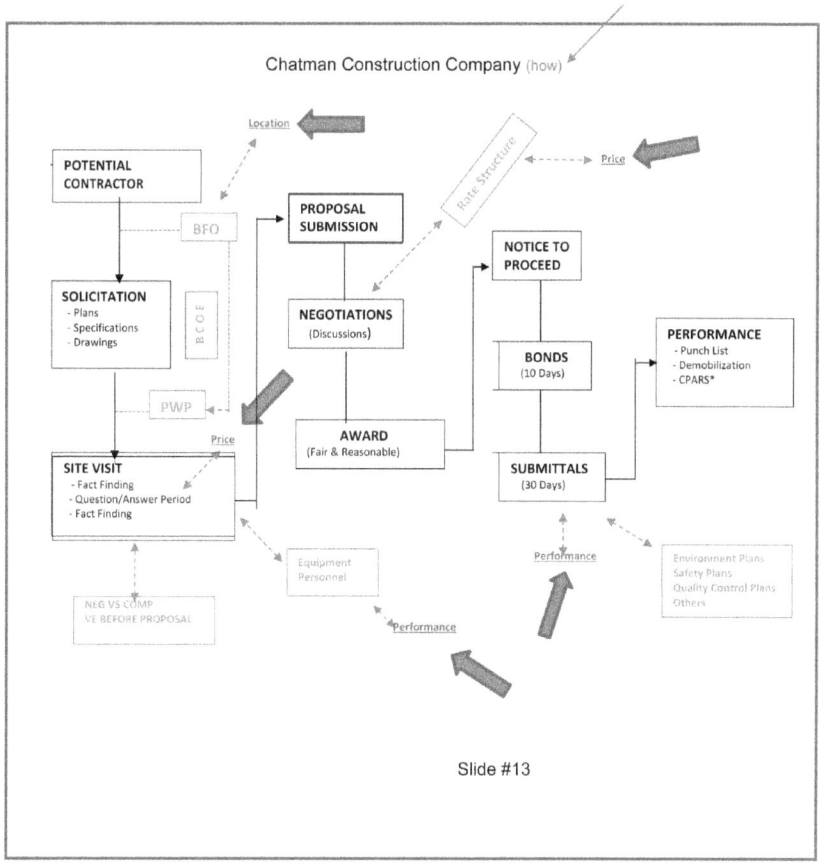

Slide #13

Slide #13 Discussion Notes:

Title: Again, the key area of the four sections of your Agenda is the "how" segment. Furthermore, the most important slide in this section is the one above. This provides your audience a composite snapshot of your knowledge, skills, abilities and addressing those three important questions…performance, price, and location. Do not get into detailed discussion of each of the areas. You are only relating to your target audience that you are knowledgeable in the steps identified.

Before we dissect the above slide, it must be noted this information is combining the last two modules of this reading:

- Potential Contractor through Contract Award…<u>Business Preparation Module</u>
- Notice to Proceed through CPARS*…<u>Business Functionality Module</u> (discussion is based on a business presentation however in-depth analysis is contained in each individual module)

Contractor Performance Assessment Reporting System (CPARS) – In simple terms, each contractor who perform work as a Prime Contractor receives a rating relative to performance. This is a grading system that consist of several levels in relation to performance. *

Organization Key Functions and Processes:

- Potential Contractor: For presentation purposes, you immediately alert the audience once you have been notified your firm is the selected 8(a) contractor for negotiations, you are prepared and ready to go to work. The critical point is to clearly explain the course of action to be followed. This is the beginning of putting a lot of the information, knowledge, and data you have learned in to use.
- Bona-Fide Office (BFO): Immediately state your intentions on identifying and opening a Bona-Fide Office within the local jurisdiction of your target market or within the boundaries of the project or job site. Based on regulations, each firm must open this type of office to ensure (if needed), verification can be made at any time by the SBA's representative. How difficult is it to have a place or office location prior to receiving potential notification? The smart firm will think ahead so this doesn't become an issue. The strategy is based on identifying your target market but search for a place that is affordable but at the same time is an acceptable place of business. This may appear to be a small issue, but to your target audience, it shows you have done your homework and you are prepared by opening a BFO.

  This is the first area addressing the question of location.
- Solicitation: Detailed discussion will be made later regarding solicitation, plans, specifications, and drawings; however, the key focal point is the area that is called BCOES.
- BCOES: This acronym stands for a process that determines whether a project is "Biddability, Constructability, Operability, Environmental

and Sustainability". There are some organizations who used this process to ensure certain proposed government projects meet a minimum set of guidelines. A brief description of this process is:

"This includes the most current construction practices, the newest configurations, and the most recent ingenious methods, which are captured to support the BCOES process…This management process can potentially play a role in reducing conflicts, claims, and disputes can inversely affect the successful outcome of a project. The BCOES review results are to be incorporated into the procurement documents for all construction projects"[25]

This briefly describes this method, which includes a plethora of internal processes.

The BCOES is an internal process that normally does not include the contractor. That is until now! This is when you recommend to your audience, of including your firm as a part in the review process. As defined by the above definition, your involvement is a wonderful opportunity to provide input and thoughts prior to formulation of final plans, specifications, and drawings. There's a potential cost saving to the government by sharing ideas and improvements to the development of the project. Over many years of working in the federal government, the contractor has never been a part of this process. (Note: 8(a) attendance to BCOES is recommended for a negotiated, sole-sourced actions. The BCOES process can be used for other procurement methods and processes)

- Performance Work Plan (PWP): This is a perfect opportunity to introduce your own PWP prior to submission of your proposal. Your entire goal is show how focused you are relative to self-performing. This is the biggest concern with contracting, project management, construction, and the entire organization. If this is a standard project you can basically self-perform, then clearly use the tools in slide #11 and slide #12 to your advantage. There are projects that you can perform 60 or 70% of the work and there may be times your performance level may be substantially less. In either case, provide the work breakdown analysis of what and how your company will start and complete this effort.

This is where you are addressing the self-performance process.

- Site Visit: This area is highly critical and quite often overlooked. During my days in contracting (in various capacities), I (100%) felt all necessary personnel needed to be included as a part of the site visit. (note: do not get into detailed discussion of the parameters of the site visit. *The following is a brief explanation for the contractor only.*) Most site visits are held at the job site or within walking or driving distance. As an 8(a) firm, this is your opportunity to clarify, ask questions, and provide alternative methods and processes to the construction of the project. It is imperative the government Cost Estimator is a part of this group. Believe it or not, there have been instances when this key individual was not present.
  - Observation #1: Ensure the right personnel are present. (Don't be afraid to ask the question as to who is going to be at the site visit.)
  - Observation #2: Ensure the first part of the site visit is held inside a building or structure thus in an environment where each of the line items can be discussed. (It is recommended that the first part of the site visit is held in this format.)
  - Observation #3: This is when preliminary Fact Finding is critical. Go over each line item of the bid schedule; ensure line items that are quantity based are clear; ensure production rates and other parts of the solicitation are clear and understood. Take your time and go over anything you think is critical and may make a difference in price, schedule, and/or performance. The bottom line is to ensure you and the government (especially the cost estimators) are reviewing the solicitation in the same way (e.g., apples to apples and oranges to oranges). In many areas within the federal organization a meeting of this nature is held although it might be called by a different name.
  - Observation #4: The second part of the site visit is held at the project location. This may appear to be a function that is automatic. I been in situations where a site visit did not occur or if it did the right personnel was not present. Don't make this mistake or allow it to happen. At the site visit, again raise all sorts of questions. There is no such thing as a dumb question. As shown in this slide, a second phase of Fact Finding can and should occur.

The main objective is to streamline and identify those areas that are ambiguous and requires clarification. Remember your proposal has not been submitted nor finalized at this point and neither has the government estimate been completed (the estimate can be modified based on additional information and changes). This process has a direct bearing on price and the final negotiated effort. This is another juncture in the acquisition process where price can be affected and again is directly related to the second question that was raised – soaring prices submitted by the 8(a) firm. Hopefully, it is obvious why this slide is ultimately important and must be clearly explained as a part of your presentation. (detailed information on the importance of the site visit will be discussed in the business functionality module)

Let's take a closer look at the site visit and the differences between the firm whose doing it the right way and the firm who's not:

- Right way firm –
    • The team is leading the discussions.
    • The team is asking pertinent questions (mobilization/equipment/personnel) The team is note taking and is attentive to details of the communication exchange.
- Wrong way firm –
    • The subcontractor's POC is leading the discussions. The subcontractor is asking all the pertinent questions.
    • The subcontractor is taking notes and is attentive to details of the communication exchange.

The question is: Who is running the show? Is it the Prime contractor who is self-performing with his equipment, laborers and operators or is it the major local subcontractor performing 90% to 95% of the effort? This point must be mentioned repeatedly because it is the primary number one concern with 8(a) contractors, which is related to the lack of performance. This issue has clearly distorted the image of the 8(a) firm.

- Negotiations vs Competitive (Value Engineering before Proposal submission)/BCOES: This section of the slide was added after the Site Visit and prior to the submission of your Proposal for a unique and specific reason. Normally, when an effort is based on competition, no firm will reveal any of his or her secrets at the Site Visit. Sure, there will be basic discussions, but nothing in the manner that is going to reveal or result in a lower price. There is a contract term or process called Value Engineering (VE) utilized during the acquisition process between the government and a contractor. (It's not necessary to get into finite details of what, when, and how VE is used).

For training purposes, the basic definition of VE is: a systematic method to improve the "value" of goods or products and services by using an examination of various processes. Value, as defined, is the ratio of function to cost. Value can therefore be increased by either improving the function or reducing the cost. Value Engineering is normally utilized when 30% (approximately) of the plans and specifications are complete. The government may call it VE; I call it working together, communicating together, sharing ideas and processes for the well-being of both parties.

The purpose of adding this area is to illustrate by working closely with the 8(a) firm at the beginning of the BCOES; during the Site Visit; and allowing various Fact-Finding sessions will and often result in a cost savings to both parties (either in cost or improved performance). This is a fantastic opportunity to seek clarification, unifications and ensuring that plans, specifications, and drawings are in concert with the viewpoint of both the government and contractor. The government does an excellent job working with contractors but adding this process of inviting the firm to the BCOES and to various meetings will improve and perhaps reduce the overall cost of the project.

A major difference using this tactic can result in a cost savings shared by both parties. Inviting the 8(a) firm to the BCOES should be a standard practice when negotiating one on one. This is a key process when the concern of soaring prices can be reduced simply by communicating and working together. Somewhere in society this has been a lost art. Earlier during the Business Theory Module, discussion occurred regarding the importance of communication. From a personal standpoint, many of our problems would be reduced or eliminated if we learned the art of communication, resulting in not hearing what people say, but what they really mean.

- Proposal Submission: If the previous processes are implemented to the slightest degree, the proposal submitted by the contractor and the cost estimate developed by the federal government will be in concert. Do not misinterpret, there are other cost factors that may affect the variation of differences between the government's cost estimate and contractor's proposal. Negotiations will ensue, but I can assure you there will not be a wide variation in cost. Government contract law reveals negotiations cannot occur if there is a variation of more than 25% difference between the government estimate and the contractor's proposal. If the above areas within this slide are followed, there is little chance of a 25% cost difference occurring. Again, let's take a closer look at the cost/price of those same two 8(a) firms; e.g., one who's self-performing (doing things the right way), in comparison to the firm who's doing things the wrong way:

  - Right way firm (1)
    - √ Self-performing the job (25% - 40% in most cases)
    - √ Mobilizing own equipment, laborers, and operators
    - √ Doesn't include over inflated subcontractor cost
    - √ Doesn't include leased equipment cost when in fact those cost is already included in subcontractor's proposal
    - √ Bona-Fide Office (BFO) is established
  - Wrong way firm (2) –
    - √ Self-performance limited to QC Manager/Superintendent only
    - √ Only mobilizing QC personnel (no equipment/laborers, and operators
    - √ Proposal includes inflated prices by Prime and Subcontractor
    - √ Proposal includes prices contained by both Prime and Subcontractor for same or similar cost
    - √ No BFO established

In the basic analysis of the two firms, which one will provide a lower, cheaper cost to the government? The only way the second firm can submit a lower cost proposal is based on the local firm (subcontractor to the 8(a) Prime) performing practically the entire job. Logically, whenever there are multiple layers of cost, there is a disparity of work performed by the Prime and Subcontractor. In this case, the Subcontractor is driving up cost, as well as affecting performance by the prime contractor. By now, if the differences and level of importance between an 8(a) firm who is following the rules and regulations relative to performance, price, and location, verses those firms who are breaking these basic rules isn't clear; stop close the book and find something else to do! Let's add clarification, there are those 8(a) firms who are trying to work with subcontractors and are giving a great effort. There are those subcontractors who are sincere in trying to help those 8(a) firms as best they can. Not all small 8(a) firms have the capability and capacity, therefore, they must start somewhere. We understand this situation, but the training point is simply this: It only takes one bad apple to ruin the entire barrel.

This entire slide is based on what happens when the image of the 8(a) firm is distorted or tarnished. You can't change your first impression (you've heard this statement before). The common denominator and belief among most organizations is a high degree of misuse and abuse. For every 8(a) firm (and subcontractor) trying to follow the rules, there are many more 8(a) firms (and subcontractors) who are circumventing the rules. You can believe this statement or not—your call!

- Negotiations: This part of the flowchart is very important. At this juncture, you are going to reveal something that is critical toward the composition of your basic proposal. The basic factors regarding negotiations will be discussed later in the next module, but for presentation concerns, you will provide and discuss the makeup of your "rate structure." I've asked many firms this question: "What is your rate structure?" Practically, 99% of all firms gave the deer in the head light look. By definition, rate structure is a combination of the following:

  - Profit
  - Direct Cost
  - Overhead (home/field)
  - Bond*

During your presentation, your goal (by revealing this information) is to show you have a clear understanding of how to put your cost proposal together, based on the above elements. At this point, only explain the basic contents of those four areas (do not get into detailed specifics of the below areas):

- Profit – Since this is a negotiated requirement and based on my experience (for proposal cost less than $2 million), an acceptable profit margin is between 8% and 10% and for proposal cost between $2 million and $4 million an acceptable margin is between 6% and 8%. The development of profit margins for negotiated contracts is based on a process called "weighted guidelines." This is a specific process that look at various independent, but related factors.
- Direct Cost - Direct cost is based on actuals. No detailed discussion needed.
- Overhead (O/H) – Overhead is an area that is very sensitive to most federal contracting personnel. There are guidelines that are applicable in the determination of overhead rates such as laws stated within Defense Contract Audit Agency (DCAA).[26] Clearly state the composition of cost factors that determine your O/H rate. This also includes home and field overhead rates. As an example, your home O/H rate is 5% and field O/H rate is 8% for a combined total overhead rate of 13%.
- Bond* – The key point is your bond rate should not exceed 3% for construction efforts (per my knowledge and experience). This is the maximum amount allowable. If your rate from your bonding company is 1%, 2% or something else, identify what it is. (Bond cost is related to only construction efforts.)

The finite details of negotiations and each of the four areas comprise your rate structure. This area will be covered in the Business Preparation Module. Until now, the areas discussed in the matrix centered around performance, price, and business location. Thus far, these processes are the basis for reaching a fair and reasonable price, which is the goal of the federal government. To most 8(a) firms, the basic composition of their rate structure and its importance is like a foreign language. These are the small nuances that are somewhat hidden and not understood by small businesses.

There is another facet to the development of rate structure that's related to the Prime contractor working, or teaming with another subcontractor. If you are not dedicated to self-performing as much as possible, the subcontractor based on the composition and submission of their rates will inflate your proposal costs. In this case, your proposal is now highly overpriced. Your subcontractor is now your worst enemy. This is a major concern among most government contracting officials. Remember, your prices are too high! Again, more to come on this topic.

- Award: There is not much to discuss (at this point) other than everything above resulted in reaching a fair and reasonable price. At this time, you should feel confident and proud. A fair and reasonable price has been reached. It also shows the above thought processes were implemented correctly...good job!
- Bonds: Normally, a contractor has ten days to obtain and submit necessary bonds as required by the terms and conditions of the contract. Again, this section is just a teaching point regarding the time frame and a requirement under the terms and conditions of the contract.
- Submittals: This step in the matrix is very important. Submittals are required documents outlining the contents, laws, regulations, and understanding areas applicable to Environmental Plans, Safety Plans, Quality Control Plans, etc. There may be a variety and high number of Submittals required by your target firm. The important thing to understand and remember, it's your responsibility to complete these documents in a timely manner. Most firms have limited experience and knowledge in this area. The level of effort required in completing these actions are extreme and can be quite complicated. The majority of 8(a) firms rely on the subcontractor (who is performing the majority of the work) to complete these requirements. However, 8(a) firms who are willing to learn this process displays a prominent level of competence and self-confidence. This level of effort indicates you have the necessary tools to be a successful Prime contractor. Be aware of this process regarding Submittal preparation and completion.

In most cases, firms understand performance of a contract is important, but the ability to handle the administration of a contract is equally important.

We have heard the term "Red Tape" within the federal government; e.g., various internal functions that slow a process that appears to be simple in nature. As an example, in the past, receiving payment from the federal government took a prolonged period. This was a prime example of this stumbling block called Red Tape.

Furthermore, you have thirty days to submit and obtain approval of your Submittals. There are known situations, when the contractor could not complete these documents in an acceptable manner which caused delays in project start time but rarely resulted in a contract being terminated. Submittal completion is a process that one must learn to perform regardless if you are self-performing some or the entire project. Never, and I mean never, rely on a subcontractor to complete these documents. At worst case scenario, work with the subcontractor as much as necessary until you have mastered this skill. There's a major difference between trying to learn a process or function, rather than doing nothing at all. The objective is to increase awareness of the Submittal process and it's level of importance.

- Notice to Proceed (NTP): The NTP is a letter submitted to you indicating a specific time to begin construction effort and other general information relative to contract award. Again, this section is to alert you of a step within the acquisition process and is not intended to cover details about the specifics of a NTP notice and other information contained in this document.
- Performance: The final leg of your presentation is performance. You must continue to stress how your capabilities meet the needs of your target market. As a part of your discussion, you covered the three basic areas:

  √ Punch List Items – Small list and/or group of minor functions must be completed prior to demobilization. This is nothing critical in your discussion other than indicating your knowledge level of the project effort.
  √ Demobilization – Nothing critical in your discussion
  √ Contractor Performance Assessment Reporting System (CPARS) – This is an area that requires further discussion. CPARS is a system used to retain contractor evaluation reports after the project has been completed.

This is the final area within your presentation to reiterate the importance of performance and doing the best job possible.

This is one of the most important slides regarding your presentation. As shown, it provides a correlation between performance, price, and location. In addition, it indicates you truly understand (to a certain degree) the acquisition process from the federal governments perspective, and from your own vantage point. Again, this is a modified version of the acquisition process, which includes many more steps and processes. Historically, there are very few firms (large and small businesses) who have a mental and visual understanding of how an organization functions, from identifying a potential contractor to completion of work in the field. I don't expect 8(a) firms to fully understand all these processes, but certainly have (at a minimum) knowledge and understanding of those sections within this matrix.

Chatman Construction Company (why)			
Top 8(a) Problem & Issues			
8(a) Contractor Concerns/Issues	Risks Assessment		Chatman Resolution
1. Pass-through	H Risk	N Risk	1. Self-Performance
2. Price	H Risk	L Risk	2. BCOE/Site Visit/Rate Structure
3. Prime/Subcontractor	M Risk	N Risk	3. Chatman Prime
4. Joint Venture	H Risk	N Risk	4. No J/V
5. Teaming Arrangement	M Risk	N Risk	5. Chatman/Chatman
6. Equipment/Personnel	H Risk	N Risk	6. Own Equipment/Personnel
7. Bonding	H Risk	N Risk	7. Indemnification
8. Negotiations	H Risk	N Risk	8. Rate Structure Provided Upfront
9. Submittal/Administration	M Risk	N Risk	9. 100+ Federal Project Experience
			Slide #14

Slide #14

Slide #14 Discussion Notes

Title: This part of your presentation now focused on the "why" aspect of the Agenda.

This slide summarizes various problems and issues that confront most 8(a) firms. Again, this is a fantastic opportunity to pinpoint the differences between your firm and other 8(a) firms. Earlier discussions covered each of these areas, but you must continue to reinforce and reiterate why your company would like to have an opportunity based on facts. The hardest distinction to master as a federal employee (Small Business Program Manager/Contracting Personnel) is to decide what's real about an 8(a) firm and what is false. It may sound strange, but the future of the 8(a) contractor hinges on the ability of federal government representative(s) to make this determination. It doesn't matter how prepared you are but whether you have convinced the government you have done the right things when it comes to capabilities and understanding of rules, regulations, and the needs of the federal government. On this slide, be clear but brief when covering each area indicated. Do not overstress these areas, but consistently remind everyone why you desire an opportunity. Look how emphasis is given to the phrase "desire an opportunity" verses <u>deserve</u> an opportunity. In most instances, we fail to understand you may desire something based on what you think your capabilities are, but the reality is you are only as good as others perceive you to be. Most individuals and firms believe that certification results in a proclamation they now deserve an opportunity. This is a crucial factor in the short and long-term success working for the federal government. Don't ever wait on someone to give you anything, but do whatever needs to be done (within the regulation) to assist and make that decision easier by those who are the decision makers. (You've heard this statement before.) Here's a brief overview of the top 8(a) problems based on risk perception of 8(a) contractors:

- Pass-through – This is the number one concern and problem. Your key talking point is to focus on your PWP by outlining equipment, personnel, and mobilization of these elements. You are fully committed to self-performing following the processes indicated above (no risk to the Chatman firm based on performance – high risk to competitors).
- Price – Clearly provide your understanding of putting together the proper rate structure and transparency in revealing how your proposal is constructed. Here, too, self-performance results in lower proposal cost. Reiterate how working with government personnel during BCOES, site visits, and fact-finding sessions ultimately creates a win-win situation for

both parties. (No risk to Chatman firm based on understanding of rate structure; self-performance; transparency; and other factors indicated in previous slides – considerable risk to non-performing outside contractors who are teaming with local subcontractors.)

- Prime/Subcontractor – No risk to Chatman firm since self-performance is the major driving principle of the company – Moderate risk to other 8(a) firms who are operating as a Prime/Subcontractor. In most cases, the work will be completed in a satisfactory manner, but cost is higher.

- Joint Venture – Stress how you do not believe this is the best course of action based on your desires as performing as a prime contractor. Remember, you have covered why JV isn't the right or best course of action for your company. This ties back into factors discussed in performance, price and providing the government with a better product by not taking this course of action. (No risk, against Chatman's firms core principles. As stated earlier (Business Theory module), this process can be an effective way of performing, but in some cases, is misused relative to misrepresentation by some firms).

- Teaming Arrangement – Point out to your target audience how your company will only work with the same subcontractor. The key is to indicate how most 8(a) firms work with multiple contractors to fit their own personal needs. Communicate to the Government how your teaming partner is dedicated to each other on a reciprocal basis (discussed in Business Theory module). (No risk, against Chatman's firm core competences and only used in unique situations – Moderate risk to competition based on the contents and lack of trust found between both organizations. Historically, when a Teaming Agreement cover any, and everything, there are obvious concerns with lack of trust and understanding of what is required by both parties.) It's appropriate to indicate that most 8(a) firms will use different subcontractors to satisfy their own needs based on the nature and location of the project.

- Equipment/Personnel - This section reverts back to the areas of performance, price, and location of the contractor. It's been established when contractor's come from other locations, there is a direct correlation between those three key issues mentioned above. The major distinction between the Chatman company and the other organization is the ability to mobilize key personnel relative to performance, which invariably reduces contract price. The ability to own and mobilize your equipment and personnel is the underlying difference between both firms. Most firms will provide a superintendent/project manager and rely on a subcontractor to furnish those elements key to performance. (This area of providing equipment/personnel is no risk to the Chatman firm and high risk to the other outside contractor.)

- Bonding – This is a very tricky topic to understand and how important it is to any contractor. Bonding will be fully discussed in the Business Preparation Module, but for presentation purposes, emphasis is made to the amount of bonding capability you have as a company. In review of slide #3, key members of your firm were shown. One of those individuals was the Bonding Agent. He clearly provided an overview of your Bonding capability and the ability to obtain necessary coverage when needed. The main point is the ability to obtain a certain amount of bonding without the aid of a subcontractor. This is a wonderful time in the presentation to reiterate there shouldn't be any concern with indemnification from any subcontractor or outside source. Remember, every potential opportunity comes your way may not be a great one for your firm. The relationship developed with your Bonding Agent is important going forward. It is critical to ensure that you do not obtain projects that exceed your bonding capability. Some Bonding companies will provide you support beyond your capability to handle multiple efforts. Always pay close attention to your company's internal ability to perform or handle several projects. This is a part of staying on top of your own infrastructure. Always maintain a clear balance between personnel, equipment, cash flow, outstanding debt, as well as the number and type of projects not completed as well as started. (No risk for a company who has strong bonding capability such as the Chatman firm. High risk for those firms who cannot provide a sound bonding strategy for current and future projects.)

- Negotiations – At this juncture, briefly restate those blocks in slide #13 that covered processes prior to entering negotiations. This is a good place to test your memory. Specifically, state how important it is to work together as one unit during the BCOES, site-visits and fact-finding sessions. Even referring to the submission of the performance work plan and rate structure further indicates your understanding of the federal process and your commitment as a potential firm. (Chatman firm indicates none to very little risk (potentially) reaching a fair and reasonable agreement by following those steps above. Contrary, there is a high risk working with those firms who are relying on subcontractors and little regard for self-performing as required by the federal government.)

- Submittals/Administration - There are many problems in the administration of a contract. There are two basic areas with the execution of a contract, which are: (1) Performance and (2) Administration of a contract. Contract administration includes a multitude of functions that can be simple to execute and, in some cases, very difficult (contract administration will be covered later). In this case, the crucial factor is the completion and submission of Submittals in an accurate and timely manner. Historically, most 8(a) firms rely on subcontractors or some other mechanism in the completion of these documents. At this point, a clear distinction can be made by your company in comparison to those who do not perform this function and most importantly they do not try. This is a major part of performance and another way to separate yourself from those firms who are pretenders. (Chatman firm completes and submits all Submittals in comparison to those firms who do not perform this function).

The main purpose of this slide is to reiterate those major problems and issues that separate the 8(a) firm who is performing in a proper manner and those firms who are not. This information provides you an opportunity to clearly indicate the elements that are hurting the 8(a) Business Development Program, those firms who are desperately doing the right things and the federal government whose confident levels regarding 8(a) firms are diminishing.

Chatman Construction Company (why)

Contract Title:	Lovejoy Street & Sewer Repairs WXXXXX-17

Category	Grading Criteria	Rating
Quality:	Technical data/report; Standards; Timeliness	(E)
Schedule:	Compliance with contract delivery/schedules	(E)
Cost Control:	Contractor reasonable/cooperative	(E)
Business Relationship:	On-site management; Knowledge/expertise	(E)
Utlization of Small Business:	Meet Terms/Conditions of the Contract	(E)
Regulatory Compliance:	Maintain environment of safety	(E)
Other:	Would you hire/work with this firm again?	(E)
		Slide #15

Slide #15 Contractor Performance Assessment System (CPARS)

Slide #15 Discussion Notes:

CPARS: This rating is given to the contractor by the federal government after the completion of a project. There are various levels of grading that exemplifies how well the contractor performed in various areas. In this example, there are seven categories reviewed and rated, which may vary depending on working with the Army, Navy, Air Force, or some other branch of service. There are up to three Other Areas may be assessed as deemed necessary in the rating process. In the Federal system, the grading system ranges from Exceptional, Very Good, Satisfactory, Marginal and Unsatisfactory.[27]

The purpose of showing this slide is two-fold:

(1) This is an opportunity to show a rating based on completing a project in support of the organization you are currently presenting. Hopefully, this effort was won on a competitive basis, if not, a negotiated requirement will suffice just as well. The key area on this slide is the final rating received. Just ensure you have a <u>hard copy of the rating if verification</u>

is requested. It's better to be safe to have back up documentation. If you don't have a rating from a project that is organizationally related, use a rating from another organization indicating similar, or the same type work. It's understandable most 8(a) firms fall into a Catch 22 when it comes to prior or current ratings on previous or any project. There are times when owners are totally confused about the entire federal process. By this, I'm referring to the problem with the lack of experience at the federal government level. However, most organizations are looking at past experience as an evaluation tool. We've talked about this before and the only way to mitigate this problem is competing for actions on a continuous and consistent basis. (This issue will be discussed in the next module.)

(2) The second crucial point is the information directly stated on this slide and the impact the rating has on current and future efforts. CPARS rating comes at the completion of the project. (This, too, will be covered in the Business Functionality section.) One of the first things an organization will do is take a close look at your previous ratings in the system. Those individual areas breakdown the effort required in the completion of a project and dissects your company's performance in those areas. Therefore, your past ratings are highly critical throughout the entire time period working at the federal level. Question, is your rating crucial on future projects? It's true each independent contract stands on its own merit, but your performance ratings are available in this one repository, which follows your company for a certain period of time. Your end goal is to obtain the highest rating in each of the individual categories resulting in a final overall rating, which hopefully is 'exceptional.' Each of the rating categories are important, but the most critical area on any job site is "safety/security." Safety is the one area that can end your federal career as a potential contractor. This, too, is a topic for later discussion. Always add this type of slide to your presentation (if possible).

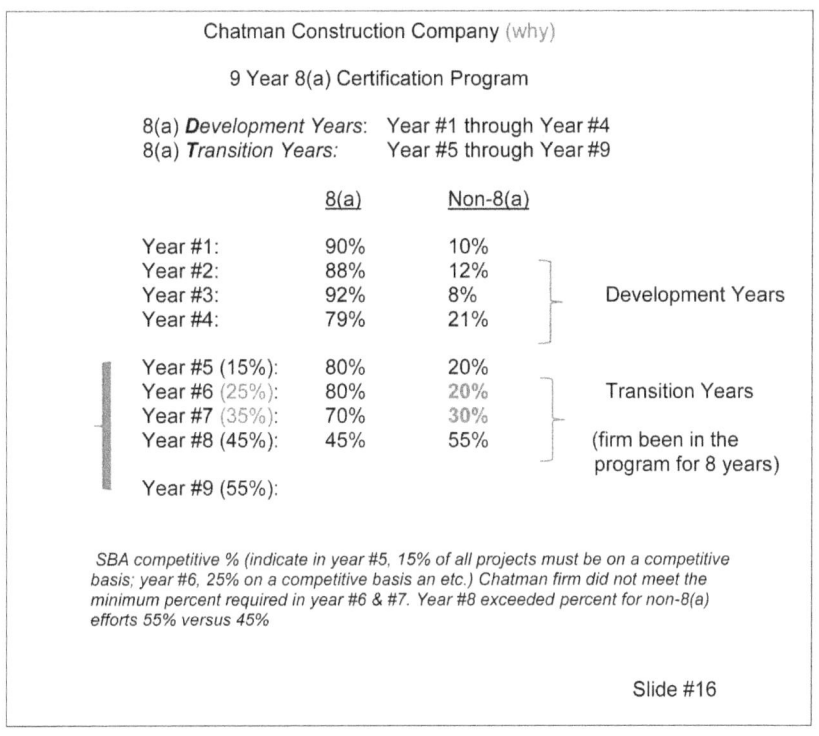

Chatman Construction Company (why)

9 Year 8(a) Certification Program

8(a) *Development Years*: Year #1 through Year #4
8(a) *Transition Years*: Year #5 through Year #9

	8(a)	Non-8(a)	
Year #1:	90%	10%	
Year #2:	88%	12%	
Year #3:	92%	8%	Development Years
Year #4:	79%	21%	
Year #5 (15%):	80%	20%	
Year #6 (25%):	80%	20%	Transition Years
Year #7 (35%):	70%	30%	
Year #8 (45%):	45%	55%	(firm been in the program for 8 years)
Year #9 (55%):			

SBA competitive % (indicate in year #5, 15% of all projects must be on a competitive basis; year #6, 25% on a competitive basis an etc.) Chatman firm did not meet the minimum percent required in year #6 & #7. Year #8 exceeded percent for non-8(a) efforts 55% versus 45%

Slide #16

Slide #16 Discussion Notes:

This slide is important to your target audience because it depicts performance based on the percentage of projects awarded that were 8(a) versus non-8(a) category. I must reiterate, projects can be obtained on an 8(a) negotiated or 8(a) competitive basis. Non-8(a) projects refer to those other projects obtained on a competitive basis, which doesn't fall under the auspices of the 8(a) negotiated/competitive process. Despite the participating program year, this data reveals you are fully trying to follow 8(a) rules and not solely relying on the benefits and rewards of the 8(a) Business Development Program. Conversely, companies failed to understand the importance of competing on all actions that are within their capabilities. Throughout the years of working with 8(a) firms and witnessing many presentations, I have yet to see a slide of this nature.

For training purposes only, this slide shows the Chatman Construction Company has been in the 8(a) Business Development Program for eight years and is entering the ninth year. Let's take a closer look at the slide and further provide insight on what the information means:

- Development Years: By definition, the first four years in the program, the contractor can use this time frame to obtain all and any type of projects that can be awarded to them. This means 100% of projects can be: 8(a) negotiated efforts; 8(a) competitive basis; or projects awarded on a competitive basis (unrestricted/small business set-aside). This slide reveals in the first year the firm was awarded 90% of their projects through the 8(a) processes either negotiated or competitive. The remainder of their contracts (10%) were awarded based on some form of competitive process. The same analysis is used through the remainder of the next three years. Is there a potential problem brewing in the graph for years one through year four? Do you see a trend that could potentially cause a major problem? There are two facts that must be noted:
  o Point (#1): entering the fifth year, 15% of all contracts awarded must be of the non-8(a) variety. The chart reveals the first three years, your ability to meet or exceed 15% of non-8(a) efforts is low. The end of year four indicated you have increased your competitive efforts to a high of 21%.
  o Point (#2): Once entering or the start of the 8(a)-program, preparation should begin *as if* you were leaving the program during the same timeframe. Although the Development Years is for learning and growth development, it is a period when most firms rely too much on the federal government's generosity in awarded negotiated projects. Always take the competitive route while in addition of trying to obtain negotiated efforts. Don't take these four years for granted! (Don't waste time.)
- Transition Period: The Transition Period (fifth year through the ninth year) is the start of a review process by SBA analyzing your ability to obtain competitive projects (along with other factors) based on the percentages indicated in each of the remaining years. The reason for this type of progressive goal is to prepare your firm for exiting the program occurring at the end of the ninth year. There are many instances when a firm leaves the program at the end of the ninth year

and shortly thereafter is no longer in business. This process was developed for the purpose of ensuring that during the entire remaining five years, a concerted effort can be made to increase the solvency and stability of the small business. Further review indicates the firm had a profitable fifth year and 20% of contracts awarded were of competitive basis, which clearly exceeded the 15% required by SBA. As shown in the slide, each of the following years the percentage of non-8(a) efforts increased by 10%. By the end of ninth year, approximately 55% of contracts received must be competitive. As shown, in the sixth and seventh years, the Chatman Company did not exceed the competitive percentages for each of those two years. In the eight year, the firm rebounded and exceeded the 45% as required by regulation with a whopping 55% non-8(a) contract awards.

Chatman Construction Company (why)

One Final Question?

How Did You Get To Where You Are Today?

PROFESSIONALISM!   INTEGRITY!   EXCELLENCE!

Slide #17

Slide #17 Discussion Notes:
This is the final slide of the presentation. In many ways, various messages are sent and received by individuals in unknown ways. Sometimes, when people

are given the same paragraph to read and by the time the same message is passed from individual to individual, its final interpretation is totally different from the original message. Throughout the entire reading, the essence of the information and data presented was to provide the reader with something to think about relative to business situations. So, the question as stated is: "How did you get to where you are today?" There are many reasons why some people are successful while others appear to struggle. It depends on how one views and defines the term success. When this question was proposed to many people, I received various answers, but the top three responses were:

(1) "I'm just lucky! I am where I am today because of just being plain lucky."
(2) "Well, I don't really know, but I have an uncle or cousin who put in a good word for me. We all know how nepotism work. So, there are those who had someone internal who pulled some strings."
(3) "There are those who respond that they are just plain good at what they do. I was at the top of my class and I am the best at this job or position."

These are the top three answers (lucky, nepotism, and greatness). If this question is asked directly to the group you are talking to, I'm sure you will get some combination of responses and probably a litany of other answers. But the answer to this question is plain as day: Somebody, someplace, somewhere gave you an opportunity. These are the optimum words defining who we are and how we got to where we are today. The word opportunity is the link to the success and failures of our careers and lives.

The Catch 22 is what did you do with that opportunity or the opportunities received? As stated earlier, you can have an opportunity and not be successful, but you cannot be successful without having an opportunity.

Take a moment and reflect about your own life. Think back when you were in grade school, high school, your first job, marriage or whatever the situation may be. There was always, and I do mean always someone, someplace who believed in you and took a chance on giving you an opportunity. All you (as an 8(a)-business owner) want is a chance to prove you can produce; you can be a successful contractor to the federal government; you do have something of noteworthy to give to society. The Presidency of our country is the highest and most powerful position anyone can hold. How did he or she get to where they are today? The Generals of our Army, the CEO of companies were given some type of opportunity. Those of you who are married, did your spouse agree to matrimony? Ask this question to the audience and look at the facial expressions as they embellish the question asked. There was once an individual who talked about getting to the Mountain Top. This, too, is the goal of every individual who was born in this world today. However, somewhere things became too difficult and the challenges to great. Is this the problem and issues facing small business owners today? (Opportunity – more to discuss)

This concludes detailed discussion on the Business Presentation Module. The critical teaching tools of this segment is analyzing:

(1) The time when you first meet with your target market
(2) Doing your presentation

The underlying factor(s) determines your ability to convince and ultimately work with the federal government is predicated in the amount of preparation, coordination, and communication of those factors discussed within this module. This slide presentation provided may not be the ultimate way of presenting your organization to your target market, but there are critical elements that must be addressed.

Regardless of the method you chose to implement, the basic three questions regarding the perception of some 8(a) contractor's must be addressed in one way or another. The issue of (a) lack of performance, (b) higher prices, and (c) location, are the main concerns confronting 8(a) contractors. Those questions must be clearly answered to an elevated level of satisfaction. The sample presentation was provided to pinpoint some of those concerns by providing direct information in four areas: "who, what, how, and why."

Those four categories (who, what, how and why) provide clear information to your target audience relative to your companies' ability to perform, as well as your understanding of the federal government and major problems critical to your success. There is a twist to those four areas you have addressed. The government representative can ask those same questions to you during your initial visit to their office. This area of the module has provided both entities a process that can be used by either side. As a former Small Business Program Manager, I asked the same four questions to every firm I met as a formal process in determining their level of knowledge, skills, abilities, and capabilities as a potential contractor. In actuality, the basic presentation (provided above) can be used as a method of determining your level of strength and weaknesses.

One final note, regardless of what method used, ensure the three questions are answered using the four areas identified above.

CHAPTER 3

(Negotiated Contract That is Fair and Reasonable)
BUSINESS PREPARATION (Module #3)

This module is very important to 8(a) contractors. This is an area most minority small business owners fail to fully understand. First, let's go back and re-define what is meant by "Business Preparation":

"The Business Preparation module is a tool developed to provide guidance, direction, knowledge and explore hidden aspects of government solicitation/proposal preparation and negotiation practices used throughout the federal sector. These are traits many 8(a) firms clearly overlook either due to a lack of understanding or knowledge relative to the importance of working with the federal government. This area provides in-depth insight the 8(a) firm need to know prior and during the acquisition phase leading up to contract award."

To be a little more specific, the above explanation is the theoretical interpretation and definition of Business Preparation; however, I'm referring to a phase occurring after the government entity has decided to enter into a negotiated contract. However, for discussion purposes, let's assume this is a negotiated requirement with an 8(a) firm. So, you (the 8(a) firm) has pulled off the most "improbable or unthinkable" ...obtain a negotiated contract from the federal government! Wait! Let's digress for a moment, and review (briefly), how we got to this point.

The first two modules are Business Theory followed by Business Presentation Modules. In simplistic terms, you as the owner of the 8(a) firm, has done, or overcame a major obstacle; e.g., got that first negotiated opportunity. In relations to the first two modules, you clearly had to exhibit a high degree of knowledge when it came to the theoretical aspects of business as defined in the Business Theory module. Secondly, you and your company representatives must have clearly displayed a prominent level of knowledge and understanding of your target market as defined in the Business Presentation Module. Remember, the basic three concerns of working with the 8(a) firm at the federal level was related to performance, soaring prices, and business location. As defined in this section, you basically "did your homework" prior to setting up the appointment. So far so good, and well done! Let's not rest on our laurels on this accomplishment because I'm promoting opportunities, which should first be obtained on a competitive basis. You must understand in a clear and positive manner, one of the major benefits of the 8(a) Business Development Program is the dollar threshold for negotiated opportunities. In reality (in the long run), the key of surviving in the business world is built on competition. I know this through you off guard. Later during this book, I shall reveal how "competition" can be a detriment to the survival of 8(a) contractors. Take a minute and let's talk about a true situation that occurred during my career as Small Business Program Manager. This is the scenario:

- I was scheduled to participate in a workshop given by the Association of Procurement Technical Assistance Center (APTAC), which is an organization designed to assist small businesses learn, grow, and understand various government functions with the objective of working or doing business with the federal government (more to come on this organization). The day prior to the workshop, I was reviewing the status of how the District was doing in meeting/exceeding our goals in each of our mandated small business areas; e.g., small business, small disadvantaged business, woman-owned small business, hubzone small business and service-disabled veteran owned small business. As covered in the earlier section (Business Theory), a percent of every dollar (minimum) must be awarded to a small business entity in any combination of the aforementioned small business categories. Something was very unusual with the report I was reviewing. The dollars obligated in the Service Disabled Veteran Owned Small Business area, was exceeding the goal percentage by an unusually high dollar/percentage amount. I didn't know why, nor did my assistant. Further review and analysis revealed several contracts were awarded to a company on a competitive basis that happened to be classified/certified in three of the five small business categories. They were small business, small disadvantaged business and service disabled veteran owned small business. In addition, they were certified as an 8(a) firm. The name of this firm is not important at this time. I knew I had never met representatives of this company, either in my office, or anywhere, during my involvement in outreach activities.

- The day of the workshop came and as usual I did my part as a guest speaker, and hopefully provided the audience something they needed and could use to help position their company in a positive manner. After the workshop concluded, I was mingling with the audience talking business, exchanging business cards, and trying to encourage everyone with positive comments. A representative of one company introduced himself and indicated he had done business with my organization and was greatly thankful for the opportunity. One comment lead to another, so I asked for the name of his company and what certifications he had achieved, if any. I was stunned at his remarks...his company was the same company that received contracts in the Service Disabled Veterans Owned Small Business category I discovered earlier, which impacted my small business goals. I immediately scheduled a meeting with his company in my office for the very next week.

- When entering my office for the meeting, again I was bewildered! He was dressed in a light blue shirt with light blue trousers…company name embroidered. He was accompanied by his Field Manager, Office Manager, and subcontractor. All other personnel were dressed in dark blue shirts, trousers and company name embroidered. Formal introductions were made and he (company owner) proceeded to introduce his team members, as well as company background, history, organizational structure, bonding capability, etc.

- He basically covered everything contained in the first two modules. This was the only time during my career anyone completely covered the elements I have thus far discussed in this book. Totally amazing! For the first hour of the meeting I didn't say one word…I listened.

- The most unique thing about this meeting was discovered at the end of his presentation. His company totally relied on obtaining work on a competitive basis; self performs over 50% of all work; was familiar and completely understood the parameters of the 8(a) Business Development Program but viewed that as an alternative way to develop and grow a company. His company's philosophy was team first with unity, coordination, and precision as their guiding principles.

Only once during my career has any company of any size was so well-organized and fully understood its role in the small business community regardless of its 8(a) status.

This defines my point (every small business must understand), there are situations when you must rely on internal fortitude and a total willingness to succeed on your own merit. There are too many times when the newly formed 8(a) firm or small business is looking for complete assistance from the federal govenment rather than learning and developing skills the right way. This statement may seem harsh, but it's the truth.

Throughout this discussion, I want to reiterate and fully ensure the following mindset is engraved in your way of thinking, which is: Do not assume since you have been granted certification from SBA as an 8(a) firm anyone owes you anything…especially a negotiated contract. There is a major difference between being certified and actually being qualified. This is a fatal mistake the majority of 8(a) firms make on a continuous basis. Since this landmine has been uncovered, and is now clear, let's proceed with exploring various processes of business preparation.

Before we analyze the complexities of solicitations, negotiations, and associated areas of concerns, you must understand the basic principles of what I refer to as 8(a) Contracting 101. "To understand the federal process, you must have someone within your organization who has direct experience in government contracting." A former Chief of Contracting, KO, Contract Specialist, or someone who has a procurement analytical perspective (Government) is the type of skillset needed. The individual that possess this type of skill, knowledge, and ability, is an invaluable asset to you and your company. It is not impossible to be successful at this level without having an individual with this type of background. However, the effort required for you, or anyone in your company to fully grasp the many facets of the government contracting/operational process, will take an enormous amount of time. This is an example of not wasting time trying to learn and understand government functions but redirecting your efforts and investing in personnel who meets your overall objective of being successful in the government process.

This is another example of being proactive rather than reactive in understanding the individual qualities to interact with the federal government. What I'm saying is quite simple: "Surround yourself with people who are knowledgeable/experts in areas you are less knowledgeable". This thought process is based on an earlier concept called the Power of Critical Thinking; using the 'outside in approach' utilizing skillsets of personnel to meet the needs of the business market. As stated earlier, if you want to be a prime contractor, you must act as a prime contractor; if you want to work in the government sector and be a viable contractor, then you must know and understand (to a certain degree) government functions. You don't have to be an expert by any stretch of the imagination but develop a level of competence in understanding the interrelationship of government contracting processes.

There are many books, pamphlets, seminars, and workshops on contracting, negotiations, and the entire spectrum of the acquisition world as it is applied to government contracting. However, I'm referring to the underlining avenues of areas that will make a significant difference on how you interface with the government from an acquisition/business perspective.

The federal government's (DoD) acquisition processes is governed by the Federal Acquisition Regulations (FAR), which covers a wide spectrum of terms, conditions, processes, and topics applicable to government contracting. This document is sometimes referred to as the "bible of DoD Government contracting" and can be reviewed at your leisure. (See below graph for outline of FAR document – exhibit #10) One word of caution, the FAR is not a tool that can be memorized but knowing how to use the FAR as a reference guide is the key. After approximately forty years in contracting, I only used this tool as a guide and didn't try to know its entire contents as it relates to the procurement process.

When there is an area in the acquisition process that is unclear, ambiguous, and/or need clarification relative to contract terms, conditions, and processes, the FAR is the right tool of reference. It might be a great asset to download this guide on your laptop, desktop, and any quick electronic device used. Better yet, someone in your organizational structure should obtain as much knowledge in the utilization of this tool as you proceed forward in the acquisition community at the federal level.

FEDERAL ACQUISITION REGULATION SITE
https://www.acquisition.gov) [28]

Section		Title
"01	-	FAR Acquisition Regulation System
02	-	Definition of Words and Terms
03	-	Improper Business Practices and Personal Conflicts
04	-	Administration Matters
05	-	Publicizing Contract Actions
06	-	Competition Requirement
07	-	Acquisition Planning
08	-	Required Sources of Supplies and Services
09	-	Contractor Qualifications
10	-	Market Research
11	-	Describing Agency Needs
12	-	Acquisition of Commercial Items
13	-	Simplified Acquisition Procedures
14	-	Sealed Bidding
15	-	Contracting by Negotiations
16	-	Types of Contracts
17	-	Special Contracting Methods
18	-	Reserved
19	-	Small Business Programs
20	-	Reserved
21	-	Reserved
22	-	Application of Labor Laws to Government Acquisition
23	-	Environment, Conservation, Occupational Safety, and Drug Free Workplace
24	-	Protection of Privacy freedom of Information
25	-	Foreign Acquisition
26	-	Other Socio-Economic Programs
27	-	Protest, Data, and Copyright
28	-	Bonds and Insurance
29	-	Taxes
30	-	Cost Accounting Standards Administration
31	-	Contract Cost Principles and Administration

32	-	Contract Financing
33	-	Protest, Disputes, and Appeals
34	-	Major Systems Acquisition
35	-	Research and Development Contracting
36	-	Construction and Architect – Engineer Contracts
37	-	Service Contracting
38	-	Federal Supply Schedule Contracting
39	-	Acquisition of Information Technology
40	-	Reserved\Section Title
41	-	Acquisition of Utility Services
42	-	Contract Administration and Audit Services
43	-	Contract Modification
44	-	Subcontracting Policies and Procedures
45	-	Government Property
46	-	Quality Assurance
47	-	Transportation
48	-	Value Engineering
49	-	Termination for Convenience
50	-	Extraordinary Contractual Actions
51	-	Use of Government Services by Contractors
52	-	Solicitation Provisions and Contract Clauses
53	-	Forms

APPENDIXES

AP – AA:	Sources Selection Supplement
AP – CC:	Army Procurement Management Assistance Program
AP – EE:	Government Purchase Card Operating Procedures
AP – BB:	Management Control Evaluation Checklist
AP – DD:	Subcontracting Evaluation Guide
AP – FF:	Plan for Control of Non-Standard Clauses"

(https://www.acquisition.gov) [29]

Exhibit #10

First order of business. Let's make a clear distinction between two organizational structures that presides over the entire spectrum of business within the United States.

Those two major entities are (1) Government Public Sector and those businesses in the (2) Private Sector. Everything that happens relative to business is centered as a part of (1) the U.S. Government, or is related to the (2) Private Sector. Specifically, when it comes to contracting, whether construction, supply or service contract, the basic concepts and principles are very similar; however, there is one major, and I do mean, major difference.

In private sector contracting, the main goal is driven by several incentives; however, there is one that clearly distinguishes the two organizational entities. This major distinction is centered on "profit margin." The private sector is driven by achieving maximum profit margin that can be obtained during negotiations, or when submitting a Sealed Bid, or Request for Proposal. Conversely, the federal government is concerned with negotiating a contract or entering into a contract considered "fair and reasonable" to both the government and contractor. Therefore, why is this a focal point leading into this module of this book? At some point you (as an 8(a) contractor) will either enter into a Joint Venture (JV) or act as a prime contractor with a major subcontractor as a part of your teaming arrangement. Both subjects JV and/or prime/subcontractor relationship was discussed in the "Business Theory" section. The element of the underlying essence of "why" Government verses Private sector contracting is distinctly different. The main point you need to understand is teaming with any contractor (whether it's a large or small business) can have a tremendous effect on your ability to put a proposal together that is fair and reasonable. Specifically, its related to the amount of profit (or overhead) your business partner (subcontractor) has in their part of your final cost proposal. Let's remember there is no privity of contract between the government and subcontractor. The word privity means no direct contractual relationship between a third-party contractor. The contract is between you (the prime) and the government. This relationship will be further discussed at a later point.

Let's discuss the relationship of profit driven relative to being fair and reasonable. Within the government contracting arena, one of the main jobs (among many) of the Contracting Officer is to ensure at the end of negotiations, both parties can walk away from negotiations feeling there was a "win/win" situation for the government and contractor. This can only occur if a final agreement can be reached during negotiations. If you are teaming with a contractor who (1) doesn't have your best interest regarding your business agreement and (2) primarily concerned with making as much money as possible, then an agreement may not be able to be reached due to these factors.

Let's review this true scenario:

- ABC Construction Company (fictitious name) is an 8(a) contractor who doesn't have any additional certifications such as woman-owned, HUBZone or SDVOSB. So, in terms of meeting the mandated goals of the federal government, his business is classified as Small Business, Small Disadvantaged Business and certified as an 8(a) firm. As discussed earlier, a firm certified as 8(a) is automatically classified as a Small Disadvantaged Business, but a company who self certifies himself as a Small Disadvantaged Business is not automatically certified as 8(a). I wanted to reiterate how this process work.

- The owner of ABC company was contacted by the Forrest Department (fictitious name) and inquired about entering into a negotiated contract (any requirement less than $4 million can be a negotiated effort/without competition). The estimated range of this effort was between $800,000 and $1.2 million. The contractor was asked to provide a proposal to their KO at a specified date. The owner of the 8(a)-firm had a good idea of his estimated cost, which he projected to be in the $700,000 range. For this effort, he determined he could perform approximately 60% of the requirement due to the amount of dirt removal and other excavation efforts needed to complete the project. The job was similar to other efforts he had performed, which increased his overall confident level. This project was perfect for him as a prime contractor. The only thing missing was finding a subcontractor who had the additional skills and qualifications to complete the project. He had the perfect subcontractor in mind to complete his team. The subcontractor resides right there in the same location where the Forrest Department's project was located. Everything was perfect!

- The prime contractor (ABC Construction) requested a proposal from the subcontractor after which he would combine both cost proposals and submit the final cost document to the Forrest Department. One major problem ensued! The subcontractor's proposal was approximately

$1.3 million to complete their portion of the job. The owner of ABC Company was furious with the cost proposal that was submitted by the subcontractor. The prime contractor asked for a complete breakdown of the subcontractor's proposal, so a determination could be made as to why their proposal was so out of character and high in cost. The subcontractor refused to disclose any further cost data and basically insinuated either the 8(a) firm take their offer or find another subcontractor. Oh, there was one other major problem…it was the end of the fiscal year and the Forrest Department funds must be obligated prior to the end of the year, which was less than four weeks away. (The fiscal year for the federal government ended on 30 September and all funds not obligated on contract can be lost.)

- WHAT SHOULD YOU DO AS AN 8(a) CONTRACTOR WHOSE REPUTATION IS NOW ON THE LINE?
- To make long story short, the owner of ABC Construction Company went back to the Forrest Department and disclosed what happened between he and his subcontractor. In addition, he revealed the total price of his proposal, which was a combined total of $2 million. The KO (Forrest Department) was rather understanding and appreciated the honesty of the owner of ABC Company. The owner of the 8(a)-firm asked for a few more days to contact an alternate subcontractor and provide a proposal that was fair and reasonable. There was a meeting later that week with the Government, Prime Contractor, and new Subcontractor to have a fact-finding session reviewing the plans, specifications, and drawings of the required effort. The government had the right individuals at the meeting including Contracting, Project Management, Cost Estimating, Construction, etc.
- The meeting proved to be beneficial to both parties and a clear understanding of the basic requirement and other things both groups (Government/Contractor) overlooked due to ambiguity contained in the plans and specifications.
- Results of this potential disaster ended with both groups reaching an agreement that was fair and reasonable to both parties.

Of course, there are several other issues involved within this scenario, but for discussion and training purposes, there are real live fire lessons to be learned.

This is a true situation that tested the internal fortitude of the 8(a) contractor from many aspects. In direct discussion with the owner of ABC Construction Company, I concluded several mistakes were made in choosing this subcontractor. Our verbal exchange of why and what went wrong with this situation centered on the following questions (not in any order of precedence):

(1) Did the initial subcontractor of choice have any prior experience in performing government contracts?
(2) Why wouldn't the subcontractor provide a complete breakdown of the subcontractor's cost?
(3) Did the subcontractor have your best interest at heart?
(4) Was the subcontractor trying to take advantage of your 8(a) status?
(5) Did the Prime Contractor due diligence prior to selecting this type of subcontractor (explore and research the relationship this company has with other 8(a) firms working with the Forrest Department or work on other government contracts)?

These are questions that could be asked given this type of situation, but the real question is related to the damage this subcontractor could have had on the image and reputation of this 8(a) firm if there hadn't been enough time to find another subcontractor. I mentioned this in the previous business module—you only get one opportunity to make a first impression. Every contract stands on its own individual merit.

You must take this type of an approach every time you enter into a contractual agreement. This scenario will be further explored during this section as we cover the prime contractor's proposal rate structure.

The "profit" area will be fully discussed later in this section; however, the major point presented is examining the major difference between a contractor functioning in the private sector, and those contractors whose target market is the federal government. By the end of this section, it will become clear as to why all profits from the prime, first and second tier contractors (subsequently all subcontractors) included in your proposal must be controlled relative to profit and overhead costs. There are many areas similar and different between government and private sector contracting. Your primary focus is targeting government contracts. Now that the true meaning of "fair and reasonable" concept in comparison to "profit driven" has been established, let's fully explore this module referred to as Business Preparation. Before we get engulfed with obtaining a government contract, there are a few concepts that must be understood. In government contracting there are five basic areas (I consider are critical contracting processes) are applicable to the acquisition process under the auspices of various methods used by the contracting officer. Those areas or acquisition processes/methods used are:

- Request for Quotes (RFQ)
- Invitation for Bid (IFB)
- Best Value (with tradeoffs)
- Best Value using Lowest Price Technical Acceptable (LPTA) process
- Request for Proposal (RFP)

In addition, you must have a basic understanding of the Type of Contracts as covered in FAR Part 16. There are other acquisition methods used, but it's important to understand the basic processes you are most likely to encounter when working with the government. (Note: This is not a course on contracting but identifying key areas so that you have a better understanding relative to working with the federal government.) For clarification purposes as stated within the FAR, examples of various contracting methods and contract types are:

Subchapter C – Contracting Methods and Contract Types
FAR Part 13 - Simplified Acquisition Procedures (Request for Quotation, RFQ)
FAR Part 14 - Sealed Bidding (Invitation for Bid, IFB)
FAR Part 15 - Contracting by Negotiation:
(Best Value w/Trade Off; Best Value Lowest Price Technical Acceptable; Request For Proposal)
FAR art 16 - Types of Contracts (Fixed and Cost Type)

[Again, it is important to understand these processes or someone within your organization who has this type of experience is at a premium – at your leisure review the above areas within the FAR.]

Each one of the contracting methods is applicable to the type of process used to receive and evaluate a contractor's proposal and/or bid. These methods have unique characteristics in determining the correct process to obtain any good or service. We will explore the definition of each method, but also beware…there are hidden factors contained in each process completely overlooked by most of the small business owners. Don't worry, we shall reveal those characteristics as each area is reviewed. Again, there are many acquisition processes used within the federal government, but these are the areas an 8(a) firm should focus on.

Early in the acquisition process, the contracting activity may solicit a "Sources Sought" by synopsizing a request for small business participation in Federal Business Opportunity (https://www.fbo.gov).[30] [This is a web site where jobs are posted for interested contractors looking for federal job opportunities] By definition, the Sources Sought process is an effort to identify the availability of large/small businesses who have a level of interest to perform the requirements as stated in the solicitation (prior to being released). A Sources Sought must be conducted every six months regardless of the time frame of an award for a specific good or services procured by that contracting activity. As an example, if a good or service is procured (1 Jan 2017) during a particular time frame, a "Sources Sought' must be done for the acquisition of that same effort if is procured six months or anytime thereafter (1 July 2017). This process is to ensure changes are captured relative to existing and new contractors entering into the business market are known. This is due to some small businesses may become classified as a large business or in some cases, a business may become debunk. Over the years, I personally feel the true meaning of obtaining a Sources Sought has been improperly used by some government contracting officials. Some KOs have used this tool as a way of determining acquisition strategy such as unrestrictive or using one of the small business set-aside methods. In some cases, this information was used to evaluate (by a committee) and determine the capability of a firm. However, it is the prerogative of the KO to use the results of a Sources Sought to determine acquisition strategy in some capacity. From a personal standpoint, a Sources Sought should only be used for determining a level of interest of firms in the marketplace, to possibly bid on that effort at a later date.

It's imperative to understand the meaning and intent of each of the above acquisition processes. It has an enormous impact on the way to formulate a proposal regardless whether the requirement is a competitive or negotiated effort. Since these processes are described in the Federal Acquisition

Regulations (FAR), let's provide an <u>excerpt</u> of the text book responses of each definition:

"(1) RFQ. (FAR Part 13)

Definition (FAR 13.001): Document used in soliciting price and deliver quotations that meet minimum quality specifications for a specific quantity of specific goods and/or services. RFQs are usually not advertised publicly and are used commonly for: (1) standard, off-the-shelf items, (2) items built to known specifications, (3) items required in small quantities, or (4) items whose purchase price falls below sealed-bidding threshold. Suppliers respond to a RFQ with firm quotations, and generally the lowest-priced quotation is awarded the contract.

Purpose (FAR13.002): The purpose of this part is to prescribe simplified acquisition procedures to:
(a) Reduce administrative costs
(b) Improve opportunities for small, small disadvantaged, women-owned, HUBZone, and service-disabled veteran-owned small business concerns to obtain a fair proportion of government contracts
(c) Promote efficiency and economy in contracting
(d) Avoid unnecessary burdens for agencies and contractors

Policy (FAR 13.003):
(a) Agencies shall use simplified acquisition procedures to the maximum extent practicable for all purchases of supplies or services not exceeding the simplified acquisition threshold (including purchases at or below the micro-purchase threshold). This policy does not apply if an agency can meet its requirement using –
     (1) Required sources of supply; e.g., Federal Prison Industries, Committee for Purchase from People Who are Blind or Severely Disabled, and Federal Supply Schedule contracts)
     (2) Existing indefinite delivery/indefinite quantity contracts
     (3) Other established contracts
(b) Acquisitions of supplies or services that have an anticipated dollar value exceeding $3,000 ($15,000 for acquisitions as described in 13.201(g)(1) but not exceeding $150,000 ($300,000

for acquisitions described in paragraph (1) of the simplified acquisition threshold definition at 2.101) are reserved exclusively for small business concerns and shall be set aside.

(c) See FAR 13.003 – Policy for additional information"[31]

Teaching point: When there is a requirement procured as an RFQ, it proposes the determining factor of the award will be based on price. There are other factors such as product availability, lead time, terms and conditions, and other related factors, but the important thing to remember the lowest price submitted is usually the basis for award. Therefore, when bidding on products, and/or goods or services, the key element of price is the focal point of submitting your quote. [Again, this area of discussion is to increase awareness of the diverse types of solicitations you will be confronted with, and to provide a basic knowledge and awareness of the key factor, relative to this type of requirement.]

"(2) Sealed Bidding, IFB – (FAR 14.101-14.105):

(a) An IFB or "Invitation for Bid" is the method used for the sealed bid process.

Typically, an IFB includes a description of the product or service to be acquired, instructions for preparing a bid, the conditions for purchase, delivery, payment, and other requirements associated with the bid, including a deadline for bid submissions.

(b) Each sealed bid is opened in a public setting by a government contracting officer, at the time designated in the invitation. All bids are read aloud and recorded. A contract is then awarded by the agency to the lowest bidder who is determined to be fully responsive/responsible to the needs of the government.

(c) Government-wide IFBs are available daily for review in the Government's online listing service, Federal Business Opportunities (www.fbo.gov). This electronic service, which is discussed in detail later, also provides direct links to available IFB invitations. The above information is basic characteristics of an IFB; however, there are other elements of the acquisition process that is equally as important:

- Responsiveness of bids (FAR 14.301)

- Bid submission (FAR 14.302)
- Modification or withdrawal of bids (FAR 14.303)
- Submission, modification, and withdrawal of bids (FAR 14.304)

Each one of these areas are specific in nature relative to the requirements necessary to execute any one of these processes. (Review each for a complete in-depth overview of its significance to IFB utilization.)"[32]

Teaching point: This process is based on lowest responsive/responsible bid submitted by a contractor. When there are various efforts that are being considered under the IFB process, the award is predominantly going to be made based on the lowest bid submitted. There is one very important process that occurs with IFBs that most companies fail to understand the level of importance. IFBs are based on bid openings. This means all bids are read aloud occurring at a specific time, place, and location. If possible, it is critical to have a company representative present at these bid openings. This is a time to obtain information on the bidding process of those companies who not only submitted a bid and related price, too. This pricing information can be very useful for efforts that occur later. This provides an opportunity to determine how your bid compared to other bids submitted. If you are teaming with another contractor (subcontractor), it is imperative to ensure your price and the subcontractor's price are reasonable from a total cost basis. The only shot to win this effort is based on initial price submitted by your company (barring other related factors). In addition, an IFB relates to a competitive situation involving other contractors. This point may seem mundane to some but to many 8(a) firms who are new to government contracting, this information is critically important.

"3. Best Value with Trade Offs (FAR 15.100)
    What is Best Value?
    Best value is the expected outcome of any acquisition that ensures the customer needs are met in the most effective, economical, and timely manner. It is the result of the combination of: the unique circumstances of each acquisition; the acquisition strategy; choice of contracting method; and the award decision. Best value is the goal of sealed bidding, simplified acquisition, commercial item acquisition, negotiated acquisition, and any other specialized acquisition method, or combination of methods.

Negotiated acquisition techniques used to obtain best value may span a "continuum" from low priced technically acceptable, to trade-offs between price, past performance, and the technical solution.

What is the Best Value Continuum?
A recognition the government always seeks to obtain is the best value in negotiated acquisitions; using any one or a combination of source selection approaches, and that the acquisition should be tailored to the requirement. At one end of this continuum is the low priced technically acceptable strategy, and at the other end is a process by which elements of a proposed solution can be traded off against each other to determine the solution that provides the government with the overall best value. All such tradeoffs are conducted according to the source selection factors and sub factors identified in the solicitation. An agency can obtain best value in negotiated acquisitions by using any one, or a combination of source selection approaches. In several types of acquisitions, the relative importance of cost or price may vary. For example, in acquisitions where the requirement is clearly definable, and the risk of unsuccessful contract performance is minimal cost or price may play a dominant role in source selection. The less definitive the requirement, the more development work required, or the greater the performance risk, the more technical or past performance considerations may play a dominant role in source selection.

Tradeoff process (FAR 15.101-1):
(a) A tradeoff process is appropriate when it may be in the best interest of the government to award to other than the lowest priced offerors or other than the highest technically rated offerors.
(b) When using a tradeoff process, the following apply:
   (1) All evaluation factors and significant sub factors that will affect contract award and their relative importance shall be clearly stated in the solicitation; and
   (2) The solicitation shall state whether all evaluation factors other than cost or price, when combined, are significantly more important than, approximately equal to, or significantly less important than cost or price.

(c) This process permits tradeoffs among cost or price and non-cost factors and allows the government to accept other than the lowest priced proposal. The perceived benefits of the higher priced proposal shall merit the additional cost, and the rationale for tradeoffs must be documented in the file in accordance with 15.406.

Oral presentations (FAR 15.102):

(a) Oral presentations by offerors as requested by the government may substitute or augment written information. Use of oral presentations as a substitute for portions of a proposal can be effective in streamlining the source selection process. Oral presentations may occur at any time in the acquisition process, and are subject to the same restrictions as written information, regarding timing and content...

(b) The solicitation may require each offeror to submit part of its proposal through oral presentations. However, representations and certifications shall be submitted as required in the FAR provisions at 52.204-8 or 52.212-3(b), and a signed offer sheet (including any exceptions to the Government's terms and conditions) shall be submitted in writing."[33]

Teaching point: In simplistic terms, Best Value is used when there are a variety of known or unknown factors that have a significant impact on the overall development of goods or services required. Normally, it takes time to complete the evaluation process reviewed by a Source Selection Evaluation Board. When there is a requirement based on Best Value (with Tradeoffs), the lowest price is or does not have to be the determining factor. There are other factors such as elements known as Evaluation Factors that have various impacts on the completion of a project.

The key teaching point is that price alone is not the determining factor, and there are other elements stated in the solicitation that plays a key role in who ultimately gets the award. Evaluation Factors may include areas such as Past History/Experience, Management Staff assigned to the project, Price, Technical Capability, and other elements the procuring activity may deemed applicable to that project. The main issue relative to Evaluation Factors is to ensure you answer each of the elements as succinctly as possible with information directly related to each factor. This is a mistake many companies make relative to solicitations evaluated under this type of acquisition process. The Evaluation Factors will be ranked in order of precedence, or the order of importance for review and analysis purposes. Do not overlook this key area based on level of importance. Pay close attention to the solicitation! It will provide clear instructions on completing and submitting your proposal based on guidelines utilizing Best Value method.

"4. Lowest Price Technical Acceptable (LPTA) (FAR 15.101-2)
The lowest price technically acceptable source selection process is appropriate when best value is expected to result from selection of the technically acceptable proposal with the lowest evaluated price.
LPTA is appropriate when:
(1) The evaluation factors and significant sub factors that establish the requirements of acceptability shall be set forth in the solicitation. Solicitations shall specify that award will be made based on the lowest evaluated price of proposals meeting or exceeding the acceptability standards for non-cost factors. If the contracting officer documents the file pursuant to 15.304(c)(3)(iii), *past performance* need not be an evaluation factor in lowest price technically acceptable source selections. If the contracting officer elects to consider past performance as an evaluation factor, it shall be evaluated in accordance with 15.305. However, the comparative assessment in 15.305(a)(2)(i) does not apply. If the contracting officer determines that a small business' past performance is not acceptable, the matter shall be referred to the Small Business Administration for a Certificate of Competency (COC) determination, in accordance with the procedures contained in subpart 19.6 and 15 U.S.C.637(b)(7)).
(2) Tradeoffs are not permitted.
(3) Proposals are evaluated for acceptability but not ranked using the non-cost/price factors.
(4) Exchanges may occur (see 15.306)."[34]
It must be noted the technical proposal is evaluated first determining technical capability and acceptance subsequently followed by opening the cost proposal. At that time, whoever has the lowest price wins the award (assuming all things equal).

Teaching Point: Throughout my career within the federal government, LPTA method was predominantly used (within my organization) when procuring requirements that exceed the Simplified Acquisition Threshold relative to larger procurements. Please note things may have changed since this time frame.

However, the bottom line is clear under this method. Each company must be determined to be technically acceptable to be considered for award. Therefore, step one is to meet/exceed technical qualifications stated within the solicitation. In the development of your proposal, the most important thing to remember under the LPTA process is to ensure your company fully address the technical qualifications as stated within the solicitation. Again, do not provide extraneous data in answering the information regarding your technical competency. There are many cases, when companies provide information that does not specifically answer the questions asked relative to technical competency. If you are not successful in getting past step #1 (Technical), there is no step #2. Under the assumption your company is considered Technically acceptable, the follow-on process, is opening the cost proposals and low bid wins the award. Therefore, the pitfalls discussed ensuring your price is fair and reasonable in a negotiated process still is applicable under this type of competitive process. The prices submitted must still follow all the guidelines and compilations required in the development of cost. Hopefully, it is now clear the difference between Best Value (Trade Offs) and Best Value (LPTA).

"5. RFP (FAR 15.203)

   (a) Request for Proposals (RFPs) are used in negotiated acquisitions to communicate government requirements to prospective contractors and to solicit proposals. RFPs for competitive acquisitions shall, at a minimum, describe the:

     (1) Government's requirement,

     (2) Anticipated terms and conditions that will apply to the contract,

        (i) The solicitation may authorize offerors to propose alternative terms and conditions, including the contract line item number (CLIN) structure, and

          (ii) When alternative CLIN structures are permitted, the evaluation approach should consider the potential impact on other terms and conditions or the requirement (e.g., place of performance or payment and funding requirements)

    (3) Information required to be in the offerors proposal, and

    (4) Factors and significant sub factors that will be used to evaluate the proposal and their relative importance.

b. An RFP may be issued for OMB Circular A-76 studies

c. Electronic commerce may be used to issue RFPs and to receive proposals, modifications, and revisions. In this case, the RFP shall specify the electronic commerce methods(s) that offerors may use.

d. Contracting officers may issue RFPs and/or authorize receipt of proposals, modifications, or revisions by facsimile

e. Letter RFPs may be used in sole source acquisitions and other appropriate circumstances. Use of a letter RFP does not relieve the contracting officer from complying with other FAR requirements. Letter RFPs should be as complete as possible and, at a minimum, should contain the following:

    (1) RFP number and date

    (2) Name, address, and telephone number of the contracting officer

    (3) Type of contract contemplated

    (4) Quantity, description, and required delivery dates for the item

    (5) Applicable certifications and representations

    (6) Anticipated contract terms and conditions

    (7) Instructions to offerors and evaluation criteria

    (8) Proposal due date and time

    (9) Other relevant information: incentives, variation in delivery schedule, etc.

(f) Oral RFPs are authorized when processing a written solicitation would delay the acquisition of supplies or services to the detriment of the government and a notice is not required under 5.202. Use of an oral RFP does not relieve the contracting officer from complying with other FAR requirements.

(1) The contract files supporting oral solicitations should include –
    (i) A description of the requirement
    (ii) Rationale for use of an oral solicitation
    (iii) Sources solicited, including the date, time, name of individuals contacted, and prices offered
    (iv) The solicitation number provided to the prospective offerors
(2) The information furnished to potential offerors under oral solicitations should include appropriate items from paragraph (e) from the above section."[35]

Before we proceed, let's refresh our memory. The definition (modified version) of (1) Acquisition Strategy is determining whether a project will be advertised by the procuring agency as (1) unrestricted; (2) small business set-aside; (3) 8(a) competitive; or (4) 8(a) negotiated. Under the small business set-aside arena, the project may be restricted to one of the following categories woman-owned; HUBZone; or SDVOSB (if needed refer to Business Theory Module for detailed definition/analysis).

(2) Acquisition Process and/or method (whichever you prefer) is whether a project will be advertised/synopsized as utilizing one of the five methods identified above; e.g., RFQ, IFB, Best Value with Trade Offs, Best Value (LPTA), and RFP.
(3) The third area that you must be aware is the two types of contracts, which are: Firm Fixed Priced and Cost-Reimbursement Contracts.[36]

In the above reading, the basic definition and key areas were covered regarding the five areas RFQ, IFB, Best Value (Trade Off), Best Value (LPTA) and RFP. This is an appropriate time to briefly touch basis on the two types of contracts; e.g., Firm Fixed Price and Cost Reimbursement. The following is a brief excerpt answer for both areas:

Firm Fixed Price Contract:
"General 16.201. Fixed-price types of contracts provides a firm price, or, in appropriate cases, an adjustable price. Fixed-price contracts providing

for an adjustable price, may include a ceiling price, a target price (including target cost, or both). The contracting officer shall use firm-fixed-price or fixed-price with economic price adjustment contracts when acquiring commercial items…

Description 16.202-1. A firm-fixed-price contract provides for a price that is not subject to any adjustment on the basis of the contractor's cost experience in performing the contract. This contract type places upon the contractor maximum risk and full responsibility for all costs and resulting profit or loss. It provides maximum incentive for the contractor to control costs and perform effectively and imposes a minimum administrative burden upon the contracting parties…

Application 16.202.2. A firm-fixed-price contract is suitable for acquiring commercial items or for acquiring other supplies or services on the basis of reasonably definite functional or detailed specifications when the contracting officer can establish fair and reasonable prices at the outset, such as when –

(a) There is adequate price competition;
(b) There are reasonable price comparisons with prior purchases of the same or similar supplies or services made on a competitive basis or supported by valid certified cost or pricing data;
(c) Available cost or pricing information permits realistic estimates of the probable costs of performance; or
(d) Performance uncertainties can be identified, and reasonable estimates of their cost impact can be made, and the contractor is willing to accept a firm fixed price representing assumption of the risks involved.[37]

"Cost Reimbursement Contracts: General 16.301. (No Text)
Description 16.301-1. Cost-reimbursement types of contracts provide for payment of allowable incurred costs, to the extent prescribed in the contract. These contracts establish an estimate of total cost for the purpose of obligating funds and establishing a ceiling that the contractor may not exceed (except at its own risk) without the approval of the contracting officer.

Application 16.301-2. (a) The contracting officer shall use cost-reimbursement contracts only when –

(1) Circumstances do not allow the agency to define its requirements sufficiently to allow for a fixed-price type contract; or

(2) Uncertainties involved in contract performance do not permit costs to be estimated with sufficient accuracy to use any type of fixed-price contract.

(b) The contracting officer shall document the rationale for selecting the contract type in the written acquisition plan and ensure that the plan is approved and signed at least one level above the contracting officer."[38] The below chart shows the basic definition and use:

- Firm Fixed Price (FFP) – Allows buyer to budget fixed price; requires seller to detail scope and accurately estimate price; very common
- Fixed Price Incentive Fee (FFIF) – includes incentive to motivate seller to produce at greater speed
- Fixed Price Economic Price Adjustment (FF EPA) – compensates for year to year economic changes
- Time and Materials (T&M) – typically used for small initiatives
- Purchase Order (PO) – typically used for commodity items
- Cost Plus Fixed Fee (CPFF) – typically variable costs are cost-plus and predictable costs are fixed fee
- Cost Plus Incentive Fee (CPIF) – actual costs plus incentive to motivate seller to produce at greater speed
- Cost Plus Award Fee (CPAF) – actual costs plus award based on customer satisfaction with agreed criteria
- Cost Plus Percent of Cost (CPPC) – actual cost plus % of actual; the higher the cost; the higher the fees

---

Exhibit #11

Note: For practical contracting purposes, most acquisitions are under the firm-fixed-price umbrella. Remember, this is not a book on contracting. For further detail understanding, and analysis: "What document are you going to refer to? The answer is the FAR!

"Tell me and I forget. Teach me and I remember. Involve me and I learn."

Now we have refreshed our thought processes with a few important terms and concepts, let's proceed directly into the centerpiece of this module, which is: "Bid Preparation and Negotiations." Additionally, you will see how the above processes defined play an important part leading up to negotiations with the government team.

For training purposes, the KO advertise a requirement as an 8(a)-negotiated effort. In accordance with the FAR and contract law, each valid requirement must be advertised or synopsized for public review and awareness. The acquisition strategy was internally approved as a negotiated effort with one 8(a) firm. So, in response to the solicitation, the KO ask for a Request for Proposal (RFP) to be submitted by a closing date. Again, for informational purposes, IFBs and RFQs have bid opening dates in correlation to RFPs, which have proposal closing dates (again referred to FAR document for further guidance/information).

The below chart (exhibit #12) was used in the Business Presentation Module to indicate the firm's knowledge of the acquisition process from an internal perspective but shows the steps used in the proposal preparation and submission process. The area in the square is related to steps used in the Business Preparation Module. It's should become clearer and clearer how each module overlaps in knowledge, data, and level of importance.

Chatman Construction Company (how)

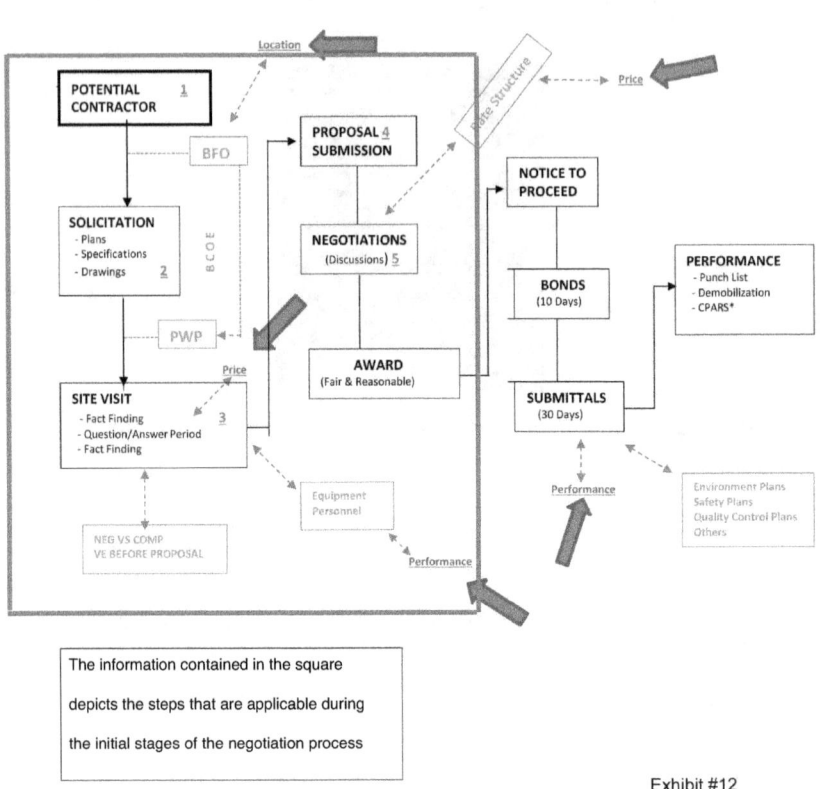

Exhibit #12

Negotiations

Let's define the art of negotiations and the correlation of various elements that are critical toward reaching a fair and reasonable price with the government. The basic definition of negotiations is "mutual discussion and arrangements of the terms of a transaction or agreement, the act or process of negotiating."[39] There are many courses offered by the government and private sector on the art of negotiations. They both identify similar and sometimes different tactics used during this process. Regardless of where you take a course on negotiations, there is one and only one word to define this process, which is "preparation". Throughout my career, taking many variations of negotiating courses, all centered on the degree of time, effort, and dedication used prior to entering the negotiation process with your opposition.

Since preparation is the key element toward success in negotiation, we will explore each function on an independent basis that results in an agreement between the government and you. Each of the five sections circled in the above graph are based on how well you have prepared yourself to lead up to negotiations. In most cases, one might think preparation is developing a strategy relative to compiling your proposal. This is the underlying difference when taking a course on negotiations in comparison to this segment of this module. Text book teaching on negotiation strategically stresses preparation in this regard. Preparation from our viewpoint starts with (1) being selected as a Potential Contractor, (2) Solicitation Preparation, (3) Site Visit, (4) Proposal Submission, and (5) actual Negotiations leading up to the Award. This is looking, reviewing, understanding, and strategically combining the information and data discovered during your preparation process is highly critical. The easiest way to teach this module is to identify those key areas; define those key areas and show how together they will improve your opportunity for a positive and successful negotiations creating a "win/win" situation for both parties. The definition of preparation and the integration of those areas contained in the square defines the contents of your proposal as it relates to the contents of the solicitation.

The following are those key elements:

Solicitation: Initially, you received a Request for Proposal (RFP). The Solicitation is the main document used to create the RFP. The Solicitation (and eventual contract) is based or follows the Uniformed Contract Format (exhibit #13), [40] which includes sections and titles of information required as a part of your proposal submission. Let's keep this simple...you have received a RFP from the government that meets the format, outline and criteria that is stated within the solicitation.

The first concern I witnessed over the years was based on contractors not fully reading and grasping the information stated within the solicitation. In many situations, questions were directed to the contractor specifically related to various areas of the solicitation, but the contractor was unable to correctly provide the right answer or response in their proposal. Therefore, if you are unaware of the contents of the solicitation, how can you begin to prepare a proposal that is sufficient leading up to actual negotiations? This is an impossible feat to overcome. As a potential contractor, you have failed before you started. Look how devastating this can be to your company but, more importantly, to the federal government.

UNIFORM CONTRACT FORMAT

PART I - THE SCHEDULE

   A. Solicitation/Contract Format

   B. Supplies or Services and Prices/Costs

   C. Description/Specifications/Statement of Work

   D. Packaging and Marking

   E. Inspection and Acceptance

   F. Deliveries or Performance

   G. Contract Administration and Data

   H. Special Contract Requirements

PART II - CONTRACT CLAUSES

   I.   Contract Clauses

PART III - List of Documents, Exhibits, and Other Attachments

   J. List of Attachments

PART IV - Representations and Instructions

   K. Representations, Certifications, and other Statements of Offerors or Respondents

   L. Instructions, Conditions, and Notices to Offerors or Respondents

   M. Evaluation Factors

Exhibit #13

By definition, a solicitation is the practice, or act, or an instance of soliciting especially; entreaty, importunity; a moving or drawing force; incitement, allurement. The Solicitation includes sections I, II, III, and IV as stated in the Uniformed Contract Format. The final negotiated contract does not include Section IV (Representations and Instructions) but incorporate Section K by Reference. Specifically, the Solicitation contains information that covers:

   i - Name, address, location of issuing activity, including room/building where proposals or information to be submitted

   ii - Solicitation #

   iii - Date of Issuance

   iv - Closing date and time

   v - Number of pages

   vi - Requisition or other purchase authority

vii - Brief description of item or services

viii -Requirement for offeror to provide its name complete address

ix - Offer expiration date [41]

It is clear relative to the contents of the RFP/Solicitation and what is to be included. The government has ensured the information needed for negotiations is provided in a manner that can be easily reviewed and understood. Anything provided to the contractor by the federal government is done so that little room is left for misinterpretation. One word that I want to introduce is "Ambiguity or Ambiguous." For now, anything relative to Plans, Specifications, Drawings, Solicitations, Contracts, Synopsis, submitted by the government to the contractor that is ambiguous in any way is the responsibility of the government to fix and/or acknowledge. This factor is critical in situations regarding 'bid protest' under competitive actions. In most cases, factors that are unclear are resolved during the negotiated effort or prior to negotiations.

Many contractors fail to fully review and analyze the solicitation in its entirety. Throughout my career, it is safe to say the government doesn't have the internal personnel/manpower to clearly perform the detailed analysis needed to ensure plans, specifications, and drawings (which are the key areas of the solicitation) include information that is 100% accurate. My experience in the private and government sector supports this statement to be true. In most cases, there's a limited number of personnel assigned and/or responsible for covering many projects. In your case (as a contractor) may have multiple project efforts but have more flexibility when covering a specific project. This doesn't mean the government is inept in any stretch of the imagination, but its management and assigned resources are limited relative to the high volume of actions that has to be executed/awarded. When a contractor receives an opportunity whether it is negotiated or on a competitive basis, the manpower needed is totally allotted to that requirement. I feel confident to say the advantage should go to the contractor regarding knowing, understanding, and applying necessary resources to analyze and breakdown the solicitation prior to submitting their cost proposal. This may sound impossible since the government wrote the solicitation and its contents. One note to understand, many projects funded (after the federal budget has been passed) are efforts that have been sitting on the shelf for months, or even years. Once funding has been allotted and approved for that project, it is now subject to time constraints or a period during the fiscal year when the money must be obligated. In most cases 30 September (based on the funding appropriation) is the end of the fiscal year for funds to be obligated. Let digress a little and cover several factors affecting solicitations, proposals and ultimately contract award!

- Project/Funding: The government is based or operates on a fiscal year cycle that start 1 October and ends 30 September of that next calendar year (example start 1 October 2015 ending 30 September 2016). Normally, the federal budget is passed somewhere during the second quarter (January thru March) and it does vary from time to time. Since "monies" are sporadically funded, the federal government then operates on what is called a "Continuing Resolution" basis.

  Congress appropriates a limited amount of funding to operate the federal government for a limited amount of time. This really hinders some federal agencies from making sound decisions on whether a project can go forth during that fiscal year due to funding uncertainty. There are many projects that are ready to proceed forward in the acquisition cycle but cannot due to lack of funding. In some cases, the plans/specifications are not up to date and cannot be reviewed until the budget has been passed. There's one huge dilemma relative to funding. Most projects (construction/supplies/service) are funded utilizing one-year funds, meaning dollars approved for a particular project must be obligated (awarded on contract) prior to the end of the fiscal year (30 September). There are exceptions to this analysis when some agencies may be funded on a two-year basis or beyond the initial one year authorization/allocation of funds. As a contractor, you can continue to strategize and prepare your organization, so at that crucial moment, you are in full position to perform once funding becomes available. Based on this type of funding process, private sector contractors have a huge advantage over most federal government agencies. (the above is a modified excerpt of the federal government budgetary process)

- Project Management: The Project Manager Team assigned to that effort has a tremendous problem associated to available funding. The government has many projects that are 60% or 70% finished and may need minimal work to ensure plans and associated documents are completed. During this period of waiting on budgetary decisions to be made, personnel assigned to the PDT (project delivery team) remain idle, and only work on projects that have carryover funds or is covered under some other funding stream. Personnel included on the PDT are individuals responsible for review, completion, and coordination of the plans, specifications, and drawings. When there's a multitude of projects (plans/specs/drawings finished/unfinished); limited resources available to perform functions necessary to ensure maximum accuracy; no available funds; abbreviated time frames to complete acquisition cycle prior to the end of the fiscal year results in errors relative to documents that are included in the solicitation. This result in solicitation documents and support information that may be inaccurate or ambiguous in some areas. The government, overall, does a tremendous job with project efforts but having necessary tools to reduce errors that streamlines efficiency are limited. In many cases, these are minor errors that are contained in the solicitation and can be easily corrected. By the time the federal budget is passed, there is a short window of opportunity for projects to be awarded prior to 30 September. By the time the budget is approved, there may be five or six months remaining to complete that acquisition process. Again, there are many efforts that are forced to be reviewed, coordinated, and provided to the contractor and subsequently negotiated.

Hopefully, you can understand how much undue pressure the federal agency is under. Therefore, each contractor should be as complete and thorough as possible in understanding the parameters of the solicitation.

- Contracting: The KO is responsible for initiating and providing the RFP/Solicitation to the contractor. However, he or she is not _fully_ responsible for the contents of the plans, specifications, and drawings. This individual is under tremendous pressure with a high volume relative to workload. This may sound a little harsh, but it's everyone's responsibility relative to the accuracy and the contents of these documents. It's true the KO has final responsibility and authority to ensure all documents are accurate and concise, but it's easy to understand how information can be unclear. To provide further insight, the KO does not have the technical qualifications needed to ensure all documents are as accurate as they should be. There are many internal meetings within the organization that covers various contents of acquisition documents and data; however, the factors discussed play a significant role on determining accuracy of related documents. Many of my counterparts and co-workers may highly disagree with my assumption, but that's okay. Sometimes it's okay to agree to disagree!

- Another factor that affects this process is the acquisition timeline regarding competitive verses negotiated acquisitions. It takes approximately 75 days and in some contracting organizations up to 90 days to complete the competitive acquisition process. This is the timeline from start to finish in the award of a project solicited on a competitive basis. The KO may use an additional 15 days (up to a total of 90) depending on the nature of the requirement, dollar value, complexity and other factors could affect contract award.

- For projects that are negotiated, the designated timeline is approximately 45 days for contract award (start to finish). Therefore, from the time the federal budget is completed and approved, ultimately has a tremendous effect on contracting personnel. Contracting personnel are affected more so than any other department/personnel who is involved with the acquisition cycle of any project that is awarded.

- Let's assume the federal budget is approved in March, appropriations are release and at the lowest level funding has been received. It's now April and projects have to be revisited for accuracy and validity (still a viable needed project); personnel have to be assigned or reassigned based on availability; all projects have to be in contracting prior to July 15 (those that are to be advertised on competitive basis) needing a minimum of 75 days for contract award; projects received after this date must be done on a negotiated basis (again, a negotiated effort can be done within a 45 day period or less).

It's imperative to understand as an 8(a) contractor, you have been fortunate enough to be in this position and is one that must be taken seriously. The information covered in the above area is information most contractors have little to no knowledge.

Let's get back to the solicitation function and continue to explore each of the key areas. You should have a better understanding of the composition of the Solicitation and sub areas that are included. Each part in the Solicitation area stated in the Uniform Contract Format are important.

For further discussion and teaching purposes and from my viewpoint there are four areas critical regarding the knowledge, data, and overall comprehension of understanding. Those areas are (1) Bid Schedule, (2) Plans/Specifications, (3) Drawings, and (4) Statement of Work. Do not misunderstand, everything in the Solicitation is important, and has a significant role in the success or failure of any contractor. Those contractors who do not fully read the Solicitation, surely lack confidence and adequate understanding of the contents of that document. Why do you think I referenced these four areas? The answer is, or should be, obvious: "The heartbeat of your proposal is based on understanding, analyzing and comprehension of these specific areas." Again, for the hundredth time, this is not a book on contracting, but these are areas overlooked and misinterpreted.

Let's assume a construction project will be negotiated, and you are putting your proposal together. The key area in the solicitation is the contents of the Bid Schedule. Your proposal will be compiled from information contained in this section.

Bid Schedule: Therefore, let's analyze this area called the Bid Schedule.

Depending on the agency, the Bid Schedule may be found upfront in the solicitation. (Section B - Supplies or Services and Prices/Cost). The Bid Schedule contains a list of Line Items that depict those areas of the project or efforts needed by the agency. Normally, the first area or Line Items is titled Mobilization/Demobilization (construction effort), which requires a cost relative to movement of equipment, personnel and other elements associated to this function. In most cases, 60% of cost associated with this Line Item can be billed upfront as compensation associated with these costs. There may be a variety of other Line Items covering rock cost, clearing, and grubbing, as well as other requirements. Information on each Line Item in the Bid Schedule is further defined (in complete scope) in the plans, specifications, and drawings section. The teaching point is anything stated in the Bid Schedule has a complete and detailed description of its functions; quantities; locations; and concerns.

The Bid Schedule (in the solicitation) is the area that identifies and describes the parameters or line items to be performed. In addition, each Line Items provide an Item Description and Unit of Measure (UM). This is an important fact that one must comprehend, which is: Each bid schedule contains specific Line Items that correlates directly to the Statement of Work that identifies (in details) the requirements of each Line Item; furthermore, is defined in the plans, specifications, and drawings. The key point is to fully review each Line Item as it relates to the Plans, Specifications and Drawings. In general, the Statement of Work (SOW) defines project-specific activities, deliverables and timelines for a contractor providing services to a client. The SOW typically includes detailed requirements and pricing, with standard regulatory and government terms and conditions.

SOLICITATION
PROPOSAL
COVER SHEET
BID SCHEDULE
LINE ITEM PRICING
PLANS & SPECIFICATIONS
DRAWINGS
STATEMENT of WORK

Let's take a closer look at this process:

(1) Receive the Solicitation (clearly analyze from front to back)

(2) Somewhere after the front cover sheet, locate and review the Bid Schedule (Section B)

(3) Each Line Items states what is to be reviewed, analyzed, delivered, and most importantly identified relative to cost; e.g., how much are you willing to pay and considered to be fair and reasonable.

(4) Turn to the area within Section C identified as Plans/Specifications, Drawings and Statement of Work. Each Line Item stated in the Bid Schedule may be identified by the same number stated in the Plans, Specifications, & Drawings. This may not necessarily be the case. The information in the Plans, Specifications will cover in detail the requirements of each Line Item within the text. The bottom line is to read all the information completely.

(5) The Plans and Specifications will provide in-depth description of the independent Line Item including a complete technical overview of functionality, technical, and performance requirements of that Line Item.

(6) All Drawings are applicable to this effort will provide a graphical representation of the data and functional aspects of each Line Item as it relates to the description, plans, specification, and Statement of Work.

(7) The Statement of Work will define various activities, deliverables, and timelines relative to completing these tasks within a required Period of Performance.

In a bid schedule, each Line Item is described in a unit of measure (EA, JB, LB, TN) as an example; unit price; and an extended price based on the description of that Line Item. There's one crucial factor you must be aware that's related to the unit of measure stated in the Bid Schedule. The one area constantly overlooked is the unit of measure identified as "JB," which stands for "JOB". This area was previously called "Lump Sum". This area is critical! In most cases, the government is asking the contractor to provide pricing for this Line Item, based on functions, processes or efforts, somewhat unknown or better yet, not clearly defined (in my opinion). The Plans and Specifications define the intended needs of the agency. In actuality, (if you look very closely to the information) there is room for speculation that may lead to a higher priced line item. In other words, each Line Item have a correlating section in the Plans/Specifications/Drawings area, which explains the details required by each Line Item. Therefore, pay close attention to any Line Item with a unit of measure of "JOB." Be prepared to ask questions relative to this Line Item. This is an opportunity to reduce ambiguity thereby reduce cost.

The teaching point in this area is quite simple. Review, understand, and analyze each Line Item as defined in the Plans/Specifications, Drawings, and Statement of Work areas. Thereafter, develop a preliminary negotiation strategy based on potential problems, issues, and concerns, that need to be addressed during follow-on discussions with the KO. This is a major part of preparation prior to entering actual negotiations. In some instances, these documents (plans/specs/drawings) are outdated (in some areas) and do not include information in a manner that reduces uncertainty in areas that are unclear. This may appear to be a government oversight to issue ambiguous specifications/documents, but any advantage is a major advantage when it comes to establishing your negotiation position. It's never the intent of any government entity to issue anything ambiguous, but given factors such as timing, funding, personnel shortage, and workload, results in documents that are not clearly defined. Most importantly, you are now assisting the agency with information that could result in a proposal closer to being fair and reasonable to both parties. This is not intentionally done by the government but does occur on a periodic basis.

At this point, you have an adequate understanding of what is included and required within the Solicitation and the key areas to focus. There is a new area added called BCOES (Biddability, Constructability, Operability, Environmentally and Sustainability review). Full discussion occurred in the earlier section describing the purpose of this group of individuals and the importance of this function. To reiterate, this group is comprised of several key personnel from different departments within the organization whose objective is to review the contents of the Plans, Specifications, and Drawings. This group covers a variety of critical aspects of the solicitation and pinpoint potential issues and concerns that need to be addressed prior to finalizing the contents of the solicitation and prior to submission to the contractor. [As a reminder, a BCOES may not be a function that is applicable to all areas within the federal sector but could have a different name or title.]

The purpose of identifying this group is to provide the government and contractor an opportunity to participate together in this process. There are three critical areas the government and contractor can benefit in clarifying the contents of a Solicitation. Those areas are BCOES, Site Visit, and Preproposal Conference.

BCOES: During my entire tenure as Small Business Program Manager, there has never been a time when the contractor was invited to participate in the BCOES meeting. The reality of a contractor to participate in the BCOES is applicable to negotiated actions with an 8(a) contractor who has been selected for a sole source action. Things may have changed, but this is a golden opportunity that should occur between both entities. Earlier discussion occurred regarding potential opportunities for ambiguity to exist within Plans, Specifications and Drawings. What if the contractor could be a part of the BCOES at the correct time that does not include any discussion relative to pricing? What if the contractor could be at the discussion table early during the beginning of this meeting for the sole purpose of providing insight as to how they viewed the construction of the project effort? There are many times during the development of a project that the government and contractor are kept at opposite ends of the spectrum until the Site Visit. If there are areas within certain documents applicable to the BCOES that does relate to pricing, redact those areas so discussion can continue between both groups. The main goal of any negotiations is to reach a price that is fair and reasonable. With this mindset, it makes perfect sense to have the contractor on-board as soon as possible, especially at this meeting. There isn't a law or rule that says the contractor cannot be a part of this meeting. In fairness, the contractor's role is to assist the government in those areas that clearly could cause a disparity in pricing. Again, the purpose of this group meeting is for clarification purposes, that results in both parties viewing the project in the same manner or perspective. This is an opportunity to see things in the same manner or sometimes what is referred to as understanding the solicitation as "Apples to Apples and Oranges to Oranges." Specifically, the government and contractor should analyze the solicitation in the same manner. This doesn't mean the contractor should disclose all his/her trade or project secrets, but certainly must be open to participate in a manner that is productive and beneficial to each group. Due to this type of group arrangement, final Plans, Specifications and Drawings have been edified to the point the government and contractor feel confident with each other's understanding of the requirement. Most of the hidden problems have been resolved, at least at this stage of the project. This shows the contractor is willing to provide insight that will help the government, and the government is willing to accept the input of the contractor. This is a fantastic opportunity that results in a better formulated government cost estimate, and a proposal from the contractor that is accurately prepared. This does not mean there won't be areas that require detailed negotiations, but it certainly removes those hidden problems otherwise would not have been discovered until negotiations. I would highly recommend those government organizations who have BCOES, or any type of preliminary meeting of this sort include the contractor for discussion purposes. This is a win/win situation for both parties.

Site Visit: The basic definition and its intent of this effort is just as it is stated…a Site Visit. During the end of my career in the federal government, I was a staunch supporter, and believer that every project must have a quote/unquote a "Site Visit." In all honesty, I was shocked (early in my career) every project did not require a visit to the potential job area for the sole purpose of covering two distinct efforts, which are: (1) covering the contents of the solicitation and (2) proceeding to the actual area that outlined the project effort for further discussion. There were some organizations during my career regarded a site visit as unimportant. It depends on the government organization, the type of goods/services procured and the thought processes of the KO. If you think participating in a BCOES is important, then you have no idea how important it is to have a Site Visit as a way of seeking clarification and reducing unknown ambiguity within the solicitation. It's imperative that a Site Visit is held, but better yet, it's "who" attends the meeting that dictates the value and level of success that is achieved by having this group session.

I never understood why the KO did not require a meeting of this sort in every given situation. I'm not speaking for some of the KOs to make this decision, but I'm referring to why 100% of all KOs at every government level make this a total prerequisite prior to going forward in the acquisition process.

During my tenure within the federal government, I can assure you this was not the case. There were many instances when a Site Visit was not a part of the process. Does this mean it was a mistake on behalf of the KO? Was this meeting not needed? I am purporting this meeting was not a 100% prerequisite. Let's discuss why I feel this is the case.

The Site Visit is composed of various processes to clearly, and conclusively discuss the contents of the Solicitation in its entirety or to a certain degree. The contents of the bid schedules as it relates to the plans, specifications, and drawings, must be discussed from the beginning to the end (without question)! Let's assimilate the situation: The Site Visit starts at 9:00 A.M. at a designated location (in the area of the project effort). The agenda of the site visit is simple, which is to start at a particular time and cover the solicitation for the first four hours (or however long it takes) and secondly, followed by a visit to the job location (however long it takes). The essence of this statement is to ensure time is not of importance but to cover the contents of the solicitation and the job site is the apex of the meeting. Remember, don't ever allow any project to continue without having a schedule Site Visit, covering the administration/data information of the solicitation followed by on-site coverage of the job location as it relates to the plans, specifications, and drawings. If the government does not require a Site Visit, make it your responsibility to 'request' this meeting! As a part of the administration of this meeting the following areas are covered in detail:

(a) The first phase of the Site Visit is to ensure the right personnel are present. As a contractor, you want the following personnel present (as a minimum):

- Owner
- Project Manager
- Subcontractor (if applicable)
- Cost Estimator*

(b) Secondly, you want to ensure the following personnel is available from the government's perspective (as a minimum):
  - KO or Contract Specialist
  - Project Manager
  - Administrative Contracting Officer (ACO)
  - Cost Estimator*

The key personnel concerns are the presence of the cost estimators from both parties. You must understand negotiations are based on the composition of the government's estimate, and the estimate of the contractor's proposal*. The critical factor to reach a settlement that is fair and reasonable hinges on how the government and contractor view relative cost. This is a good time to throw in the critical need for attending the BCOES and Site Visit. It can be agreed that information is relative to understanding and reaching an agreement. Therefore, communication exchange between the government and contractor must be done in a clear and precise manner.

One must not disregard the need for communication and understanding of the information translated among both groups. This statement is not solely relevant to the relationship between the government and the contractor, but this is one of the keys to success or failure, and a part of the building blocks of establishing world peace.

Therefore, as a minimum, ensure that the following is covered (not necessary in any sequence):

- Cover the Solicitation from beginning to end (to a certain degree).
- Cover each line item as it relates to the plans, specifications, and drawings.
- Ensure all issues, questions and concerns are documented.
- Require all issues and concerns identified in the first meeting are brought forward to the actual job site for further discussion.
- Require as part two of the Site Visit, all concerns at the job location are documented as it relates to the plans, specifications, and drawings.

- Establish specific thoughts/concerns relative to "Differing Site Conditions"

Differing Site Conditions (in layman's terms) are those problems, issues and concerns are discovered below the surface after construction has begun. There are contract terms/conditions that are associated to unknown factors. These are hidden, unknown factors, that may result in additional costs for the contractor to continue the construction effort. The government was not aware of these issues and certainly were not a part of the solicitation as it relates to plans, specifications and/or drawings. In some cases, a Differing Site Condition may result in a reduction in costs and not necessarily increased cost to the contractor. [The bottom line is there may be unknown occurrences at the job site once construction begins.] Discuss potential Differing Site Conditions although they are not known at this time. As an example, a construction effort was located near a railroad. There was a question regarding the potential existence of underground cables which were not identified on the drawings which were slightly outdated. The point is to briefly discuss this area that may or may not be of concern until a later date.

- Remember, whatever the case may be, the Site Visit may result in an Amendment (change) to the Solicitation that can, or cannot, result in a delay or extension to the submission of your final proposal. This delay can be an advantage to both parties.

The key to this process is to allow for additional "Fact Finding" efforts that may also reduce ambiguity in plans, specifications, and drawings, as well as provide an increased opportunity for both parties to reach an agreement that is fair and reasonable later during negotiations. The basic definition of Fact Finding is self-explanatory! This is the process of exchanging ideas, concerns, views, and potential resolutions, beneficial to everyone. Fact Finding is not only applicable to construction projects but is very useful process in any situation. Never jump to conclusions without first analyzing the facts, as well as being cognizant of those hidden issues that could possibly surface later. In most cases, failure to use common sense, results in failed attempts relative to reaching success. In other words, look before you leap! In a court of law, a person is innocent until proven guilty; therefore, all the facts are pertinent prior to making a final decision.

The final part of this area is to ensure everything is documented and exchanged among those individuals who have a "need to know." In contracting, there is one key factor (among many) …information discussed must result in fully documenting all facts. All questions and answers should be captured in written form, so there is no misinterpretation of what took place. This should be done prior, during, and after the Site Visit. I cannot reiterate how important documentation and exchange of information regarding data, or anything relevant to the project. Anything agreed by both parties that changes the initial contents of a Solicitation or even a contract must be documented in writing. Do not accept guidance from those who are not authorized to do so; e.g.. accept changes only from the KO, or the Administrative Contracting Officer (ACO).

Remember, the ACO can only act within the confines of his or her authority. Per regulation, "the ACO receives contracting authority through the issuance of a Standard Form 1402, Certificate of Appointment, also known as a warrant. The warrant is set at a specific dollar limit and a specific purpose… In addition, the Procuring Contracting Officer (PCO) must delegate the authority to administer a specific contract to the ACO." [42] Do not be limited in your thinking when it comes to Fact Finding. This is your right to ensure you clearly understand the contents of the Solicitation and any document, or process, relative to the project. The bottom line is to ensure a clear understanding is reached by both parties before proceeding forward.

The teaching point is to request a Site Visit and at a minimum cover the areas discussed above. Never agree to proceed into the depths of a project without including this very important step. This ensures both parties have an understanding and exchange of information that can save the government thousands of dollars (if not millions) and provide you (a contractor) an opportunity to show your willingness to be a team player. There's no price tag that can replace openness and sincerity of a contractor who's willing to go the extra mile as a potential contractor to the federal government. There is something to be said about those individuals who are open and honest when it comes to working with the federal government.

A Site Visit and Fact-Finding ventures increases the ability of the government and contractor to have a better understanding of the parameters of the project. The essence of both processes is full documentation by the government, and exchange of this information to the contractor. As a precautionary measure, someone from either party should recap those things discussed to prohibit any misunderstanding. It's also recommended someone from your organization capture those changes as they occur. During these conclaves, there is no discussion relative to price, but only discussion regarding processes are captured. The fact of the matter is, both the government and contractor can benefit from detailed communication and working together. This mutual relationship fosters a process that improves the efficiency of the project, as well as potential lower cost to both entities.

We have covered a wealth of the information needed to establish your negotiation position. However, there is another critical meeting that cannot be overlooked, and that process is called Pre-proposal Conference.

- Pre-proposal/Pre-bid Conference: This area is a key period during the acquisition process that is critical from the standpoint of identifying, discussing, and coordination of differences. This is another opportunity to review the plans, specifications, and drawings as it relates to each Line Item. You may want to ask the question, "Why is this meeting so important?" Normally the Pre-proposal Conference is held two weeks prior to Proposal Closing. The Pre-Bid Conference is held two weeks prior to Bid Opening. Again, this meeting is normally for competitive actions with potentially many contractors involved in the bidding process. Remember, you may be involved with actions that are competing with other 8(a) firms, or in other competitive processes with other large or small businesses. This meeting is done prior to the submission of the proposal by the contractor. This function is not noted on the graph but is a process critical to the government and contractor. Some KOs may not require this type of meeting. In most cases, these meetings are done for competitive acquisitions, and not used for sole source requirements. In any case, it's the decision of the KO to hold this type of meeting.

    [Note: refer to the FAR for detailed parameters on Pre-proposal Conferences and Pre-Bid Conferences.

Pre-proposal Conferences - Proposal Closing
Pre-Bid Conferences - Bid Opening]

- The purpose of this meeting is to discuss the contents of the Solicitation as it relates to the job site and it can be done in a variety of
  ways. Some KOs may decide to meet at the job site, (only) and discuss concerns the contractor may have (based on their analysis) of
  the solicitation.

I want to reiterate this is my own interpretation of the acquisition process
relative to when, where, and how the Site Visit, Fact Finding, Questions/An-
swers and the Pre-proposal Conference are interrelated. Others (KOs) may
decide to have a formal meeting with contractors (in the morning) and go over
each Line Item discussing any issues, problems or concerns as it relates to the
Bid Schedule and Plans, Specification/Drawing section…or, in reality, any
problem that needs to be discussed. At this time, you have not finalized your
proposal for submission. This type of meeting is highly encouraged. During
my career, I've been in situations when the KO has determined that a pre-pro-
posal/bid meeting is not necessary. For your awareness, some KOs use this
type of meeting in conjunction with the "Site Visit." Regardless, there should
always be some sort of discussion (first) to go over the contents of the Solicitation and (secondly), followed by an official site visit at the location where
the work is to be performed. Do not forget this area is oriented toward preparation, and this function is one that some organizations fail to include prior to
proposal submission. You may view the Site Visit and Pre-proposal conference
as synonymous, or entirely different, nevertheless, it's critical to hold these
types of meetings.

Another formal meeting most KOs utilize prior to the Pre-proposal/Bid
meeting, or even the Site Visit, is called the "Technical Meeting," between the
government personnel and contractor. The Technical Meeting is designed for
discussion of the Solicitation and for clarification purposes. This meeting includes various government representatives from the PDT group, representatives from the contractor, and subcontractor (if necessary). It's great to have
certain personnel present, but it should be mandatory the Cost Engineer (person responsible for putting the in-house government estimate together) is included from both parties.

I have been involved in many technical meetings with one, or both individuals absent. This is a path for destruction, meaning the Government's IGE and the contractor's proposal may be thousands of dollars apart. Normally, the KO will decide who should attend the meeting representing the government's position but, in most cases, will not object from anyone who feels they have a specific need to know to attend. From the contractor's perspective, it is a clever idea to have your technical folks available even if it includes personnel from your subcontractor. This type of meeting is highly recommended for projects that may be complex, high dollar value, include multiple lines items, and/or in most cases just for general purposes. There is no discussion of price/cost, therefore is another opportunity to identify any area that is ambiguous, needs clarification, and most importantly, results in the government and contractor obtaining a better understanding of the contents of the solicitation. It is imperative this meeting become a major part of the preparation process, prior to finalizing the cost/price proposal. From historical purposes, by doing these small but crucial functions, contractors usually provide proposals in line with cost, identified in the Government's IGE. Therefore, from your vantage point, you must ensure that the following meetings occur somewhere during the acquisition process:

- o   Request attendance to BCOES
- o   Request a Technical Evaluation meeting
- o   Request Fact Finding sessions
- o   Request Site Visit
- o   Request a Pre-proposal/Bid Conference (if necessary) or, in some cases, a Pre-solicitation meeting (all of these meetings are similar in nature, purpose and content). The main focus on each of these meetings is to discuss and exchange information relative to the contents of the solicitation which hopefully reduces future problems, concerns and issues. These meetings are designed to reduce ambiguity resulting in a better final negotiated cost between the government and contractor.

Let's continue down the road of information and data identification relative to this module. We have discovered and covered some very important elements of Business Preparation such as the Solicitation, Site Visits, Fact Finding/Technical Evaluation Meetings, the Pre-proposal/Bid Conference,

Uniform Contract Format, Line Items, and Plans/Specifications. All of these areas are important toward elevating your preparation level prior to entering negotiations with the KO. Again, we cannot cover all areas that are factors in this section but increasing your awareness of key areas is the objective of this information. As stated earlier in this reading, "Information is knowledge; knowledge is power; power to make a better-informed decision." If all else fails after reading this book, please remember this statement and use this as a platform for everything that is done in your business endeavor, or even in life. So, if you now have mastered these areas, you should have a better understanding how important these factors are.

It is now appropriate to reveal some other key areas contained in the compilation of your cost proposal. As a contractor entering negotiations with the federal government, your "Proposal Rate Structure" is the heartbeat of your proposal. I'll explain in depth at the end of this section.

Proposal Rate Structure: The Proposal Rate Structure (my own definition) is defined as the basic elements used to develop your negotiation position with the government. This sounds simplistic in nature, but is often overlooked, unknown, and foreign to the majority of 8(a) firms. The basic definition and contents of your "proposal rate structure" was briefly covered in the Business Presentation module. Over the final sixteen years of my government career as Small Business Program Manager, it was astonishing to reveal that 99% of business owners I met did not know and understand what is meant by this title and/or name. It sounds unbelievable but, sadly enough, true. Your Proposal Rate Structure includes four basic areas, which are: (1) profit, (2) direct cost, (3) overhead (home/field), and (4) bond cost. [Note: the teaching point is from the standpoint of a construction project and not supply/services effort] Oddly enough, when the components of the rate structure are revealed, nearly every contractor would respond "I knew that!" They didn't know these critical components that is known as 'rate structure.' As a litmus test, walk up to any contractor whether they are a large or a small business owner, and ask that basic question: "What is your proposal rate structure?" I guarantee 99% of all responses will either include one or at most two, of the four elements. Write this down and put it in your memory bank.

The composition of all proposals will always include three of the four areas, which are: profit, direct cost, and overhead (home/field). Bond cost are applicable only to construction projects, and not for the acquisition of commercial supply/services. This is applicable for federal, state, and local (city and county) contracting. Let's take a closer look at each of the following:

(1) Profit (FAR 15.404-4): There are many ways to determine the profit margin that is acceptable, or desirable, regardless of the type of goods or services provided. As a reminder, government contracting is based on reaching a settlement that is considered "fair and reasonable" to both parties and private sector contracting is based on "profit driven" or obtaining the greatest amount of profit (within reason). Most contractors have established a certain percent of total contract price for profit. This mindset is used throughout their business lives and in some cases has reached a certain level of success. It must be noted survival in business is the underlying driving force of all businesses, regardless of the size and socioeconomic classification of that business entity. That's the normal way of thinking for most organizations; however, does this result in success and increased longevity of that business? You must be very careful in developing your profit margin in relation to public, and private sector contracting. For training purposes remember this rule about profit (from my vantage point); the acceptable range for establishing profit for a government construction contract is between 6% and 10%. This is applicable for efforts such as Construction (only), for Research and Development and Supply Contracts; profits margins can be as high as 15%. Architecture and Engineering (A&E) and some Service contracts vary, depending on the type of services rendered and whether it is a public, or private sector requirement. For purposes stated herein, the main reference is focused on Construction contracts containing your profit between the 6% and 10% range. As a rule of thumb, the higher the anticipated contract price, or the estimated dollar value of the project, the lower the profit margin. The lower the anticipated project cost, results in a higher allowable profit margin. The relationship is as follows:

HIGHER PROJECT COST =   LOWER PROFIT MARGIN
LOWER PROJECT COST =   HIGHER PROFIT MARGIN

This is a small but highly important factor to remember when establishing your profit margin in your proposal. There have been many situations when the KO may allow a contractor as much as 10% profit and even at the low end of 6% profit (or lower). So, it depends, but at least you now have an acceptable range going forward. In the development of profit for a negotiated effort, there is an analytical process called "Weighted Guidelines"[43]

Weighted Guidelines: This method is used to establish a reasonable profit value, and should be used to determine profit for contracts that include profit.

(a) To properly reflect differences and among contracts and the circumstances relating thereto and to select an appropriate relative to profit/fee in consideration of these differences and circumstances weightings have been developed for application by the contracting officer to standard measurement bases representative of the prescribed profit factors cited in 48 CFR 15.404-4(d) and paragraph (d) of this section. This is a structured system, referred to as weighted guidelines. Each profit factor or sub factor, or component thereof, has been assigned weights relative to their value to the contract's overall effort.

(b) The weighted guidelines shall be used in establishing the profit objective for negotiation of contracts where cost analysis is performed.

(c) The negotiation process does not contemplate or require agreement on either elements or profit elements. Accordingly, although the details of analysis and evaluation may be discussed in the fact-finding phase of the negotiation, process to develop a mutual understanding of the logic of respective positions, specific agreement on the exact weights of values of the individual profit factors are not required and need not be attempted.

(d) The factors set forth in the following table are used in determining profit objectives (modified version - weighted guidelines chart) is rated from 0.03 to 0.12.

(1) Degree of risk: Where the work involves no risk or the degree of risk is very small, the weighting should be 0.03; as the degree of risk increases the weighting should be increased up to a maximum of 0.12. JOB items will have, generally, a higher weighted value than unit price items for, which quantities are provided. Other things to consider include the portion of the work to be done by subcontractors; the nature of work; where the work is

to be performed; the reasonableness of negotiated costs; the amount of labor included in the costs; and whether the negotiation occurs before or after the period of performance of work.

(2) Relative difficulty of work. If the work is difficult and complex, the weighting should be 0.12 and should be proportionately reduced to 0.03 on the simplest of jobs. This factor is tied in to some extent with the degree of risk. Some things to consider include technical nature of the work; by whom work is to be done; location of work; and time schedule.

(3) Size of the job. Work not in excess of $100,000 will be weighed at 0.12. Work estimated between $100,000 and $5 million will be proportionately weighted from 0.12 to 0.05. Work from $5 million to $10 million shall be weighted at 0.04 and work in excess of $10 million at 0.03.

(4) Period of performance. Jobs in excess of twenty-four months are to be weighted at 0.12. Jobs of lesser duration are to be proportionately weighted to a minimum of 0.03 for jobs not to exceed thirty days. No weight is given when additional performance time is not required.

(5) Contractor's investment. Jobs are to be weighted from 0.03 to 0.12 on the basis of below average, average to above average of contractor investment. Things to consider include amount of subcontracting; mobilization payment item; Government-furnished property; method of making progress payments; and front-end requirements of the job.

(6) Assistance by Government. Jobs are to be weighted from 0.12 to 0.03 on the basis of below average to above average, things to consider include use of Government-owned property; equipment and facilities; and expediting assistance. (sample Weighted guidelines profit sheet below, exhibit #14)

WEIGHTED GUIDELINES CHART

Project: _____   Estimated By: _____

Contract No: _____   Checked By: _____

Change Order No. _____   Date: _____

Profit Objective Fro: (Prime Contractor, Subcontractor)

Factor	Rate (%)		Weight		Value
				(0.03 - 0.12)	
1. Degree of Risk	20	x	_____	=	_____
2. Difficulty of Work	15	x	_____	=	_____
3. Size of Job	15	x	_____	=	_____
4. Period of Performance	15	x	_____	=	_____
5. Contractor's Investment	5	x	_____	=	_____
6. Assistance by Government	5	x	_____	=	_____
7. Subcontracting	25	x	_____	=	_____

COMMENTS: (Reasons for Weights Assigned):

1. _____

2. _____

3. _____

4. _____

5. _____

6. _____

Weighted Guidelines Exhibit #14

(this is a modified version of the contents of this process and a visual chart of how it is composed)

Profit Margin - Indefinite Delivery/Indefinite Quantity (IDIQ), Task Orders (TO): I completely feel it is necessary to address profit as it relates to IDIQ contracts and subsequently follow-on TO. [44] Again, this is not a book on contracting, but is subliminal information needed to increase your awareness in certain basic critical areas. In layman's terms, the simple definition of IDIQ Contract is an acquisition method used by the KO when a project has:

(1) Lack of funding [in most cases] ...Project Manager (PM) does not have full funding to complete the effort, but additional funds are expected either during the remaining of the fiscal year or it may be included in next year's budget.

(2) The project may need to be completed in phases due to the complexity of the effort or lack of information known to fully complete the project until the first phase is completed.

(3) Rather than issuing a new contract, the KO issues Statements of Work against the existing contract in the form of Task Orders. For those individuals (public/private) who have experience in contracting may view this information as irrelevant but for those 8(a) contractors who don't know about this process is highly important. You may be confused as to the point I'm trying to convey. That's okay because this information is directly correlated toward making a better-informed decision...remember that statement? This is the training point example:

Scenario: The basic contract (IDIQ) was awarded to an 8(a) firm for $3 million. The parameters of the contract were base (one year) with two option years; firm fixed price; negotiated effort; PM only has (for the first fiscal year) a total of $500,000. The negotiated profit margin was 7%; overhead rate (home/field) was 13%; bond cost 1.5%. Task Order (TO) 0001 was issued for the entire $500,000. Everything is going smoothly, and the contractor completes TO 0001. Additional funding is received and TO 0002 is issued for another $500,000. However, during this phase of the work, the contractor runs into a problem when digging a trench. The problem encountered is outside the scope of the original contract, which is called a "differing site condition". In this case the contractor encountered a subsurface or latent physical condition at the job site which differed materially from those indicated in the contract (unknown physical conditions at the site).[45]

This is a potential problem: There was a discussion or an attempt to negotiate a new rate structure for the differing site condition...new profit, new overhead rate, bond cost stays the same. Contractually, this is incorrect and should not happen. Always remember, the rate structure agreed during initial contract negotiations is the same rate structure used throughout the life of the contract regardless of the differing site condition encountered. The negotiated price for this situation uses the same rate structure originally negotiated. This is an usual situation that occurred but sometimes mistakes are made. The bottom line is the error was found and corrected. Just beware of this type of situation! The rate structure negotiated and agreed by both parties remain unchanged during the life of the contract.

However, getting back to the example, if the KO exercises the first option year of the contract, a percent increase in cost to the initial contract is allowable for the second and third year of the contract term. As an example, the total contract price is $3 million. The base year of the contract the government indicates that a total of $1 million may be obligated for the initial year (pending funds). Each of the following two years, it's anticipated that $1 million may be awarded for each of the remaining years. The KO should allow (up to 3%) increase per unit price of each of the line items in the contract for each option year executed by the KO. If there are ten-line items each of the line items are increased on a unit basis by 3% (or whatever is negotiated during the initial phase/agreement) of the contract. This is basic contracting protocol but an area that is sometimes overlooked by government contracting representatives. Just remember the KO has final decision on all contracting issues, problems, and concerns. However, oversights are sometimes made!

(2) Direct Cost: The second element of the proposal rate structure is Direct Cost. In some cases, there are discrepancies between the government and contractor when negotiating those elements that are classified in this area. Direct cost can be associated to Labor, Equipment, and Materials. These are cost that are fixed, have a direct bearing on the outcome of the project and can be substantiated either by history on performance, published price list (commercial items) or any related cost identified. Specifically, Direct Costs are those costs, which can be attributed to a single task of construction work. These costs are usually associated with a construction labor crew performing a task using specific materials for the task. Labor foreman costs should normally be considered as a direct cost. Subcontracted costs should be considered as direct costs to the prime contractor in estimates.

Direct Labor Cost: Defined as base wages plus labor cost additives including payroll taxes, fringe benefits, travel, and overtime allowances paid by the contractor for personnel who perform a specific construction task. In addition to the actual workers, there are generally working crew foremen who receive an hourly wage and are considered part of the direct labor costs.

Indirect Cost: Those costs, which cannot be attributed to a single task of construction work. These costs include overhead, profit, and bond. Indirect costs are also referred to as distributed costs.

Indirect Labor Cost: Wages and labor cost additives paid to contractor personnel whose effort cannot be attributed to a specific construction task. Personnel such as superintendents, engineers, clerks, and site cleanup laborers are usually included as indirect labor costs (overhead).

(3) Overhead Costs: Costs which cannot be attributed to a single task of construction work. Costs which can be applied to an item of work should be considered a direct cost to that item and are not to be included in overhead costs. The overhead costs are customarily divided into two categories:

(1) Job office overhead, also referred to as General Conditions or Field Office Overhead.
  a. Job overhead costs are those costs at the project site, which occur specifically because of that particular project. Some examples of job overhead costs are:
     (1) Job supervision and office personnel
     (2) Engineering and shop drawings/surveys
     (3) Site security
     (4) Temporary facilities, project office
     (5) Temporary material storage
     (6) Temporary utilities
     (7) Preparatory work and laboratory testing
     (8) Transportation vehicles
     (9) Supplies and maintenance facilities
     (10) Temporary protection and Occupational Safety and Health Administration (OSHA) requirements
     (11) Telephone and communications
     (12) Permits and licenses

(13) Insurance (project coverage)

(14) Schedules and reports

(15) Quality control

(16) Cleanup

(17) Taxes

(18) Equipment costs not chargeable to a specific task

(19) Operation and maintenance of temporary job site facilities

(2) General home office overhead, commonly referred to as General and Administrative (G&A) costs. Home office overhead expenses are those incurred by the contractor in the overall management of business, associated with all costs at the home office. Since they are not incurred for any one specific project, they must be apportioned to the entire project. Typical categories of home office overhead are:

(1) Main office building, furniture, equipment

(2) Management and office staff, salary, and expense

(3) Utilities

(4) General communications and travel

(5) Supplies

(6) Corporate vehicles

(7) General business insurance

(8) Taxes

(4) Bonding: The fourth and final area of the proposal rate structure is cost associated to Bonds. There are basically three types of bonds required by the government (again related to construction contracts), which are: (1) Bid Bond/Bid Guarantee, (2) Performance Bond, and (3) Payment Bond. Traditional definition of the three Bonding processes are:

o   Construction Bonds: Also known as contract bonds, represent a type of surety bond. They provide a financial guarantee that the bills on a construction project will be paid. The issuing insurance company or bank guarantees the project's completion by a specific contractor. Construction bonds protect the assets of the investor or project owner against shoddy work or non-completion of the project.

o   Bid/Guarantee Bonds: "The bid bond protects the project owner if the bid is not honored by the principal, such as a contractor. The owner is obliged under the bond and has the right to sue the principal and the surety (the issuer of the bond) to enforce the bond. If the principal refuses to honor the bid, the principal, and the surety (the insurance company or bank insurer of the bond) are liable for any additional costs incurred in contracting a second time with a replacement contractor.

This type of bond provides an assurance that the bidder will not withdraw his (her) bid within the specified period for acceptance and will execute a written contract and furnish the required bonds if the bid is accepted."[46]

o   Performance Bonds: "A contractor, or principal, uses a Performance Bond to guarantee that it will complete the contract in accordance with its terms. If the principal defaults, the owner may call upon the surety to complete the contract. In such a case, the surety will have to hand the contract to a new contractor or pay the costs for the owner to complete the contract. It does not shift responsibility for administering the contract to the surety. A performance bond provides a financial guaranty for the work and provides the contractor with a method of freeing his (her) working capital, and other assets, which might otherwise be tied up by other forms of security such as certified checks, retainage, or deposits."[47]

o   Payment Bonds: "A Payment Bond guarantees all payments that are due to subcontractors and others from the principal. Beneficiaries of a Payment Bond are the subcontractors and suppliers. The owner benefits from such a bond because it provides a substitute to Mechanic's Lien if as remedies for non-payment."[48]

Normally, there is a limit on the amount that can be charged for bonding cost per regulation. Over the years, the maximum amount allowable is not to exceed 3% for bonding. Some organizations may calculate this charge in a variety of ways. Within my organization (at that time), bonding was established during negotiations and the actual bonding cost was added as an additional line item at the end of the final negotiated contract price. One reason why this was done in this manner was to ensure the contractor could determine exact cost associated to bonding and could be provided to the Bonding Company in a clear and precise manner.

One important note relative to bonding, is related to this cost under an IDIQ (Task Order). Under an IDIQ contract, utilizing TOs as a method of accomplishing work, each TO have to be bonded independently. Utilizing the example (total contract award was $3 million dollars) above for an IDIQ, the $500,000 TO must be bonded in the amount of $500,000; although the proposed total contract price was $3 million. After completion of each TO, the bonding capacity for that amount ($500,000) is released by the KO back to your company. The company now has those dollars available as bonding capacity for additional TOs, or for other projects. As discussed in the Business Theory Module, the alternative to the prime contractor's ability or lack of ability to obtain Bonding, can be offset by "indemnification" ...contract bonding provided by the subcontractor. As previously determined, indemnification is, or should be used, as an alternative method of acquiring bonding. This method is not used as a "way of life" relative to acquiring bonding support. This is a total separate discussion due to the complexity and the legal parameters governing bonding. [If more information is or understanding of 'bonding" is desired, refer to the FAR, or seek additional guidance from a bonding company/agent.]

There is a real situation regarding bonding that must be shared for your own benefit. Be aware if this situation happens! All contract opportunities are not good opportunities and all money is not good money! There was a situation where a small business won a competitive requirement that far exceeded their available bonding capacity. For discussion purposes, let's say the size of the effort was approximately $30 to $40 million. After several efforts to obtain bonding, the contract was indeed awarded to that small business. Based on contract regulations all bonds must be provided within ten days after contract award. As a refresher, typically a small business is classified based on their average annual revenue and/or number of employees (along with other related factors). For a project of this magnitude, the small business had to allot their available bonding capacity to this one effort. If any other project became available this company didn't have any remaining bonding capacity. A contract of this size can have a direct effect on your size standard as a small business, as well as your ability to obtain additional bonding support. After contract award, this effort was later cancelled (reason not important). The Bonding Company (due to the cancelation) directly penalized this company and reduced their bonding limit substantially below their original amount for future efforts. It can only be assumed this was the Bonding Company's way of minimizing their risk when it comes to providing bonding support to that firm for future project efforts. The company who won the contract overlooked a very real potential "right" regarding government contracting; the government does terminate contracts for various reasons. This is a classic case of winning a contract that turned out to be an opportunity (on one hand) but not to be in the best interest of the small business. (There were other factors involved in this example; however, they are not relevant for training purposes.) There are many instances when a company may lose their bonding capability due to a variety of factors.

The key training point is to be aware of your size standard, bonding capacity, and the effect all projects may have on your ability to operate in an efficient and effective manner. Thus, be conscious of good/bad opportunities!

o In-house Government Cost Estimate (IGE/IGCE): This is another area discussed for your own awareness. The IGCE or in some cases called IGE is the primary internal cost tool the government (cost estimator) uses to establish the negotiating position for the government's negotiating team.

The government estimate is the formal, approved cost estimate prepared to support the negotiating team resulting in contract award (hopefully). This document parallels various key areas of the Solicitation such as Bid Schedule (identifying Line Item Cost); cost breakdown and individual identification of direct/indirect labor elements, material cost factors; and proposal rate structure. The IGCE is the key document the KO and government team uses to establish a fair and reasonable cost.[49]

One important factor, negotiations can only occur as long as the contractor's proposal is within 25% of the total cost stated within the IGE. There have been situations when the contractor's proposal (negotiated contract) has exceeded the IGE. Don't get too alarmed! Sometimes this happens, and (in most cases) there was a communication disconnect during the Technical meetings and/or discussions among government and contractor personnel at the Site Visit. This is one of the primary reasons why these two meetings (along with others) are essential. In some cases, the absence of both meetings can result in a wide disparity in the IGE and contractor's proposal. If this does happen, go back to the drawing board, and open technical discussions only. Normally, there will be something identified that affected the cost of either the IGE or contractor's proposal. In essence, some type of cost element was either over-priced, underpriced, or not considered by either or both parties. There are in-stances when "descoping" of the procurement effort is an alternative which reduces overall cost. There are many situations when the government over-looked elements that either reduces or increases the IGE and the same is true from the contractor's perspective. That is the beauty of negotiations, which allows for open discussions between both parties.

There has been an enormous amount of information and data shared regarding this module, and the importance of "preparation." Preparation is a key factor in determining the success of the government and contractor, prior to entering negotiations. One must remember, preparation includes various functions from the inception of the receipt of the solicitation, until the end of negotiations. I specifically wanted to identify the urgent need of preparation. The bottom line is quite simple, preparation can either en-hance or reduce the level of success obtained by the government and to the contractor.

In most cases, the government has limited internal resources to fully pro-vide the in-depth research and development necessary for analyzing all areas of a solicitation, prior to entering negotiations. This is one of the hidden dif-ferences between the government and private sector when it comes to prepa-ration. It may seem (from the outside looking in) that the government has the upper hand when it comes to allocating time, resources, and funding needed for each project, regardless if it is a competitive (unrestricted/small business set-aside) or a negotiated effort.

The government, in some cases, has a small department or limited per-sonnel assigned to perform functions in researching, developing, and analyzing the solicitation from a cost standpoint. There are many projects funded, as well as unfunded, that are available for internal review. Once Congress passes the budget for the fiscal year, each organization receives the "go ahead" for projects (funded) to proceed through the acquisition cycle, leading up to con-struction. (There is a formal process that each federal organization follows after Congress approves the budget.)

For mathematical purposes, let's envision there are fifty _major_ projects (more or less) that are funded for the current fiscal year. Let's assume there are only eight individuals assigned to the Cost Estimating Department who are responsible for providing an estimate for each of those funded efforts. The degree and level of knowledge, expertise and time required to perform one independent cost estimate is enormous. Immediately it's apparent the Cost Estimating department has a tremendous workload with performing the details of determining a cost estimate for each project. Therefore, let's take a closer review of guiding principles that personnel having this job function must, or should follow as Cost Estimators:

"Cost estimates should be prepared as though the government were a prudent and well-equipped contractor estimating the project. Therefore, all costs, that a contractor would expect to incur should be included in the cost estimate. The cost estimator should maintain this thought process throughout the completion of the construction effort. Each estimate should be developed as accurately, detailed and be based upon the best information available. This ensures that the cost estimate will in all aspects represent the "fair and reasonable" cost to the government. Key elements and functions of the cost estimates are;

- Estimating consists of analyzing the plans and specifications into definable features of work, that can be quantified in some manner. For example, earthwork is generally broken down into cubic yards; structural concrete is broken down into cubic yards; concrete flatwork is broken down into square yards; drywall and painting are broken down into square feet; and so on. This provides the cost estimator an opportunity to determine the magnitude of the work involved in a quantifiable method. In addition, historical cost data from previous "similar" projects can be used to determine the amount of effort in labor, equipment, tools, and other resources to construct a project. This type of analysis provides the quantities of various materials that is needed to purchase for the project, quantities that subcontractors will need to quote, personnel and equipment that will be needed for the entire effort.
- The cost engineer is accountable for the completeness, quality, and accuracy of the reasonableness of the cost estimate. All construction cost estimates is given an independent review by Government Cost Engineers. The purpose of this review is to check the validity and logic

used in the analysis of the construction functions. The review should always include a check of the quantities, unit prices, and arithmetic.

- Detail estimating methods are to be employed whenever adequate design information is known or can be reasonably assumed. Details can be reasonably assumed for many projects from experience in past designs, designer, and cost engineer experience, and use of various models. Historical bid unit prices can also be used in the formulation of the cost estimate.

- The degree of accuracy and completeness are critical factors in all cost estimates. An accurate and complete estimate establishes accountability with the cost engineer and enables management to place greater confidence in the cost estimate. The KO and the negotiating team is critically dependent on the validity of the cost estimate"[50]

It is apparent, the importance of a quality IGCE requires an enormous amount of time in preparation, review, and analysis per each project. In my opinion, the amount of time necessary to complete a cost estimate greater exceeds the number of government personnel assigned per each funded project. Conversely, the contractor has personnel that can be assigned to each independent project and the required amount of time to perform a higher level of review is ever-present. This is the advantage contractors have over some government agencies. Throughout my career, I have seen this to be a matter of fact, rather than fiction. Do not misinterpret the value of the job a Cost Estimator must perform. It's a matter of increased projects that requires his/her undivided oversight, which is a tremendous burden to manage on a daily basis.

Look at this issue from this perspective, the Cost Estimator must attend each internal meeting (or should attend) per each project assigned under his/her purview; analyze each project under the parameters discussed above relative to developing a cost estimate that is fair and reasonable; attend offsite project visits to discuss issues/problems and concerns regarding project cost and/or changes. This job is one of the most important and demanding functions performed by the government organization. The Cost Estimator must ensure that the cost data used to negotiate a contract is prepared in a fashion that creates a win/win situation for both parties.

There are many critical functions that requires full attention to detail by the cost estimator. The cost estimator for the contractor must also provide the same level of detail to that project. However, their time and resource availability are much greater than the government cost estimator on a per project basis. Pay close attention to those adjectives that describe the efforts associated to performing cost estimating duties:

- By regulation (all duties performed must be in accordance to regulatory guidance)
- Accountable (accountability rest with the cost estimator and cost engineering department)
- Completeness (all estimates must be done in a thorough manner)
- Quality (must be performed at the highest level of efficiency and quality)
- Accuracy (performed in a manner that limits ambiguity)
- Reasonableness (fair to both parties)
- Confirming the Validity (estimating oversight performed by cost engineering department)

The proposal fully covers all areas, relative to cost factors assigned in preparation of their cost proposal. It must be reiterated, government personnel (due to assigned workload) does not have equal amounts of time that can be allotted to each project. Therefore, you (as the contractor) must take advantage of this opportunity. I must clarify what is meant by "take advantage of this opportunity", meaning the contractor must be ultra-prepared in the level of knowledge related to the contents within the Solicitation.

This situation will occur at some point within negotiations. As a result, reference to the fact "consideration of a cost element was not a part of their initial cost estimate". This statement is relevant to comments made by the government and contractor personnel. This provides an opening for the contractor to state clearly and precisely when proven increased cost in a line item is acceptable. Conversely, lack of preparation by the contractor (in this area) can affect the line item cost in the contractor's proposal. The bottom line is no area can be considered as minor in the preparation of the proposal or performing any function in the Business Preparation Module.

Negotiations: Here is a modified version of my own personal format for entering negotiations with the government (exhibit #15):

Preliminary Negotiation Decision Points:

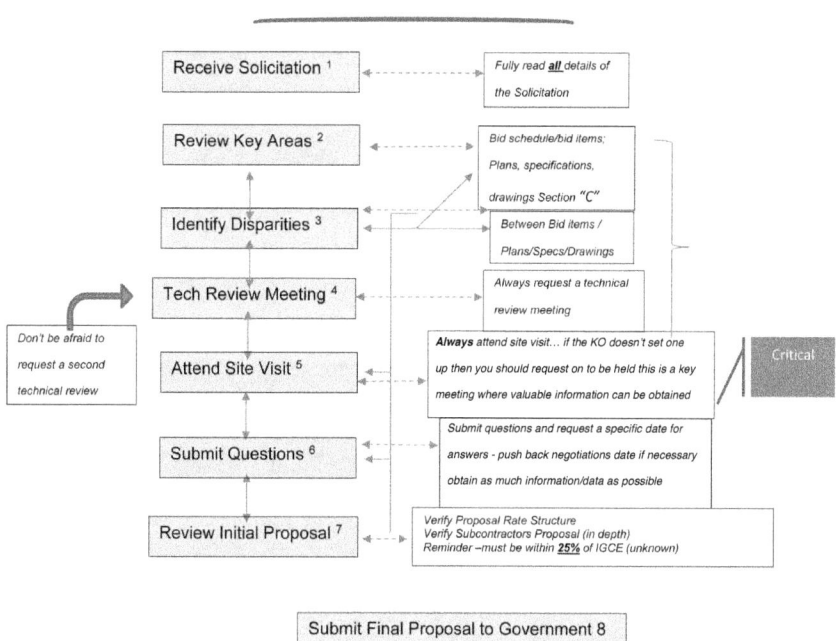

Glenn L. Chatman

Negotiations Protocol (cursive overview)

Negotiations Protocol (cursive overview)

Negotiations [8]	←→	*Always arrive early shows that you're eager and prepared for negotiations*

Contractor's Negotiation Team [9]	←→	Contractor Team: Owner, Project Manager/Superintendent, (can be one in the same), Technical Lead, Subcontractor Rep, [Key is to always bring the right personnel who can answer questions applicable to the project—there's no minimum nor maximum number of personnel assigned to your negotiation team

Introductions [10]	←→	Normal protocol is for the Government to introduce their team first followed by the contractor's introduction. Be sure to provide an overview of each member and their role as a part of your team. However, there is no set way whether the Government goes first or the contractor. [Key point is to ensure that you have the right personnel to answer Government questions or any potential question that may occur

Start of Negotiations [11]	←→	Start of Negotiations ˉone very important note...do not engage in negotiations starting on a Friday especially if you are out of town: big advantage to Government. You may be pressed for time of traveling out of town e.g. time factor BE AWARE!

Discussion/Negotiations of Rate [12] Structure / Period of Performance (POP)	←→	Always start with negotiating profit, over-head (home/field, & bond rate). This establishes and ensures that you are not working for a fair and reasonable profit and associated cost.

Performance Work Plan (PWP)	←→	After the rate structure has been agreed upon, immediately provide a clear path recommendation on how you (as the prime contractor) and your subcontractor is going to perform the work stated in the solicitation. From the first time that you meet with your potential customer.

Negotiations Protocol (cursive overview continued)

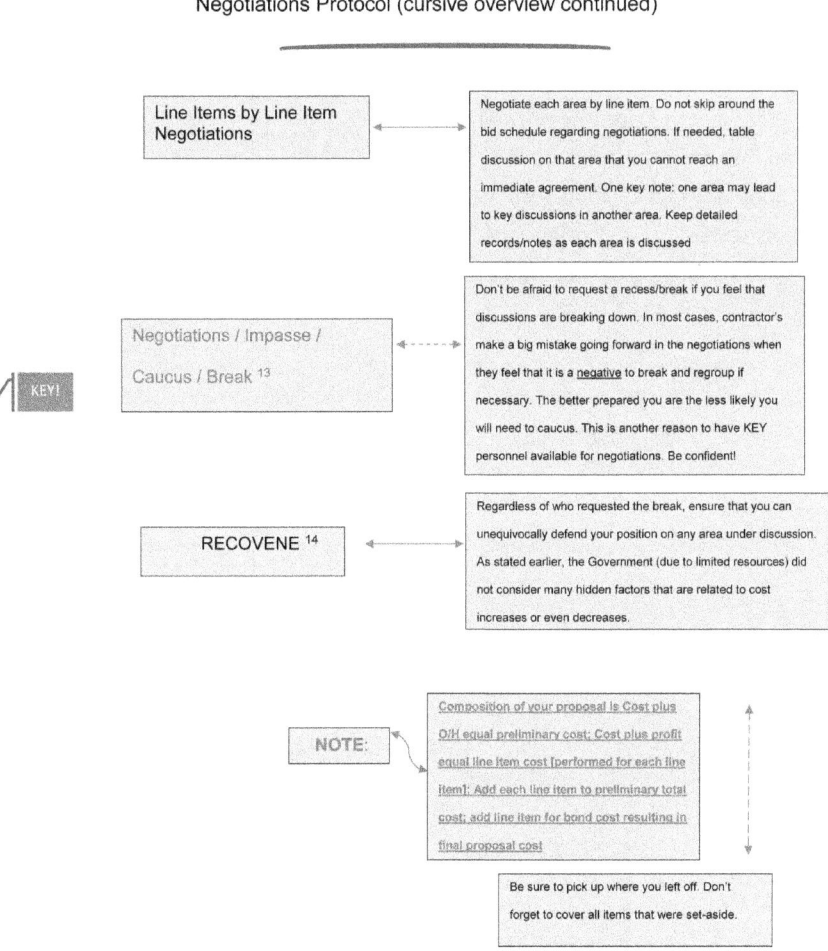

Contractor Team: Owner, Project Manager/Superintendent, (can be one in the same), Technical Lead, Subcontractor Rep, [Key is to always bring the right personnel who can answer questions applicable to the project—there's no minimum nor maximum number of personnel assigned to your negotiation team.]

Normal protocol is for the Government to introduce their team first followed by the contractor's introduction. Be sure to provide an overview of each member and their role as a part of your team. However, there is no set way whether the Government goes first or the contractor. [Key point is to ensure that you have the right personnel to answer Government questions or any potential question that may occur.]

Start of Negotiations (one very important note): Do not engage in negotiations starting on a Friday especially if you are out of town; big advantage to the Government. You may be pressed for time of traveling out of town (e.g., time factor BE AWARE!).

Negotiations Protocol (cursive overview continued)

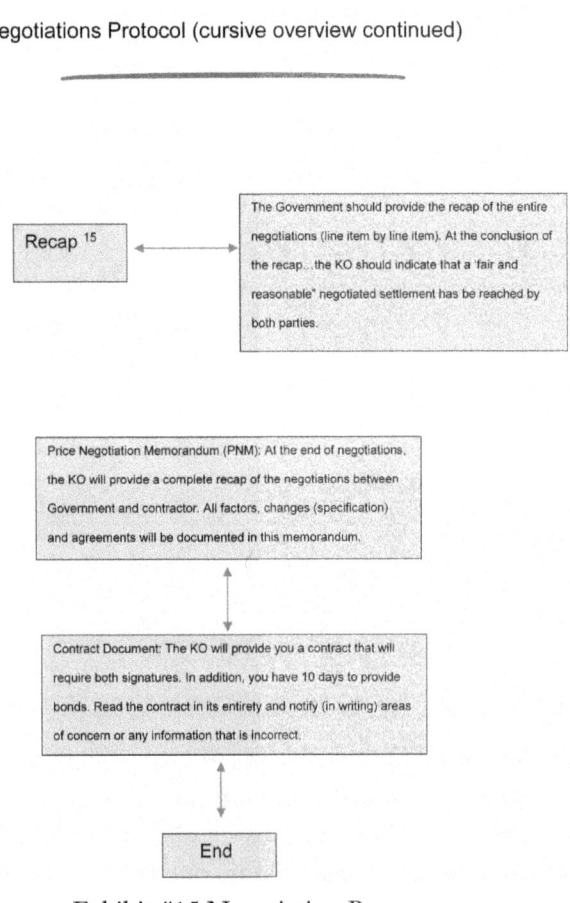

Exhibit #15 Negotiation Process

The above graph is (I repeat only) an overview of standard functions or steps included during negotiations between the government and contractor. There are other steps that may or may not be included, but these are areas (as a minimum), you must be aware and follow. There are too many situations, when the contractor overlooks one or several basic steps in negotiations that has a major impact on either the government, or contractor's ability to reach a settlement that is fair and reasonable. Each of the areas discussed in the previous graph are sections that have been defined, discussed, and analyzed in the beginning of this module. Everything that have been covered, provides a clear pathway of underlying principles of preparation that dictate the level or degree of having a successful negotiation.

Let's cover a part of the negotiations process that may appear to be minor but can result in a total disaster to the contractor. This scenario happened to an 8(a) contractor during negotiations (time, place, and location not important). I was not a part of the negotiations process, but the contractor contacted me and thus disclosed something that was totally astonishing! The preliminary steps that took place are again irrelevant. The government and contractor were engaged in a process of identifying, discussing, and providing line item costs each party viewed as fair and reasonable.

Negotiations concluded by backing into a final negotiated price, rather than following the standard (basic) steps covered in exhibit #15. It was conveyed to me, he (contractor) accepted this project at a final cost, which he later determined that the agreement included absolutely "zero profit." An agreement had been reached; negotiations concluded and a contractor basically working for nothing. Did he have any recourse of going back to the KO and ask to reopen negotiations after the fact? Is it appropriate for a contractor to work for zero profit, regardless of the oversight that took place? Is the KO responsible for what happened, although both parties shook hands and said excellent job? Was the KO unfair in this process?

These questions and more can be a part of this discussion. However, the onus is clearly on the part of the contractor to ensure some form of rate structure is discussed first and foremost, during the negotiations. Area #12 in the above graph is the solution to prohibit any contractor from accepting a final cost that does not include an acceptable profit margin. After the preliminary acts are done in the beginning of negotiations, the most critical function is contained in the negotiations of your RATE STRUCTURE. I repeat, negotiating your rate structure is the first major step of negotiations. This doesn't mean the final agreed to terms and conditions are done at this point, but establishment of these rates are presented by the contractor as a starting point. Establishing your rate structure is based on initially agreeing on the rates in terms of **percentages**. Later, during negotiations, a detailed review and negotiations of each of the individual areas will be performed relative to Direct and Indirect cost.

As an example, you (the contractor) immediately propose to the government your profit is 8%, overhead (home/field) 13%, and bond cost 2%...direct cost is a given. As stated earlier, the contractor must disclose all direct cost (including various cost obtained from at least three other sources). The KO may not require an alternate cost from three sources, or it may be from one or even two other sources. This is his or her call as a KO. If there is concern by the government these rates are not 100% acceptable (at this time), the alternative is to table these cost (table means to set aside) until later during the negotiations. This is the safest way to ensure the situation that occurred earlier doesn't ever happen to you during negotiations. One must remember, the government may have a limited amount of available funds. This is another reason to control subcontractor costs prior to submission of your proposal and certainly during negotiations can be a major factor. There are times, to reach a fair and reasonable cost, is accomplished by reducing some parts of your rate structure and in some cases reducing the rates provided by the subcontractor. It is the responsibility of the government to ensure a settlement is fair and reasonable, which certainly doesn't mean a contractor working for zero profit. If this situation does occur, and the KO is aware of this situation, I personally believe the onus is on the KO to reopen negotiations. It's within their power to do so and is clearly the right thing to do! This is the answer for any contractor working for little to zero profit. If this ever happens, clearly indicate a breakdown in negotiations that was overlooked, and concluded inappropriately. This situation was critical and had to be revealed as one that should never happen from the government and contractor's perspective.

There are many books and pamphlets that outline the art of negotiations, but I can assure you the one key denominator centers around the word "preparation." We have covered this process from an analytical and practical sense, but there is no substitute from being prepared. In business or in life, there is no one who plans to fail but failure to plan, is the biggest obstacle in determining success or failure in negotiations.

Throughout the years of training and text book learning, the follow are basic rules for negotiation success and basic tactics for creating a win/win situation. I have followed these rules throughout my career. (exhibit #16):

RULES FOR A SUCCESSFUL NEGOTIATIONS

BE PREPARED: Preparation is always essential for successful negotiations. Analyze strengths and weaknesses of your opposition and study the needs of the other party and ways to satisfy those needs.

ESTABLISH HIGH GOALS: The higher your expectations, the more successful your performance will be. Strive for a WIN/WIN outcome with expectations on both price and on non-price (contract requirements) issues. This provides room for compromise. Never accept the initial offer from the opposition regardless of how the price stacks against your proposal unless the offer is one that cannot be refused!

ALWAYS LEAVE ROOM TO COMPROMISE: Government negotiators should present an initial, fair and reasonable position below what will be the ultimate price in order to make concessions before agreeing on the final price. Remember, the initial offer by the government may be low however it should be within the realm of fair and reasonable. The same concept is applied to the contractor's position. The contractor's initial offer should be high enough but still is an offer that should be considered fair and reasonable. Basically, this provide room and leverage for both the government and contractor to compromise.

DO NOT SHOW WEAKNESSES: Never disclose information that would weaken your negotiating position or enhance the bargaining position. Respond to questions carefully by avoiding a direct response to a direct question. Carefully think before you speak. Most negotiators are adept at reading body language and various facial expressions so be cognizant of anything that will portray weakness.

USE CONCESSIONS WISELY: Compromise is a critical part of contract negotiations. Do not appear overly generous or rush to make concessions. Concede slowly and in small amounts. Do not get into a "tick" for "tac" process…you give something, you immediately want a concession at that time. Strategically ask for concessions at the appropriate time during negotiations.

BE PROFESSIONAL: Sell yourself and your ideas. Keep it simple and never personalize differences. Emphasize need for cooperation. Speak with strength and confidence. Never make negative personal comments and stay calm. Always be professional!

EXHIBIT PATIENCE: Always use patience. Patience is a major part of exuding professionalism and confidence. Again, be careful of facial expressions and body language which can portray a sense of anxiety and lack of emotional control. You can never tell whether a good negotiator is either winning nor losing the negotiations debate.

POWER OF WALKING AWAY: Always walk away from any deal that is considered a bad deal. This means to take a break, caucus, postpone negotiations at a later date after an apparent deadlock. Be aware of personal behavior and attitudes interfering with returning back to the negotiating table. The bottom line is to achieve a win/win situation for both parties.

Exhibit #16 Rules for a Successful Negotiation

As shown in the above graph, the first rule for bargaining success is based on "preparation." Put this process, function, or whatever the description may be in your memory bank, back pocket, or in your brief case. This concept is the pillow for a successful negotiation. It must be noted, that these rules (along with others) can be used and followed by the government and the contractor. These rules are universal throughout the history of negotiations and can be utilized by both groups. One other important note is the final rule as noted above: Always be prepared and willing to walk away from a bad deal. The government is committed to negotiate in a manner that is considered fair and reasonable; however, in some instances, the ability to reach an agreement may not be achievable at that moment. Be willing to step back and break away from negotiations or even to change negotiators. I've rarely seen this done during my tenure within the government, but just be aware this can be a viable option. This is when the ability to compromise and engage in meaningful concessions by both parties is crucial to reaching the final goal.

The graph below provides various tactics used enroot to establishing a successful negotiations. There are other known elements that are highly effective tools that can become a part of developing a winning strategy (exhibit #17):

DEVELOPING A WINNING STRATEGY:

FORBEARANCE: Agree to disagree and move on to the next issue without making a commitment one way or another. Search for issues where you can agree. Return to the unresolved issue later. Fully document discussion on a per line item basis. Again, this is an act of "tabling" an issue for later review. This is another area to utilize the act of patience.

QUESTIONING: Ask questions to probe the position of the other party. Ask questions such as, "What is the best you can do?" Have you considered…?" Is this project fully funded…? In certain cases, it is beneficial to repeat a question or statement made by the opposition as a means of clarifying the intent of the problem or issue.

ALTERNATIVE POSITIONS: By offering two or more alternative positions at the same time, you can indicate that you would be willing to accept more than one way of settling an issue or a group of issues. Another form of compromise. There is always room to compromise by formulating countermeasures relative to price. If applicable, this may be a great time to offer suggestions of a change in scope of the effort. Also utilize brainstorming tactics if you feel a need to provide another path to achieve a similar goal or objective.

ACCEPTANCE TIME: Increase acceptance time by making an offer near the end of the day and then allowing the Gov/Con to think about the offer overnight. Be aware of negotiations running through the end of the week. Avoid negotiations on a Friday (if possible). Both parties (gov/con) has used this time frame to their advantage pending who appears to have leverage at this point during negotiations. Negotiating on a Friday can be beneficial, if and only if you feel you are in a favorable position at that point during the negotiations.

This is a tactic used to develop alternative solutions through thinking out loud and openly discussing alternatives or ways to resolve issues. When negotiators are sincere and open to new ideas, the result is usually a win/win outcome. This method should be done openly by both the government and contractor. In some cases, it may be determined that an alternative method may be plausible due to open communication process. Keep an open mind at all times.

BLANKETING: This is designed to get all the issues on the table at the beginning of the negotiation so that everyone understands the magnitude of the negotiation task. Do not get bogged down on one issue. Table that issue and continue on with negotiations. Document those areas and come back later during the discussion process for resolution. Be careful utilizing this type of process. In some cases, withholding problems or issues until later may directly affect the outcome of another issue. This tactic can be beneficial but can also convolute negotiations with identifying too many problems early in the negotiations.

Exhibit #17 Developing a Winning Strategy

Conversely, knowing the dynamics of developing a winning strategy, there are other elements of negotiations that are just as important, relative to creating a positive negotiation atmosphere. There are appropriate countermeasures when identifying win/lose tactics. There are many times "mind games" are played when two oppositions meet. The truly successful negotiator is skilled in recognizing when things aren't going well for his organization. Things can shift in a moment during negotiations, pending the problems and issues uncovered. The following are situations identifying win/lose tactics: (see exhibit #18 below)

WIN/LOSE TACTICS

SURPRISE: This tactic is used to introduce an unexpected issue or goal during the Proceedings. Successful negotiators will sometimes withhold key issues or areas to throw their counterpart off balance. This tactic can be beneficial pending the degree of importance of the unknown and how well negotiations are going. Use this tactic relative to an area that has low to medium impact. Do not hold back information that may be considered a "bomb shell" to your opposition. The opposition can view this as a dirty tactic and may reduce their confidence level of you being open and fair. Just be careful when to use the element of surprise as a negotiation tactic.

BULLYING: When necessary, call for a team caucus to make

sure you are responding with reason and not emotion. Most successful negotiators remain calm at all times regardless of the negotiation climate. If at all possible, refrain from using the phrase "take it or leave it." If this is the position of either the government or contractor during negotiations, it may be a need to caucus, delay or ask to resume discussions at a later date. Sometimes this is used to put the opposition on the defensive. Ignore the threat, remain professional, and move on to the next issue. Be aware of the degree of threat and how it affects your ability to proceed forward. Rather than end up in confrontation, may be a great time to caucus. Take a break!

SILENCE: This tactic is generally used when the negotiator does not want to disclose weakness in their position. Do not take silence as a sign of weakness. Ask effective questions to uncover information on the avoided topic. In this case, either side is trying to gain an advantage by remaining silent as a way of showing strength. This can be a great tactic to use but do not overplay the act of remaining silent.

LIMITED AUTHORITY: This tactic limits a negotiator's authority by limited funds and required management approvals. Ask at the beginning of the negotiations if there are any issues that the Gov/Con negotiator does not have authority to negotiate. It is a great idea to determine the level of authority as well as who has the authority from the perspective of the government and contractor. From the government's perspective, the KO may not have full authority meaning their warrant limit is only at a certain level. From the contractor's viewpoint, always have the individual at the negotiations who have total power to enter into a contract with the government.

APPARENT WITHDRAWAL: A negotiator using this tactic gives the impression that his/her organization is withdrawing from the negotiations when that is not the actual intent. Inform the negotiator that you are considering alternatives. Always keep the door open from your standpoint. This tactic can benefit the government and contractor if used correctly. As a former negotiator for both the government and contractor, I have used this tactic to force the opposition to make a concession. Timing is very important relative to when this tactic should be used.

Exhibit #18 Win/Lose Tactics

This module has been intriguing, to say the least. There have been many things uncovered that are critical in reaching a fair reasonable settlement. The contractor is aware of many of these functions, but the utilization and criticality of knowing the cause and effect of these processes are mostly unknown, due to a lack of understanding. Somehow, a "bridging the gap" of these functions must take place to ensure negotiations are done in a fashion and manner fair to the government and the contractor.

We are at the point in this module that occurs right before contract award.

Throughout my career and involvement in many negotiation sessions, some contractors feel this is an opportunity to make a lot of money. It's imperative to remember the government has given you an opportunity that is priceless. Only once, during my tenure as Small Business Program Manager a contractor failed to negotiate. This was an unfortunate situation which, believe it or not, influenced opportunities for other contractors in the 8(a)-program wishing or seeking a negotiated opportunity. Do not make this mistake!

This module is just as important as the other two areas that were covered. In summarization, all areas discussed are critical in terms of knowledge, understanding and implementation of each of the sub functions. As stated, preparation is the key element prior to reaching the negotiation table. Each of the areas addressed is paramount in relation to preparation. In simple terms, the solicitation must be clearly covered as it correlates to the plans, specifications, and drawings. The need for following the rules of the Site Visit and having the right personnel is the heartbeat of developing the IGCE, as well as the proposal submitted by the contractor. If the government and contractor fail in any area regarding the importance of these sub processes, such as Fact Finding, Questions/Answers and more Fact Finding, can derail any effort of reaching a fair and reasonable agreement.

As one can see, the relationship between Business Theory, Business Presentation and Business Preparation, are as independent as a spider's web. You cannot separate and mitigate any of the functions and processes that have been covered. So as a suggestion, follow the script! Again, it is not expected of any contractor to fully grasp these tools, but the difference between being unaware, somewhat aware, and fully aware, depends on your desire to be successful, and the amount of work put into this process.

Contract Award: The last area of this module is focusing on Contract Award. The information covered is quite simple but is just as important as any topic covered so far. In many cases, due to funding availability, most government contracts are awarded during late third quarter and early fourth quarter. [Depending on the area of the government you are working with the standard fiscal year is 1 October, ending 30 September of the following year]. As stated in one of the earlier modules, negotiated contracts play a significant role due to the time frame it takes to award a sole source contract. To reiterate, a negotiated contract takes approximately 45 days and a competitive contract is anywhere from 75 to 90 days. This depends on the acquisition lead-time of the effort from the beginning to end (cradle to grave). Therefore, pay close attention to the timing of negotiations and ultimately resulting in the award of the contract. The significance of this timeframe is not based on negotiations but is based on the time the government has remaining to obligate funds on a contract that will expire (depending on the type of funds) 30 September of that current year. The time remaining prior to the end of the fiscal year, will dictate whether there is enough time to award a contract on a negotiated or competitive basis. This may not appear to be very important to most small businesses but to those 8(a) firms who are ready for this late date acquisition can obtain many negotiated opportunities. Therefore, stay focused, ready, and prepared throughout the fiscal year for these types of opportunities. It must be understood, that many opportunities are afforded to an 8(a)-contractor, due to late developments, within the government that needed a certified and qualified 8(a) contractor specifically for sole source negotiation purposes. This information is for your benefit although the acquisition timeline identified is directly an internal contracting function.

There are two areas important to Contract Award, or shortly, after Contract Award.

Let's assume negotiations went smoothly. The government and contractor felt the final negotiated price was a win/win for both groups. Negotiations were tough, and many of the negotiation tactics discussed were utilized by both groups. Subsequently, the KO prepares the contract document, and is forward to the contractor resulting in a bilateral agreement (signed by both government and contractor). All is well! There are still major road blocks that can occur even after contract award. There are two areas that needs to be addressed, which are critical factors that can delay, or even cancel a contract, after an agreement has been reached. Those two areas are submission of (1) Bonds and (2) those administrative type documents called "Submittals."

(1) Bonds: [This section is for construction efforts only – reference is not made to service/supply contracts.] The discussion relative to bonds and its level of importance was briefly discussed in the Business Presentation Module. In that area, focus was on the need of your bonding agent to be present (if possible) during your presentation to the government. The key point(s) critical to your success is to understand the following elements applicable to Bonds:

√ Ten Days: After contract award, the contractor has ten days to submit all bonds as required by the contract.

√ Required Bonds: In a construction contract (normally) there are three types of bonds that are required, which are:

"a. Bid Guarantee. Bid guarantee means a form of security assuring that the bidder will (1) not withdraw a bid within the period specified for acceptance and (2) will execute a written contract and furnish required bonds, including any necessary coinsurance or reinsurance agreements, within the time specified in the bid, unless a longer time is allowed, after receipt of the specified forms. Note: The chief of the contracting office may waive the requirement to obtain a bid guarantee when a performance bond or a payment bond is required, if it is determined that a bid guarantee is not in the best interest of the government for a specific acquisition (e.g., overseas construction, emergency acquisitions, sole-source contracts)

b. Payment Bond. A payment bond assures payments as required by law to all persons supplying labor or material in the prosecution of the work provided for in the contract.

c. Performance Bond. A performance bond secures performance and fulfillment of the contractor's obligations under the contract."[51]

d. Indemnification. This was added as a part of discussion on bonding as an alternative methods or process on obtaining bonding relative to performing a construction contract. An indemnity agreement is a contract where one party agrees to protect another party against certain future claims or losses. For example, a contract is awarded to an 8(a) contractor in an amount of $2 million. The 8(a) company only has bonding capacity not to exceed $1 million. The subcontractor can indemnify the prime contractor (8(a) firm) for the remainder of the $1 million, or in this case can bond the entire effort for $2 million. There is a written agreement between the prime contractor, subcontractor, and the bonding surety. Once this agreement is determined, the government is notified of this arrangement. Although the subcontractor is providing the bonding support, the contract agreement and related bonds are between the government and 8(a)-contractor. The bonds are submitted and signed by the 8(a)-contractor (prime) and provided within the ten-day period. Remember, there is no Privity of Contract between the government and the subcontractor. [Privity of contract means there is no contractual relationships or obligation between the government and subcontractor.]

(This information was covered earlier, but its relevancy of importance must be reiterated.)

The key training point regarding bonding is to ensure you have a solid relationship with the Bonding Company. It is understandable most newly developed firms have a real problem with bonding capacity necessary to meet the terms and conditions related to bonding. The majority of companies I worked with over the last sixteen years were oblivious to the alternative that exist in obtaining bonding from a subcontractor. As discussed earlier, its never too early in the establishment of bonding capacity with the surety company. Some companies can obtain a higher level of bonding capacity when other companies struggle. If the bonding company is concerned with risk, which can affect your bonding capacity, do not overlook the alternative of working with your subcontractor. As you can see, discussion occurred early in the Business Presentation Module relative to Bonding Agent, Surety and Bonding Capacity, but later during this module the relationship and level of importance of bonding, and the criticality of bonding is still prevalent. This section is only scratching the surface relative to bonding and its many facets. The main purpose is to increase your awareness and the level of importance of bonding and its effect it can have after negotiations have been completed. Your ability or inability to obtain bonding within the allotted time frame can ultimately affect the contract going forward. Your bonding capacity and/or ability to obtain any level of bonding is a major concern for many upstart contractors. [for more information on bonding refer to FAR Part 28 – Bonds and Insurance and your Bond Surety Agent.]

Submittals (2): It must be clear there are several types of submittals as it relates to construction, supply, and service contracts. It depends on the type of agency within the federal government who's your target market. The following are an example of various submittals:

- Shop Drawings
- Progress Schedules
- Material Product Certificate
- Test Reports
- QC Reports
- Safety Plans, etc.
- Environmental Plans

The completion of Submittals have a major impact on the administration efforts required by the contractor. There are basically two distinct areas contained under the umbrella known as business. All business organizations are divided into two functional areas, which are administration and performance. In the analysis and breakdown of any company, many functions are centered around the administration efforts that are required in the execution of a contract. The condensed version of the definition of administration is comprised of certain functions such as:

a. execution and implementation of contract terms and conditions including modifications, change orders, email exchange, etc.
b. execution and implementation of invoices and contract execution
c. management and supervision of personnel and support documentation required in support of organization and project interfaces/changes
d. execution and implementation of required submittals
e. management and supervision of all day to day functions in the operation of business processes
f. management and execution of internal fiscal management systems
g. Note: There are many other functions that fall under the umbrella of administration

The management and control of administrative functions within any organization can be totally overwhelming. Most owners totally overlook the necessity of having an in-depth understanding of this aspect of business. Administration success is as important as performance in the field. There are many instances when organizations do not have the right accounting system, or financial system, to handle the proper paperwork required by the federal government. The importance of this section is to increase the awareness of how paperwork is a big part of the government system, and there is no way around it. You have heard many times over: Working within the government sector is not worth the headache due to the red tape; e.g., paperwork and the administration thereof.

It's apparent, completing Submittals is a critical part of administration. The normal time frame for completion and approval of all submittals is within a thirty-day window. (Note: the timeframe for completing these types of documents may vary depending on the type of organization you are working within the government. There may be situations when submittals are not a part of the contracting process or may be known by a different name) The four types of submittals we are covering are:

1. Quality Control Plan (QCP)
2. Accident Prevention Plan (APP)
3. Environmental Protection Plan (EPP) and
4. Project Schedule

Most government agencies require at the very least a Project Schedule and an Accident Prevention Plan. The Environmental Protection Plan (EPP) applies to projects involved with movement of earth or in projects related to fuel storage, chemicals, gases, etc. Depending on which agency you are working with, may not require a Contractor Quality Control Plan (QCP). However, within my organization, each of the above plans were required for any construction project. Therefore, one must know the needs of the organization or target market when it comes to completion of various plans and submittals. The following is an excerpt of each of the documents:

(1) Quality Control Plan (QCP):
    The basic QCP specifies how the contractor will ensure the level of quality specified in the contract by means of a three-phase control system.
    • Preparatory (prior to starting that feature of work)
    • Initial (once a representative quantity of the work is performed)
    • Follow-up (when the work is completed but before acceptance by the government). Deficiencies can be identified in any of the

three phases and corrections can be made.

The general QCP plan will include (not limited to):

- The quality control staff along with their qualifications
- Documents from company management giving authority over the project to the quality control manager
- Identification of any testing required, frequency and the third-party testing company that will be doing the testing
- The definable features of work that constitute the list for tracking of quality control
- Forms that will be used to identify deficiencies and document that corrections have been completed

(2) Accident Prevention Plan (APP):

The APP explains how the contractor will ensure the safety of all involved in the project specified in the contract and following the requirements of the environmental manual. Generally, the plan will include:

- The safety staff along with their qualifications
- Documents from company management giving authority over the project to the Site Safety and Health Officer (SSHO)
- Project specific safety requirement, procedures, reporting
- Company specific safety policies, training, procedures, reporting, safety history, etc.
- Included is a checklist that outlines the requirements of the accident prevention plan. The checklist contains a list of plans that need to be prepared based on the terms and conditions of the contract

(3) Environmental Protection Plan (EPP):

The EPP plan explains how the contractor will ensure that environmental laws and project specific requirements are adhered to. Generally, the plan will include:

- The environmental protection staff along with their qualifications.
- Documents from company management giving authority over the project to the company person responsible for meeting the contract requirements.
- Project specific environmental protection requirements, procedures, reporting, testing, emergency contact list.

- Company specific environmental protection policies, training, procedures, reporting.
- Generally, the contract documents will contain permit information from various local and federal agencies. The plan shall address the requirements of the permits and how the contractor will ensure that all requirements are met, and violation are avoided.

(4) Project Schedule:

This entails the submission of a preliminary schedule. The contract will specify the format required. At a minimum, you can expect to prepare a Gantt Chart, outlining the sequence and durations of each phase of work. Some contracts may require very sophisticated schedules, that could require expensive software that will require a skilled scheduler to prepare.

Generally, the schedule will include:

- Logical sequence of work with durations.
- Schedule of values along with an earnings curve.
- Milestones to include completion date. Note that it is generally an innovative idea to use all of the contract days in the initial schedule so that the contractor owns the float.
- Generally, the contract documents will contain project specific scheduling requirements.

These are four, of many types of submittals, a contractor will encounter relative to the performance of a construction contract for the federal government. The key teaching point is, do not overlook the importance of administration of a contract. It requires a lot of detailed knowledge and functions. This process can easily delay a contract from entering into the construction phase, due to the contractor's inability to complete and administer the required paperwork. There's another factor that is critical. The majority of 8(a) contractors' I worked with, failed to learn the art of completing submittals required by the contract. They relied upon the subcontractor or some other source for completion of these documents. Remember, the Notice to Proceed (NTP) cannot be given by the KO to the contractor, until all submittals are submitted, reviewed, complete, and approved.

- Quick review: a prime contractor must PERFORM 15% of a construction contract and 50% of a service contract. Performance does not include the cost of material. Therefore, is completing submittals, a major part of contract administration? Who is responsible for the completion of submittals...is it the prime or subcontractor?

- The importance of the 8(a) contractors to perform this function is paramount as a prime contractor. Approximately 98% of contracts awarded to 8(a) firms rely upon the subcontractor (or some other source) to complete submittals. Remember, the contract is with the 8(a) contractors (prime).

Do not rely totally on the subcontractor to complete this function. If this process is new to you as a contractor, put this function high on your priority list of things that must be learned as a part of doing business with the government. This is your contract, and you must be aware of the contents of the various plans that are directly related to the execution of the contract. If anything goes wrong relative to the details outlined in the submittals, the prime contractor is responsible. If you can master performing this part of the contract, you have reduced your dependence and reliability on the subcontractor for future contracts regarding completion and submission of submittals.

Thus far we have covered approximately ¾% of this process called "Unfinished Business" inroads to completing this journey of hidden facts of working with the federal government. It should be clear doing business with the government includes many sections and cross sections of processes that can be truly overwhelming. It only appears that way because of the lack of information, exchange of information, and basically working together as one entity. This means developing a working relationship with the government, 8(a) contractor, and subcontractors. For the 8(a) contractors, there is one way to reach your endeavor and goals. The process is to gain as much knowledge as possible and using that information in a concentrated and concise method.

It must be reiterated that this module is heavy slighted toward government contracting functions. Many of the charts, graphs, and functions are directly identified and captured under the contractual guidance contained in the FAR.

CHAPTER 4
BUSINESS FUNCTIONALITY (Module #4)

Whatever you do give it your all. Leave nothing on the table whether it is in sports, business, or in life. Don't cheat yourself out of anything, and with that, life will be good!

Business Functionality is the last part of this incredible journey, designed to provide the small business community with a sense of understanding, relative to performance out in the field. As noted earlier, there is no real priority regarding the previous three business process modules, and this concluding section (if I had to say), is certainly the last step of fully establishing your business as a viable contractor working with the federal government. Let's recapture what has been covered thus far; first, the various avenues of Business Theory were explained providing a theoretical process of being in business; second, there was an in-depth analysis of how to market your organization through utilization of what is referred to as Business Presentation; and third, previous discussion covered the various processes of proposal preparation, and understanding key elements often over looked by 8(a) firms…called Business Preparation. In layman's terms and for simplicity purposes, you now understand (to a certain degree) business analytics (Theory), organizational marketing (Presentation), business proposal composition (Preparation) and finally to this point of working in the field (Functionality).

At this point, you have overcome many obstacles trying to understand this complicated process called government contracting or working with the federal government. This area can be difficult to understand if indeed this is the first time you have received a government contract, either as a prime contractor, or partnering in some sort of JV capacity. Don't worry, this section will cover the basic pitfalls and common functions you need to understand.

The basic meaning of Business Functionality is identifying those functions and processes related to working in the field (performing the terms and conditions contained in the contract). As identified in the previous modules, the intent (for discussion purposes) is to pinpoint those areas that appear (to the average contractor) to be minor but is detrimental to the long-term success of an 8(a) firm. Thus far, you have managed to maneuver your way through negotiations and completion of documents required by the terms and conditions of the contract. This is fantastic! Now the real trouble starts, and it is right in front of you! Once the job begins, in the field, everything you do is scrutinized and watched. The first part of this process involved working with personnel associated to contracting, project management, cost estimators, planning, environmental, and other types of individuals who were responsible for the award of the contract. The second aspect of this process deals with working with agency construction personnel in field activities and functions (Business Functionality).

Let's assume you have fully followed the script that has been discussed herein. You are ready and prepared to go forward, and to the best of your ability, wanting to exceed the terms and conditions of the contract relative to performance. Your primary goal is to complete the project ahead of schedule, within or below budget, and with exceptional quality. This is your intent, so let's cover some of those areas that are of utmost importance. Below is a chart of critical path areas that are basic functions, but if overlooked, can result in a disaster relative to the success of your performance. (exhibit #19) (Note: The areas below are not in any order rather than key discussion topics, critical to your success in the field):

Business Functionality

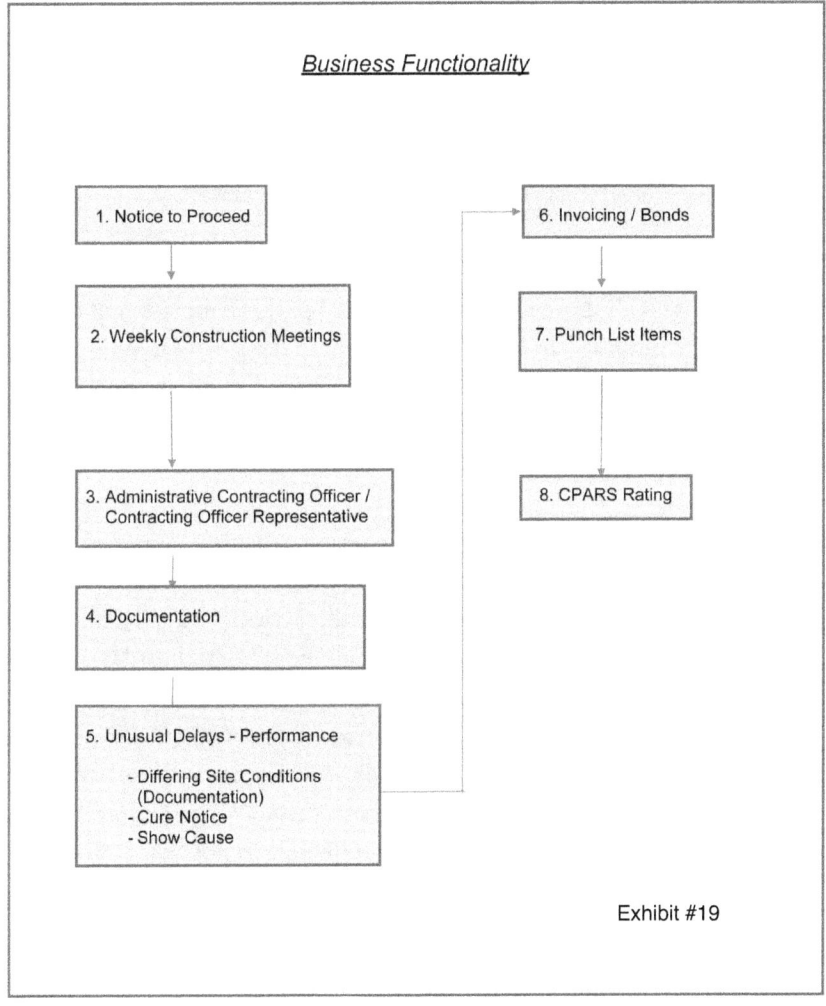

The above graph depicts some of the functions ever-present when working in the field. Let's examine the cause and effect of each of those areas indicated and the level of influence it has on the performance outcome of a contractor:

1. Notice to Proceed: Obviously, the issuance of the Notice to Proceed (NTP) signifies that all required preliminary administrative requirements (bonds/submittals) have been received and approved by the contracting

office, and therefore, authorized to mobilize. In this case, mobilization is associated to the movement of personnel and equipment, to the job site. However, pay close attention to the Period of Performance (POP). The construction time clock begins as soon as NTP is issued. As an example, if the POP is 365 days, the start of the project effort begins leading to completion. At this point, there's nothing critical to the issuance of NTP other than the project completion journey is underway.

[Note: The term Administration includes processing bonds and submittals. It also entails all those functions associated to the completion of the contract, from beginning to end. This includes management of personnel actions/functions and documents; contract related documents; financial and internal system functions; and other administration related actions.]

So far, so good!

2. Weekly Construction Meetings: The measure of any contractor's success starts during the activities covered during the Weekly Construction Meetings (WCM). In the construction industry, it is virtually impossible to have a great ending without having a great beginning! We've heard the old saying: You pretty much always end up, based on the way that you started. In most cases, I believe this statement is true, for the majority of 8(a) firms. To reiterate, the margin for error when it comes to performance for the 8(a) firm, is very slim. I'm hesitant to put a percent of error, but the room for any mishap is slim to none. This statement is not based on opinion but based on facts. There have been countless situations when the phone rings or attending a follow-up meeting, when discussion surface regarding poor performance by the 8(a) firm. You must never forget this statement: Everything done in the field is scrutinized at a much higher level for 8(a) firms verses non-8(a) contractors. This is a strong statement, but there is no need (at this point) to provide anything but the truth regarding this issue (more discussion on why this is true regarding performance).

Now the stage is set for the WCM. Let's review some of the areas that (I feel) are important during the construction effort. There are many things that occur during these meetings; some critical and some mundane related issues. The following are some of those critical areas (not in any order or precedence):

a. Right Personnel: It's imperative to have the right personnel at the WCM from the prime and subcontractor's perspective. As the prime contractor, you are responsible for everything contained in the contract…I mean everything! The subcontractor is only responsible for the guidance and instructions provided by the prime contractor (only).

    Again, there is no privity of contract between the government and subcontractor. Those individuals such as Superintendent, Project Manager, Quality Control POC, or other individuals identified during negotiations, should be present at the initial WCM.

    - Prime/Sub Contractor: Owner/President (at least at the initial meeting)
    - Superintendent/Project Manager, QC POC
    - Contract Negotiator (contract negotiation leader)
    - Admin Personnel (note taker)
    - Designated individual or individuals who will be main POC for all field and contract matters, relative to the performance of subcontractor functions

    It is crucial to show that you, the 8(a)-prime contractor, is in total control from the standpoint of performance. Take this opportunity very seriously! Do not provide any indicators your company is a pass-through firm. (pass through contractor…8(a) firm who receives a government contract either on a competitive, or negotiated basis, who has no real intent on performing very little or 0% of the work – more discussion to come on pass-through contractors). The government may have a variety of individuals at the WCM who have many functions regarding the performance aspect of the project.

    However, two key individuals from the governments perspective are the Administrative Contracting Officer (ACO) and the Contracting Officer Representative (COR), will be discussed later.

b. Cover plans/specifications and terms and conditions of the contract: In most cases, there will be, or should have been, a basic 'construction meeting' between the government and contractor prior to the WCM. During this meeting, the plans, specifications, and other specificities of the contract was again covered. Although the plans, specifications, and other areas, were previously communicated, I'm suggesting that a quick review of these documents are again discussed. It's nothing wrong with the exchange of ideas and concerns regarding these documents. In theory, this will be approximately the fourth (or fifth) time these documents are specifically covered. As a refresher, these documents should be discussed at the BCOES, Technical Meetings, Site Visit, 1st Official Construction Meeting (can be held at the government facility or at an offsite location), and now, during the first gathering of the WCM. In most cases, the government will follow this type of review process. If this is not the case, do not be afraid to bring this up to the KO, or the designated government official. There were Fact-Finding sessions that occurred intermittently, prior to contract award, regarding the contents of plans, specifications, and drawings. The teaching point is to communicate as much as possible the contents of contract related documents as often, and necessary, as possible. The more dialogue between both parties, the higher level of success will occur because of this communication exchange.

c. Performance Work Plan (PWP): If you recall, the PWP was first discussed in the Business Theory section, as well as in the Business Presentation Module. This plan is highly important in soothing the confidence level of field personnel, from the standpoint of your willingness to discuss "how" you are going to perform the task at hand. Is the PWP an important part of the entire acquisition process? Is this an important aspect of building confidence of the government that you are an important player? You must think about these questions as you develop and present your plan of performing as a prime 8(a) contractor. Remember, the image and overall impression that is bestowed as an 8(a) contractor. Anything other than portraying a positive image is highly impossible to correct.

This is an optimum time to convey (again) to the government representatives, your intent and process of acting as a prime contractor. You should clearly go over the plan of action, relative to performance. This is another opportunity to display (with confidence) to others at the meeting that you are in control. If ever, there was a situation to be arrogant (to a certain degree), this is the perfect opportunity. Earlier, there was a discussion about what happens to your image, even when one mistake is made regarding performance, or lack thereof, from the 8(a)-prime contractor. Let's digress for a moment.

Let's assume the following hypothetical scenario previously occurred:

(1) Presenting your business to your target market (presentation).

(2) Meeting with the Chief of Contracting and SBPM.

(3) Ultimately receiving a sole source opportunity.

During this process, you indicated your company was going to perform approximately 25% of the work as the prime contractor (e.g., your performance work plan explaining how your company is going to perform 25% of the job). Initially, the government was ecstatic about the PWP presented, and was highly enthusiastic about your capability regarding performance. Well, you are now at this point in the process of the WCM, and things are going especially well. The next week (or somewhere during this time frame) you are given the "go-ahead" to mobilize. Various personnel from the subcontractor start to congregate at the job site, with multiple pieces of equipment that happens to belong to the subcontractor. The first week on the job goes by, followed by the second, and third week. Suddenly, the KO is contacted by field government personnel indicating there is only one individual from the prime contractor on the job. Questions arise, and you the owner of the company, is contacted regarding lack of performance as indicated and conveyed throughout this entire process. Hopefully, you can understand where this is leading. Earlier reference was made to a contractor acting as a "pass-through." This is the belief of what happens on the majority of 8(a) contracts regarding performance. Is this the perception, or is this reality? Look, there is nothing to hide, but to state this is reality regarding the 8(a) firm's ability to actual perform or acting as a pass-through company. This is only an example and may be a little to the extreme in content, but the bottom line is this situation happens often relative to 8(a) awarded contracts. It only takes one mistake of this kind to ruin subsequent opportunities for 8(a) contractors in the future. This is one of the major problems affecting most of the 8(a)-contractor's working with the federal government. Throughout many meetings, the conversation of performance, or lack thereof, has always been a major concern. The teaching point is to adhere to the PWP presented and be prepared during the WCM to reiterate in full detail, your role and responsibility as a prime contractor. It's to your advantage to follow this course of action.

d. Project Schedule/Weekly and Monthly Milestones: During the WCM, it's imperative to fully discuss those events that are to occur during that week. It's plausible to discuss milestones for the next two weeks, or for the entire month. Communication and exchange of information for activities to be accomplished are keys to understanding, and as well as staying on schedule. Too many times, subcontractors are given this task and invariably leads to problems, issues, and concerns that results in presenting a bad image for 8(a) contractors. You cannot afford to take this risk at any point in time. There is a basic agenda that is discussed by the government representative, however, I'm implying that these are additional areas that need to be covered during these weekly meetings.

3. Key Personnel ACO/COR: Another important aspect of working with the government or in any situation, is getting to know key personnel. During the WCM, field personnel from the government will be at the meeting. Relationship building is paramount and a critical need for each party to develop a clear understanding and respect for each other. There are many situations, when attitudes, behaviors, and personal biases play a role in the success and/or failures of the contractor. It's true personalities and personal feelings should not be a factor, but this is not always the case. It's the responsibility of both entities to ensure current and "follow-on" meetings occur on schedule or when necessary. They should be conducted in a professional and courteous manner. It may not seem important to discuss relationship building, but there are many situations when the attitude of either the government representatives, or contractor personnel, can be a detriment to the overall success of the project. There were several situations during my career when certain contractor personnel were removed from negotiations, or from the field activities, due to less than desirable personalities. Do not underestimate the need to know those government personnel who are the decision makers in retrospect to authority and responsibility. This is from a contractor's viewpoint, and from the government's perspective.

There are two field government personnel, you clearly must understand their roles and responsibilities, as it relates to performance in the field. Those two key individuals are the Administrative Contracting Officer (ACO) and the Contracting Officer Representative (COR). In simple terms, the duties of the ACO and COR are assigned in the following manner:

- ACO: The ACO receives contracting authority from Headquarters, or a designated official through the issuance of a Standard Form 1402, Certificate of Appointment, also known as a warrant. The warrant is set at a specific dollar limit and for a specific purpose. The KO must delegate the authority to administer a specific contract to the ACO. Only the KO can legally bind the government to a contract, and the ACO can only act within the limits as specified within their warrant. (Refer to FAR for further definition and authority of the ACO.)

- COR: The KO routinely appoints CORs nominated by the requiring activity commander, to assist in contract administration. The CORs and the extent of their authority to act on the behalf of the KO is designated in writing. The key is, their duties are clearly defined in writing by the KO. He or she has no binding contract authority. (ref to FAR for further definition and authority of the COR).

A Contracting Officer's authority is derived from a warrant. Only a Contracting Officer can negotiate a contract with industry and contractually bind the government. The warrant may give the individual unlimited authority or may limit one to a certain dollar threshold and/or commodity. Contracting Officers must display this document in a conspicuous place to inform every one of their express authority. (FAR, Subpart 1.603-3)

The Secretary of Defense, through the Defense Federal Acquisition Regulation Supplement (DFARS), confers authority on Contracting Officers to designate Contracting Officer Representatives. This authority is extremely limited. CORs cannot change price, quantity, delivery, or any other terms, or conditions of the contract and cannot delegate their authority to another individual. The COR designation must be in writing.

The COR is designated in the letter of delegation stipulating the express authority given to that particular individual for a specific contract… under no circumstances is the COR authorized to effect any changes in the work required under the contract, or enter into any agreement that has the effect of changing the terms and conditions of the contract or causes the contractor to incur costs. "The COR shall not supervise, direct, or control contractor employees." (FAR, Subpart 1.604)

The teaching point is to always know the roles and responsibilities of the ACO/COR, as well as who has the right authority to exercise, and execute contract terms and conditions. Do not be susceptible to following instructions and directions from anyone other than those individuals who have been designated and have the responsibility and authority to provide you direction as stated within the parameters of the contract and within the limits of their authority.

4. Documentation: Throughout many years working in the private and public sectors, one of the absolute keys to working in the field for any contractor, is the degree and extent of "documentation." This refers to capturing (documenting) actions relative to the performance and execution of the terms and conditions of the contract. It must be noted that the contract contains parameters relative to performance and specifies what a contractor must and will do. The actions and functions contained within the contract are self-defined and for the most part very clear. Documentation in this case, is directed toward meetings, concerns, issues, directives given, and any process or functions that may be clear or ambiguous. In other words, know explicitly what is in the contract, as well as how it relates to daily performance, duties, and responsibilities. I've found most contractors fail miserably when it comes to documenting what appears to be minor details. In reality, you are safeguarding against any misunderstanding or future disputes, that may occur at a later date between you and the government.

In the above section, there is specific discussion on the roles and responsibilities of the ACO and COR, as well as distinct types of authority. There are actual situations when a government representative, has given direction to a contractor, regardless were it is apparent and/or implied authority, but had no real (actual) authority to do so. This mistake is not acceptable at any level. To offset this from happening, you (as the prime contractor) must know the contract terms and conditions completely, as well as know (from the government's perspective) who can provide direction within the scope of the contract. The question remains: Who's in charge from the contractor's perspective and from the government's standpoint? The onus is on you (the contractor) to figure this out and ensure to follow what is stated in the contract, or any modifications that have been provided by the KO. If everything fails, there's one suggestion that I must provide: "read the contract over and over again and ensure that all contractor field personnel are fully informed of the contents of the contract."

The art of learning when and what to document will prohibit problems and issues that may result in extensive monetary cost, unusual contract delays, and/or cancelation of a contract. This is a wonderful time to use the term 'ALWAYS' document any situation relative to performance and contract terms, and conditions that are seemingly uncommon practices, or requests. Especially, during WCM, things are said and done in a fashion that doesn't always coincide with contract terms and conditions. Do not over react to the extent and amount of documentation, but do not underestimate its level of importance. There is one individual (when in doubt) you can always revert to and that is the KO. Earlier, we talked about relationship building especially with the field ACO and COR. If there is not a good relationship, these individuals (ACO/COR) may feel you are circumventing their authority, by coordinating with the KO on certain issues. Therefore, a solid relationship must be developed with government field and office personnel. The bottom line is, do not perform any act, function, or process outside the scope of the contract and, when in doubt, document the situation and coordinate with the KO.

5. Unusual Delays - Performance: This section is not directly related or based on Unusual Delays as contained in regulatory guidance found in the FAR. An example of these types of delays are related to weather, suspensions, and other areas that fall under this topic. This section is specifically related to three critical areas associated to performance in the field that most 8(a) firms fail to comprehend. I personally feel that the following are areas that has an enormous impact related to performance. Those

three areas are (a) Differing Site Conditions, (b) Cure Notice, and (c) Show Cause Notice. I picked these three areas for training purposes due to the lack of knowledge and the level of impact on performance. There are other factors associated to field performance that are just as important as the three areas noted above. However, it's impossible to cover all those situations. Let's take a close look at each of these areas, and depict the importance of each area, and its effect on the contractor:

a. Differing Site Conditions: This topic was selected since unknown situations relative to construction, can have a direct impact on cost to the government and contractor. This clause places the risk of unknown site conditions (sometimes referred to as changed conditions) on the government as well as on the contractor. The purpose of this clause is to avoid the contractor from placing contingencies (cost) in their initial bid/proposal for unknown subsurface or physical site conditions. Based on the standard text book definition regarding Differing Site Conditions are:

   - "The contractor shall promptly, and before the conditions are disturbed, give a <u>written notice</u> to the KO of (1) subsurface or latent physical conditions at the site, which differ materially from those indicated in this contract, or (2) unknown physical conditions at the site, of an unusual nature, which differ materially from those ordinarily encountered and generally recognized as inhering in work of the character provided for in the contract.

   - The Contracting Officer shall investigate the site conditions promptly after receiving the notice. If the conditions do materially so differ and cause an increase or decrease in the contractor's cost of, or the time required for, performing any part of the work under this contract, whether or not changed as a result of the conditions, an equitable adjustment, shall be made under this clause and the contract modified in writing accordingly.

   - No request by the contractor for an equitable adjustment to the contract under this clause shall be allowed, unless the contractor has given the written notice required, provided that the time prescribed in (a) above for giving written notice may be extended by the KO.

- No request by the contractor for an equitable adjustment to the contract for differing site conditions shall be allowed if made after final payment under this contract. (FAR 52.236-2)"

In layman's terms, the essence of this clause is to allow the contractor to receive possible compensation for unknown work, at the time of contract negotiations was hidden. In many cases, the contractor is unaware of these special conditions due to lack of knowledge, and because of limited experience. You can't always rely on the subcontractor (pending on their level of involvement with performance) to recognize these changes. Over the years, most 8(a) firms (novice) have little to no knowledge of the importance of this clause and its relevancy. Before we move forward to discuss the other two topics, what was the key action stated within the above four areas outlining the Differing Site Condition action and procedure? Look closely in the very first section (a) and the answer is underlined…<u>written notice</u>. Earlier in this module, the importance of documentation was stressed repeatedly. As stated in this section, written notification (documentation) is so important. Remember, when in doubt, relative to any situation always document the action and coordinate with the KO. Don't ever assume that compensation is provided for work completed that was unknown or unauthorized. To the reader, it may seem strange to address this area as important, however, to the 8(a) contractors could have a major impact on cost and performance. This is another example of exploring hidden elements of performance. This is a contract term that most KO's will discuss at some point prior to actual performance in the field.

Cure Notice/Show Cause Notice: Although these are two distinct processes, they are directly interconnected, since a Cure Notice is first issued to a contractor for failure to perform (to a certain degree), followed by the Show Cause Notice leading to possibly termination of the contract. Throughout forty years of working in the contracting arena (in various capacities), there were few instances when the KO had to issue a Cure Notice Letter, and subsequently follow by Show Cause Notice for termination of the contract for lack of performance. It must be understood; the use of these processes was in existence but seldom invoked during my own experiences in contracting. [Depending on the area of contracting and the type of business commodities procured, may dictate the frequency a KO may invoke these contract clauses.]

b.   - Cure Notice: This notice (letter) is directly related to lack of performance or failure to make progress by the contractor. When the
KO sends you a contract cure notice (in my opinion), chances are the
government is approximately 60% ready to issue a termination for
cause. In a normal situation, the KO (or government authorized representative COR/ACO) has met with you and had many discussions
regarding inferior performance. In addition, the KO should have provided <u>written notification</u>, indicating lack of performing in accordance
within the terms and conditions stated in the contract. Again, the act
of providing written documentation of inferior performance should
have been given to you in writing. (A paper trail should be available
regarding performance or lack thereof.)

Step #1. In addition, there should be documented meetings between
the government and you discussing problems, issues, concerns, as well
as a recommended schedule of corrective actions taken by the contractor
to improve performance. From my perspective, this is step #1, *prior* to
issuing a Cure Notice. A contractor working with the government
should be done in the realm of working in "good faith." The KO is
100% obligated to go the "extra mile" working with any contractor
when it comes to performance related issues. There are some KO's who
believe corrective actions are a part of the processes contained in the
Cure Notice, but I'm a firm believer every opportunity should be given
to the contractor to get back on the right performance track. Let's be
clear about the utilization of a Cure Notice, this is the formal process
used in corrective action relative to performance. Throughout my career, for the most part, the 8(a) contractors were given many opportunities to improve performance prior to the issuance of a Cure Notice.

Step #2. Under this assumption, if the procedure stated in step
#1 is followed, and the contractor has failed to show improvement;
the next step is issuance of the Cure Notice. [For teaching purposes,
step #1 is my own personal viewpoint of the course of action but may
not be the course of action taken by the KO.] The difference between
a Cure Notice from a "Show Cause" Notice, is when the period of
performance has passed, and the government issues a Show Cause
Notice. A Cure Notice is not appropriate because the performance
period has already ended.[52]

c. - Show Cause Notice: Again, the difference between the Show Cause Notice and Cure Notice is based on the fact the period of performance has ended, therefore the Show Cause Notice may be invoked. However, the government may make a preliminary decision to terminate the contract for default, when the government believes your performance under the contract is at risk, a Cure Notice may be issued. On the other hand, if it's believed you have violated the terms and conditions of the contract, the government may issue a Show Cause Notice. In the case of a Show Cause Notice for non-performance, the government could even pursue a termination for default.[53] The main point regarding performance (or lack thereof) of the 8(a) firm is predicated on the government affording the contractor every opportunity to correct performance deficiencies and verification can be supported by documentation of actions taken by the government.

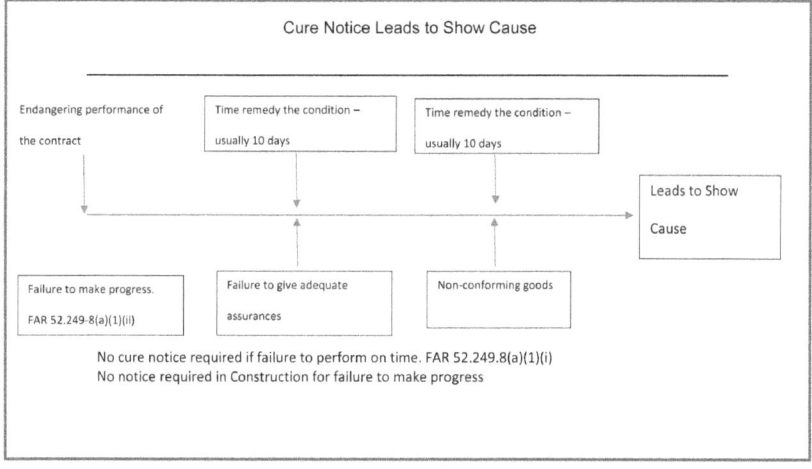

6. Invoicing/Bonds: This segment of Business Functionality is specifically targeted to efforts that are Indefinite Delivery Indefinite Quantity (IDIQ) type contracts. Normally, invoices are paid within thirty days or less, and over the recent years, has not been a problem. The government has streamlined its process and has ensured under normal processing of invoices (if submitted properly) are done in a timely manner. This has not always been the case, but now is one of the major benefits of contractors

working with the government. The question may arise as to why this section is tied to invoices and bonds? Most 8(a) firms have a major problem securing bonding capacity for current and future projects.

The topic of bonding capacity and ways to obtain bonding assistance, was fully discussed in the previous modules. As explained and discussed, any firm acting as a prime contractor through 'indemnification' can obtain bonding support/assistance through the subcontractor. Indemnification is an alternative most prime contractors don't understand in relations to obtaining bonding under certain types of contracts.

As an example, the following is the structure of a typical government contract number: "W912X2-17-C-0010." The basic composition or breakdown of this fabricated contract number is:

- "W912X2" is call the DoDAAC (Department of Defense Activity Address Code) which is a six-position code that identifies a unit, activity or organization that has the authority to requisition a good or service).
- "17" is the year that the contract was awarded.
- "C" indicates this contract is fully funded from the government perspective and the contractor (if a construction effort) must provide <u>bonding in the full amount of the contract total</u>.
- "0010" is the number of contracts awarded by this activity in consecutive order…the next contract awarded would be 0011.

For discussion purposes, let's assume this was an IDIQ type contract, therefore, the contract number (as an example) would be "W912X2-17-<u>D</u>-0001" The way to determine the distinction between the two contracts, is the "D" designation stated in the above sample contract number. The "D" indicates a contract is not fully funded, and therefore, each requirement is issued on a Task Order basis. In the case of an IDIQ type contract, the key factor is related to the completion of each Task Order issued by the contracting office. As an example, the first Task Order (or statement of work outlining the work to be completed) is in the amount of $100,000. The total contract is in the amount of $1 million. The contractor must provide a bond in the amount equal to the dollar value of the first Task Order, which is $100,000. After the completion of the work, the KO releases the bond capacity back to the contractor, to be used for the next or follow-on requirement. (The bonding process was fully discussed earlier but is relevant to performance in the field.)

This is an example of the difference between two types of contracts, and to increase the awareness to the contractor. It's important to know and understand the difference between a contract that is fully funded ("C" type) and a contract that is IDIQ, ("D" type) that requires the prime contractor to provide a bond in the <u>amount equal to the dollar value of the first Task Order</u>. Therefore, the KO fully understands these contractual guidelines and should ensure you are not handicapped based on bonding requirements, as it relates to the type of contract. This may seem like a simple process. I have known instances when this same function has been overlooked, resulting in minor harm to the contractor. Basically, the Task Order was completed, however, the relinquishing of the cost of the bond was not "released" back to the contractor. Eventually, this problem was corrected, but is a situation that a prime contractor must be aware. Regardless, if the contract is fully funded, or funded based on issuance of Task Orders, directly affects your bonding capacity. Remember, the difference in a "C" type contract and a "D" contract is significantly different, as it has a major impact on your bonding capacity and obligation. [Refer to the FAR for further clarification and discuss with the KO to ensure you understand the two types of contracts and how it affects your bonding capability. Any reference made to "C" and "D" type contract numbers are related to funding. There are only two types of contracts which are Firm Fixed Priced and Cost Reimbursement.]

7. Punch List Items: There is not much in this section, only a contract is not closed until all final requirements (regardless in size or dollar value) are completed by the contractor. There is nothing critical about this topic. However, all items must be considered complete (relative to performance and payment) by the government. If you are not aware of this term, or process, do not be alarmed regarding its level of importance, but remember, all items shall be completed by the contractor prior to submission of final payment.

8. Contractor Performance Assessment Reporting System (CPARS): This is the concluding section that will be discussed, which is tied to your overall performance rating given to your company. This area is the last step that

summarizes how well you performed in the field, and perhaps, dictate your ability to receive additional follow-on contracts with the federal government. The following question has been asked many times to various 8(a) contractors: "How do they feel about the rating received <u>after the completion of a project</u>?" It was astonishing to hear the types of responses given.

Before we proceed, please pay close attention to the above sentence that is underlined. This was done for a reason and will be explained shortly.

Here are some of the responses received over the period of years from contractors:

- I was expecting a higher rating, but I guess it's not important.
- I guess we'll try harder next time.
- I thought we were doing an outstanding job!
- This rating is wrong, but what can I do about it?
- Well, the next time we'll do better and get that outstanding rating.
- No one told us where we needed to improve, we assumed that we were headed on the right track.

 Negative or less-than-optimistic responses on and on!

Less get back on track! The importance of your final rating is two-fold. Number one is to provide feedback at the end of the project, analyzing and grading how well your company performed in accordance to the terms and conditions of the contract; and two, to assist your company with increased opportunity, based on information submitted into CPARS. What do you mean, this information is used to assist in future contract opportunities? One must understand the rating given to you by the ACO (approved by the KO) is submitted in the rating system. This information can be accessed and used by other government organizations in reviewing your capability for future projects.

As an example, the Forrest Department has a requirement and is looking for an 8(a) contractor for a sole-source award. They selected your company based on your overall capabilities, using whatever method that resulted in the selection process. However, somewhere along the line, the KO decided to extend his due diligence check and decided to obtain your past history data contained in CPARS. For some reason (unknown), your company received a marginal rating on your last job. This information obtained by the KO changes everything! Due to this low rating, he/she decides not to make a sole-source award to your company, because of this poor rating. Again, this is only an example and there were other related evaluation factors leading to this decision.

Let's look at example #2. In this case, the Forrest Department has a competitive solicitation set-aside for only 8(a) companies. As a part of the evaluation criteria, past history was one of the review or evaluation elements. The Source Selection Review Board is following the rules regarding the selection process and analyzed the ratings of those contractors whose proposals are under review considering "all other factors are equal". What do you think happened to your company's proposal once the Selection Board obtained and reviewed the information contained in CPARS? Do you think your proposal was (under consideration) reviewed in the same manner as those firms who had a much favorable CPARS rating? There are other factors under review in the evaluation process, but past project ratings can be critical to the selection authorities.

The teaching point is simple: Your overall rating matters; highly important; critical from the perspective of affecting your ability for follow-on efforts; etc. The question is: "How do you ensure you are on track and heading in the right direction toward receiving a rating that is favorable and desirable?" There's one thing for sure, every company wants an Exceptional or Outstanding rating. However, they are not sure how to obtain this level of rating although they feel that their performance level has been exceptional. There are many organizations within the government that uses a variety of methods for grading contractor's performance. The information and grading system may be different, but as a contractor, you want the highest rating possible.

I've asked this question to every contractor I ever met, and throughout my presentations: "At what time do you know the rating you are going to receive after the project is completed?" This is a simple question, with no twist or turns. At least 99.9% of all contractors answered in the same manner: "We will or won't know, until the end and completion of the project." This is the wrong answer! Let's dig deeper into why this is an inappropriate response. Let's assume you were awarded an 8(a)-negotiated contract in the amount of $2.5 million and the POP is 365 days. Everything is going smoothly, and you are performing in the field in accordance to contract terms and conditions. Oh, by the way, this is an IDIQ contract with Task Orders issued for work to be completed, based on issuance of Statements of Work. The first Task Order was in the amount of $500,000, with work to be completed in 60 days. The stage is now set, and your company is working very hard to meet/exceed the terms and conditions stated within the contract. Your goal is to be an outstanding contractor! Telephone calls are received from the ACO/COR, and the KO indicating how well you are performing. Time is passing, and the second and third Task Orders have been issued. Its 120 days into the contract term. The 365 day Period of Performance passes and finally, the job is complete. You receive your rating, which is Satisfactory. You are astonished, and now ask the question, "Why didn't my company receive a higher rating?" It's too late to a certain degree! There is a process to discuss your rating with the ACO and perhaps consideration by the KO to make an adjustment to your final rating. Some organizations don't believe in giving a company an Exceptional or Outstanding rating regardless of a firm's overall performance level. This is a fact! There isn't any rationale why some government organizations don't rate firms in accordance to, or in a manner indicating exceptional or outstanding performance.

This is the hidden answer of receiving a rating you feel is inappropriate, or, is much lower than it should be. (Remember discussion can occur with the ACO and KO prior to submission in CPARS) Using the above example with a POP of 365 days...You know there are weekly meetings, quarterly meetings, and various internal meetings between government personnel regarding your project. At the end of the first month, ask the ACO how are you doing relative to performance? Ask the following questions:

- If you had to rate my company's performance thus far, how would you rate our level of performance?
- What are areas do you consider need to be improved?
- How and what can we do as a contractor to improve on our current level of performance?
- Ask these same questions six months, nine months, and so forth, during the 365 POP
- Provide a brief email to the ACO and cc the KO each time you ask this question(s).

These are questions you periodically ask the ACO/KO regarding your performance level. The ultimate goal is to define and pinpoint the areas that require improvement. There's nothing wrong with using this approach. The rationale behind this method is quite simple in theory. Most supervisors and managers who rate their subordinates start from the lower echelon or mid-level of performance and subsequently working their way up the ladder toward obtaining the highest performance rating.

Normally, most organizations have a mid-year review for their employees. If you think back during one of these sessions, your supervisor explained your strengths, as well as things that needed improvement. Evaluating personnel in this manner is backwards. This is why I feel this way. The very next day after your final rating going into the next performance period, the question is: What have you done to decrease your degree and quality of work (assuming your rating was satisfactory or higher)? The answer is nothing. Therefore, each subordinate should start at the highest level of performance and either maintains the highest level or work themselves down the grading scale. Theoretically, you are providing the employee with the greatest amount of support and mentally has changed that employees mental approach toward developing good working habits. In using this theory in grading contractor performance in the field, the contractor starts at the highest level before one shovel of dirt is turned. As a contractor or employee, I would prefer to start at the highest level relative to performance subsequent falling down the evaluation scale; but I know at every moment what is required to climb the ladder back to success. Therefore, it is crucial to know where you stand regarding performance. If this question is asked: "What is your firms current performance rating?" At any point during the contract term, you should know where your firm stand in terms of performance. Don't ever wait until the completion of the contract, you may be surprised of your firms final rating! By using this approach, the ACO/COR and the KO increases communication between themselves and contractor personnel. This reduces various problems and issues because the government and contractor personnel are in constant discussion regarding contractor performance.

This type of communication exchange between both parties should result in improved performance and can be directly attribute to problem solving of issues that are hidden, delayed and/or obvious. Knowing your performance status during the contract term rather than waiting at the end, forces increased communication and develops a better relationship between both entities. This can only create a win/win situation for the government and contractor thereby increases the performance level of a contractor to the highest practical extent possible. One may not agree with the evaluation method presented, but it provides an optimistic viewpoint that a contractor (from the onset) could perform at the highest level. This substantiates why this firm was selected as the contractor of choice for that effort.

There have been meetings at the end of a contract period, whereby statements were made that the 8(a)-firm failed to perform. The contractor wasn't reliable, and thus, should not be recommended for future efforts. In some cases, the problem lies in the fact that there was no written documentation of the contractor's failure to perform in any magnitude. Just as discussed in the previous section on Documentation, Cure Notice, and Show Cause areas, the need for documenting these actions, or lack thereof, is critical and impacts the government and contractor's ability to complete the project. The final stage of the entire acquisition process (from award to project completion), rests with the final rating that is provided to that contractor. The contractor should have a clear understanding of how his company is performing throughout the performance period of the contract. It's clearly an advantage to both the government and contractor in understanding the pros and cons of performance in the field well in advance to contract completion. By following this process, allows the contractor an opportunity to correct deficiencies early during the contract term and provide the contractor the highest opportunity to achieve an exceptional or outstanding rating.

Now it's time to come home! The journey is almost complete. The roads were rough, and the mountains were high, but through it all, through the grace of God, I (we) made it home! So far, so good! We have now covered (almost completed) one of the most amazing journeys in the history of the 8(a) firm. This ride is one that appeared to be an uphill struggle, and at times, insurmountable. Through all the agony, trials, and tribulations, the "true grit" of the 8(a) firm stands tall. Those government representatives who have worked so diligently in support of the program and its mission also should be commended. Before we enter the final discussion phase and conclusion, we must identify the correct process of working with the federal government and some of the intriguing functions and avenues.

Throughout many years of working with the small business community, there appeared to be a certain degree of confusion as to the right process for the 8(a) firm to pursue, regarding working with the federal government. Time and time again, the phone would ring, and on the other end of the phone, would be an individual who wanted to start a business.

They wanted to set a up meeting to discuss business protocol in establishing a business or speak to an SBA representative. In many cases, an individual needed to contact SBA prior to contacting a potential target organization within the federal government. Therefore, the following is a recommended path to take in starting a business who wish to (at a minimum) work with the federal government (targeted toward construction, services, A&E, etc./exhibit #20):

Steps in Starting a Business (Working with federal government)

Step #1.   Read this Book
Step #2.   Organize your Company (use guidelines in the book)
Step #3.   Contact Small Business Administration (SBA)
Step #4.   Read this Book
Step #5.   Contact Association of Contact Procurement Technical Assistance Center (APTAC)
Step #6.   Refer to this Book
Step #7.   Set up meeting with your Target Market (Government)
Step #8.   Prior to meeting…Refer to this Book
Step #9.   Meet with your Target Market (Government)
Step #10.   Repeat steps #3 and #5
Step #11.   Always Refer to this book

Exhibit #20

The above chart is a recommended path (again at a minimum) toward starting a business, with the end goal of working with the federal government. There are many instances when new companies fail to understand there are organizations who specialize in assisting their company in many facets of working with the government. Let's take a closer look at each of the recommended courses of action, and obtain a basic understanding as to why these steps are critical in the development of your firm:

Step #1 – Read this Book: The first step in accomplishing your goal/mission is to obtain as much information and knowledge as possible. This document is certainly not a panacea for the multitude of problems, issues, and concerns you will encounter along this journey of starting and remaining in business, but you must have a solid foundation. This information, data, functions, and procedures you have read, puts you light-years ahead of those individuals who didn't understand the basic concepts of doing business with the government. There's no need to regurgitate what you have read, as long as the first thing you do, is start with reading, understanding, and digesting as much information as possible. Remember, information is knowledge; knowledge is power; power to make a better-informed decision!

NOTE: DO NOT CONTACT
THE FEDERAL GOVERNMENT POC

Step #2 – Organize your Company: Organize your company using the Outside in Approach as stated in exhibit #5 – The Power of Critical Thinking. This approach may not be the best way for all firms to follow, but it certainly reduces a lot of leg work used by hiring the wrong personnel thus targeting the wrong business market. To reiterate, this approach is designed to identify the needs within the business world; identify target market (public/private); and develop the right skillset of personnel to meet the needs of the target market. A prudent and shrewd business owner builds a company based on market demand and is surrounded by those individuals who can help him flourish. Always ensure the right people are in the right places, performing the right jobs!

DO NOT CONTACT THE FEDERAL GOVERNMENT POC

Step #3 – Contact Small Business Administration (SBA): This is the first CRITICAL step in developing your company. SBA offers a multitude of services and functions from loans, to starting a business, training, certification programs and others, too. These organization(s) are located throughout the country with regional and local offices specifically to assist anyone (and I mean anyone) who needs business assistance. In order to do business with the federal government your company must be registered in the master system named System for Awards Management Systems (SAMS). It is recommended you explore this web site, and do your homework prior to setting up the initial meeting with SBA. This organization is there to assist and provide guidance and direction; however, it is your responsibility to be prepared prior to meeting with SBA. [As you can see, the word preparation shows up throughout this reading regardless to the manner and level of importance.] This step cannot be overlooked, and you must work with this organization before doing anything else.

DO NOT CONTACT THE FEDERAL GOVERNMENT POC

Step #4 – Read the Book: The amount of time working with SBA is going to be long and arduous. This is a positive thing! Periodically, throughout your meetings with SBA, continue to refer to this document to associate things learned and how they interface with the points identified herein. The more information you obtain, the stronger your mental capability will grow, in order to deal with the physical aspects of starting a business and working with the government.

DO NOT CONTACT THE FEDERAL GOVERNMENT POC

Step #5 – Contact the Association of Procurement Technical Assistance Center (APTAC): The second organization to contact (at a minimum) is APTAC. This organization is found throughout various states within the US and offers a variety of services to small business and to anyone who have a valid need. The mission of this organization is to "assist small businesses that want to sell their products or services to the government." APTAC is sponsored by Department of Defense (DoD) and in joint cooperation with Defense Logistics Agency (DLA), Department of Commerce/Economic Opportunity, and other business organizations within each state. These entities are organized to provide assistance to small businesses. The following are some questions/answers as to the services provided by APTAC:

- What is the purpose of APTAC?
  - Familiarize clients with government procurement
  - Assist with paperwork
  - Electronic bid match service
  - Government marketing assistance
  - Pricing History
- What type of assistance is provided by APTAC?
  - Federal registrations (SAMS)
  - Federal certifications/verification

- State registrations and State certifications
- Why work with a APTAC?
  - Bridge between the business and government
  - One on one counseling
  - Training opportunities
  - No charge for services (see state regulations)
- With whom does APTAC work with?
  - Established manufacturers, service firms and wholesale companies, construction – e.g., janitorial and cleaning, printers, trucking firms, landscaping, engineers, architects, IT firms, suppliers, scientific and technical services, demolition, remediation, etc. APTACs throughout the country have provided invaluable assistance and guidance to new and existing businesses since their inception. This organization provides those functions that can save time and money to those organizations who wish to do business with the government.[54]

DO NOT CONTACT THE FEDERAL GOVERNMENT POC

Step #6 – Refer to this Book: The amount of information, direction, and assistance received from the various support organizations are beginning to mount. This is a good thing! SBA and APTAC (at a minimum) can steer you in the right direction and with the resources (and staff) to meet your (majority) every need. Do not be afraid to contact and work closely with these organizations. Go back and interject the information obtained from SBA and APTAC and associate it with the information contained herein. Take your time with organizing and integrating everything that is learned thus far with key members of your company. Communication and integration of information is paramount. {Note: There are many organizations in addition to SBA and APTAC; however, these two organizations are a great starting point.}

NOW YOU ARE READY TO MAKE THAT FIRST PHONE CALL TO YOUR TARGET MARKET…THE FEDERAL GOVERNMENT!

IT'S SHOWTIME!

Step #7- Set up meeting with your Target Market (Government): By following the first six steps, you and your company members (those selected individuals as defined in Business Presentation Module) are prepared to discuss your capabilities with the needs of your target market. This is the first step in making a first impression. All members should know their role! Your goal is to display knowledge, capabilities, and total confidence. You and your company members are both certified and qualified to meet the needs of the government. Set up the meeting!

Step #8 – Prior to meeting…Refer to this Book: Before the actual meeting with the government, call an internal meeting with your company members who are going to be present. Go back over the roles and responsibilities of each member, and fully discuss your presentation plan. There is nothing wrong with pre-rehearsal of the presentation plan of attack. Always allow each team member to discuss his/her personal opinion, relative to the upcoming meeting. Prepare! Prepare! Prepare! There's no such thing as over preparation, but certainly a lack of preparation will become obvious.

Step #9 – Meet with your Target Market (Government): During your meeting, always follow the plan and the details you have learned. There is one small tip that needs to be shared. Be aware of questions asked during the meeting. In most cases, some of the questions asked during the meeting are what is referred to as set-up questions. A set-up question (by my definition) is a question asked during a meeting to a member of your group when the answer to the question is already known. This is similar to a grand jury investigation. In most cases, the answers to the questions asked are known, based on inquiries and background checks. The only way to get through a grand jury meeting is by telling the truth. Therefore, during the meeting with the government, always answer any question with honesty and integrity. The only way this can be accomplished is ensuring each member of your company is on the same accord. Sometimes, questions are asked to certain members of the group relative to performance, past history, implementation of your performance work plan, etc. I've used this tactic throughout many meetings with companies, during my career. In every meeting held, I researched the company's background and was knowledgeable about the firms' capabilities prior to the meeting. Just beware of this type of tactic. This is nothing new and not illegal, but it is directly attributed to doing your homework as a government representative, and you as a potential contractor to the government.

Step #10 – Repeat steps #3 and #5: Once you have met with your target market, go back and meet with your SBA representative and APTAC POCs. Why do you think further coordination with these two organization is recommended? The services and guidance offered by both organizations are knowledgeable in government contracting practices and procedures, thereby providing guidance (directions) on the next course of action; if, and when, you may be awarded a negotiated action. It is highly recommended that close coordination with SBA and APTAC is done on a consistent and as needed basis. Throughout your nine-year process in the 8(a) program, you will work with both organizations on a frequent and on-going basis.

Step #11 – Always Refer to this Book: "It's almost time to wake up. The journey beneath the surface is almost complete; however, there is still Unfinished Business."

This module was the last step in discussing many things that affect your ability to become a long-term contractor, working within the framework established by the federal government. Even after the job has been completed, the level of awareness to be a successful 8(a) firm is a continuous and grueling process that never ends. Remember, each contract stands on its own merit! This means each time a contract is completed, theoretically, it becomes pass history in a figurative sense.

Specifically, each time a project is completed, you as a contractor must repeat and follow the guidelines used on the initial contract. Your ability to perform on the previous effort has no bearing on your ability to perform on future contracts. Do not misinterpret the true meaning of the above statement. The history and rating your company received is certainly used by other organizations in the evaluation process for future efforts. Your mental approach to each subsequent effort should be as if this was your first government project.

In other words, don't get comfortable or laxed in your preparation and remain focused regarding all follow-on projects. You are only as good as your performance on the last job completed. Do not become over confident or cocky…stay humble and thankful for every opportunity that comes your way!

CODE RED!
(Code Red is used to indicate a difficult or dangerous situation
has deteriorated drastically so as to constitute an emergency.)

From my perspective, the longevity and survival of the 8(a)-small business contractor is at a "crossroads." Many strides and advancements have been made to mitigate many problems and concerns that are plaguing these organizations. There are laws (federal, state, local) in place to provide guidance, direction, and in many cases, directives that govern processes design to create opportunities for socio-economic businesses. So, at the end of the day, have we (on a collective basis) met our obligations in support of these business entities? Have we done everything in our power to ensure there are opportunities for all and not for a select few? Have we leveled the playing field treating and viewing the small business owner as an equal partner? Many more questions could be raised regarding this issue, but only the future will dictate how well we have worked together regarding the fate of the 8(a) contractors or any small business. It is a known fact your history dictates your present, and your present will mold and shape your future. We all have heard this old adage: If I only knew then what I know now, then where would I be? This is the essence of why I wanted to leave the small business community this relevant and informative abundance of information.

This is my story, this is my belief! My overall goal and objective was to leave the small business community (especially the 8(a) firm), in a better position from a knowledge base standpoint. It doesn't matter what anyone does in life, or in business, if the degree of information is kept to a minimum and to a select few. It doesn't matter how brilliant one may be in certain categories relative to skills, abilities, and in the areas of preparation. It doesn't matter, if you have done everything in accordance to your upbringing or from a social, racial, or ethnic perspective. What does matter, is to give everyone a fair opportunity to achieve the American dream, even if it means from obtaining the highest level of education; becoming an actor; a professional athlete; or starting your own business. I want to reiterate the optimum word in the above equation is "fair opportunity." In many cases, there are two things in this life that cannot be overcome, which are "death and taxes" …or is this the correct assumption? From my perspective, the two most important obstacles that are insurmountable, or cannot be overcome is death and beating the system. Is it a coincidence the system controls the level or degree afforded to any individual from an opportunistic standpoint?

Let's take a closer look how opportunity plays a key role in business and in everyday walks of life. As an example, the words of our nations national anthem, "The Star Spangled Banner," are instrumental in shaping, molding our forefathers' beliefs and even today, is the trademark of who we are as a people, living in a land based on opportunity for all. As a brief history lesson, the Star Spangled Banner was originally entitled, "The Defiance of Fort McHenry," written during the War of 1812 with Great Britain.[55] [Do your own research on the history of our nation's anthem.] The key words that must be discussed is stated at the very end of the Anthem, which are: "O'er the land of the free and the home of the brave." Our heritage, and in today's society, whole heartily believe these truths to be the foundation of our past, present, and future of our nation. I strongly have a problem with the true meaning of the above phrase, especially how it affects all people within our nation. My point is this, if we indeed live in a land and country where democracy is truly the land of the free and home of the brave, then I challenge the true meaning of this statement and its real effect on society. Let's analyze the following exhibit #21:

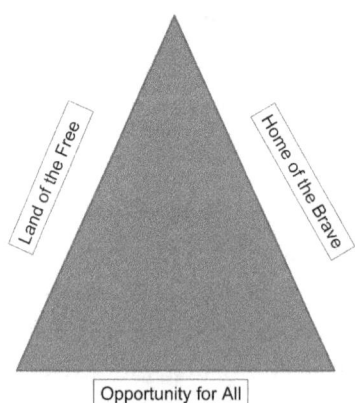

Exhibit 21

The exhibit displays the answers to many of our nation's problems, regardless of social, or ethnicity of those in our country. The question(s) that should be asked to those who really have a vested interest in the survival of the small business society are:

- What if you lived in a Land of the Free? <u>Freedom</u> for every man, woman and child, and <u>opportunity</u> for all but is lacking the <u>bravery</u> to go forth and seek the American Dream!
- What if you lived in the Home of the <u>Brave</u>? Yes, we are a brave nation with the military power to overcome any enemy in any location. We certainly live in a nation where <u>freedom</u> rings but there are <u>no opportunities</u>. Yes, you can be brave and free, but what good is it if there are no opportunities?
- What if you lived in a land of <u>Opportunity</u> for All? Yes, opportunity for all and you have the <u>internal fortitude</u> to overcome, but you are <u>not free</u> and held hostage in a time when there are those who appear to prosper.

The essence of this triad is freedom, bravery and opportunity are all synonymous. The absence of one of the three elements reduces potential of reaching success at its highest level. Ask this question to anyone, anywhere, at anyplace:

HOW DID YOU GET TO WHERE YOU ARE TODAY?

There are several answers to this question, and certainly, who am I to challenge the responses. But in most cases, the obvious answers are:

- I know or knew someone (family member/friend) who help me get to where I am.
- I just got lucky.
- I'm just good at what I do.

The answers received are probably one of the three above, or even, may be a response not stated. The truthful answer is someone, somewhere, gave you an opportunity! This is the only answer, despite if you are a businessman/woman, professor, pro athlete, teacher, or regardless of the situation. Therefore, the absence of opportunity is the missing element from our own national anthem. In parallel to the desires of the small business owner, it is apparent this is the overarching goal of this individual. Do not be misled by the desires and wants of the 8(a)-business owner. I'm in total support of those individuals, but only if their desires are played fairly and by the rules of the game! This can only mean full support should be given to those who are certified, and qualified, and anything less is unacceptable. (code red)

There were many of our forefathers who had goals, desires, hopes, and dreams, who had an impact not only on our nation but from a global perspective. Throughout our history, opportunity has not been a way of life for all, but for a select few. (code red) There are certainly individuals who paid the ultimate price fighting for those who were less fortunate, or didn't understand when humanity or mankind, was in peril and under seized.

This is a wonderful time to reflect on four instances in our history that changed, shaped, and molded the world. Something happened in:

- New Deli, India – 30 January 1948
- Dallas, Texas – 22 November 1963
- New York City, New York – 21 February 1965
- Memphis, Tennessee – 4 April 1968

For those who may not know or need to be reminded:

- Mahatma Gandhi was assassinated in New Deli, India (30 Jan 1948)
- President John F. Kennedy was assassinated in Dallas Texas, (22 Nov 1963)
- Malcolm (X) Little was assassinated in New York City, New York (21 Feb 1965)
- Martin L. King Jr was assassinated in Memphis, Tennessee (4 Apr 1968)

Certainly, there are other great leaders who paid the ultimate price fighting for what they believed and by no means is there any intent to overlook any of those great individuals. The intent is to remember each of those individuals mentioned above had strong beliefs, hopes and dreams. Although each of them took different paths preaching and teaching what they believed to be in the best interest of mankind, there were those who viewed their plight in a distinct perspective.

The commonality among each of those great individuals was they never saw their own dream become a reality. I'm not inferring they saw things from the same standpoint or in a different light, but they believed in the betterment of people in their own way.

Whether the theme of their beliefs was Separate but Equal; Integration not Segregation; and Social justice for all will not be forgotten nor perish from those who still believe their lives were not taken in vain. If it was possible to make an assumption, I'm sure their vision and dream for our country and the world, would be something that included:

"Land of the free, home of the brave and opportunity for all!"

Somewhere, I was asked this question: "Is this a book about history or is it a book on small business?" The plight of the small business person is one that is based on the dreams and aspirations of our predecessors who were teachers, preachers, actors, inventors and so forth. It doesn't matter which area of expertise that we possess, the underlying principle of success is derived from our beliefs, dreams, and internal fortitude. The final verdict of anyone with the hopes of achieving success depends on the fact that opportunity is a right for all and not a privilege for a select few.

Author's Final Words

From my own personal viewpoint, the plight of the 8(a)-program is an endangered species. (code red) The basic intent of the program was designed to provide those 8(a) contractors eligible for set-aside projects that was under and/or above the $4 million threshold. Those projects that were under this dollar amount could, and should be awarded, as a negotiated effort directly to that contractor (assuming all basic qualifications were met in accordance to required standards for those unique firms). Those efforts exceeding that dollar amount remained competitive requirements, but only for the certified 8(a) contractors. Sure, these special contractors could bid on any project available, but it's known their ability to compete on a level playing field was, and is, impossible. This was the basic reason why the program was established. Based on this belief, directed many individuals to seek the 8(a)-certification process that would (hopefully) open doors that would provide opportunities to become a potential contractor to the federal government. There have been enormous successes generated from this process and program. I personally want to say job well done to the Small Business Administration for your diligence and efforts, as the founders and gatekeepers of this program! In addition, the various organizations within the federal government should and must be commended for the support given to these contractors throughout the years. However, I'm concerned with the long-term prognostication, the 8(a) firm as it is known today won't survive if it continues to travel the same old road that was once a haven for many. (code red)

Although there are many great programs coupled with many training opportunities, there still looms a concern within the validity of those firms who are a part of the various small business set-aside programs. When you fully analyze each program, there are glaring concerns of potential fraud, waste, and abuse within the system. I must be clear when reference is made to fraud, waste, and abuse. It's directed toward those companies who are not following the rules, directives, and laws of the socio-economic program. Additionally, there is a concern whether those who represent the government fully recognize that such abuse is present. (code red)

There is a real distinction when violators of rules and regulations are known, but nothing is done to rectify such violations. If these violations are not corrected, and the violators not appropriately dealt with, a negative long-term suffocating and paralyzing effect will be experienced by all groups involved. There are rules in place to "protect the innocent" (e.g., the small business entity). However, there are clear internal efforts that are done to bend and ultimately break those rules designed to protect those businesses who are trying so hard to do the right thing. Honestly, there is no greater supporter (than I) of the 8(a) Business Development Program and the efforts of the federal government who provides opportunities to those firms. There are issues on both sides that will ultimately be the demise of the program. Wait, this is a pessimistic view of a situation that has been and is still highly successful! So, what am I really saying? Have I been contradictory implying on one hand a process has been so successful but, on the other hand, the future is doomed for uncertainty? Okay, you caught me…Let's view this from the standpoint the glass is half full and from a positive viewpoint.

Let's psychoanalyze my own observation and find out why my thoughts are either right or wrong. It's clear to me the underlying principles of the success of any program or business is the basis of its foundation, and how well each building brick is laid.

Notwithstanding, those who are involved with these processes are measured by something that comes from within their own beliefs of what is right and what is wrong. Therefore, in analyzing each of the small business set-asides, there lies a formidable problem that must be revealed. (You must pay close attention to the following analysis.)

It's a known fact, that any small business who meets the size standard and required gross annual revenue is classified as a small business (along with other requirements). In theory, any small business can bid on any project classified "unrestricted" and bid on all projects that are set-aside for only small businesses.

The key fact for "unrestricted" and set aside for only "small businesses," they are procured on a competitive basis. (discussion is not geared for actions that required a Justification/Approval (e.g., J&A). Therefore, any competitive action does not require a performance work plan (PWP). (code red) Any large or small business (under these guidelines) can formulate their business in any manner deemed reasonable. The following depicts the pro and cons of the various set-asides efforts for small business and issues associated to each:

- Program #1 – Unrestricted Procurement: Any business large or small can bid on this action. No performance plan required; the majority of work can be performed by the prime or no specified limit of work can be performed by the subcontractor) – no performance plan required. This requirement is 100% competitive.
- Program #2 – Small Business Set-aside: Only small businesses can bid on these type actions. Any small business in any of the set-aside or certified programs can bid – no performance plan required. This requirement is 100% competitive. It's important to note, there are rules relative to "Limitations on Subcontracting" that limits the amount of work that can be subcontracted pertaining to small businesses concerns and 8(a) concerns. Specifically, the dynamics of the clause implies: "(1) Services – at least fifty percent of the cost of contract performance incurred for personnel shall be expended for employees of the concern. (2) General Construction: The concern will perform at fifteen percent of the cost of the contract, not including the cost of material, with its own employees.[56] The question remains, are these businesses held accountable for the percent of work subcontracted or performed as a prime contractor?
- Program #3 – HUBZone Program: This program is (as discussed in Modules #1 and #2) for small businesses located in "Historically Underutilized Business Zone" areas.

Initially, there were many problems with fraud, regarding firms indicating they were located in these areas and major problems with verification and authentication of those small businesses. These firms are certified as HUBZone contractors. Only small businesses who are certified as HUBZone contractors can bid on these set-asides. HUBZone contractors all over the country (or restricted on a regional basis) can bid – no performance plan required. This requirement is 100% competitive only for HUBZone contractors. How much of the actual work is subcontracted in accordance with the "limitations on subcontracting" clause?

- Program #4 – 8(a) Certified Contractors: These contract actions fall under the dollar thresholds stated earlier (negotiated < $4M; competitive > $4M). These small businesses (as discussed) are certified in the

8(a) Business Development Program and be classified in any of the other classifications; e.g., woman-owned; hub zone; small disadvantaged business; and/or service disabled veteran-owned small business (not including veteran-owned certified contractors). All negotiated actions REQUIRE a performance work plan relative to performance. (code red) Award made to one designated company. This requirement is 100% negotiated. Competitive 8(a) requirements (> $4M) do not require a performance plan). This requirement is 100% competed only with other 8(a) certified companies (open on national basis or may be restricted to a particular location within certain regions).

- Program #5 – Service Disabled Veteran Owned Small Business: There were initial problems with certification and verification of those firms who were approved under this program. Projects set-aside for this category are only for those firms approved as SDVOSB. These actions are competed on a national basis (or restricted to certain regions) and do not require a performance work plan. Requirements of this nature are 100% competitive for only SDVOSB contractors. How much of the actual work is subcontracted in accordance with the "limitations on subcontracting" clause?

- Program #6 – Woman-Owned Small Business Program: Recently, this program was established as set-asides for woman who owned businesses under various commodity codes. Moreover, within the last couple of years (prior to 2017), approval was granted for requirements under the construction commodity code. [The government correct vernacular for commodity code is NAICS or North American Industry Classification System.] This system categorizes various commodities into numbered groups. Firms can designate various codes indicating the type of services they provide. The old system was called Standard Industrial Classification (SIC) system. For clarification purposes, all commodities are assigned a particular NAICS codes for identification and business classification purposes. The key point is the federal government approved actions under construction type projects (NAICS – 237990) to be a part of the woman-owned set-aside program. The expansion of designation for this type of project has a major impact on the 8(a) program (negotiated). One of the important commodities codes (NAICS – 237990) fall under the area of construction, which supports and provides key opportunities for those firms who are a part of the 8(a) Business Development Program. A performance work plan is not required.

Requirements of this nature are 100% competitive restricted to woman-owned contractors only. These actions are competed on a national basis or restricted to certain regions. How much of the actual work is subcontracted in accordance with the "limitations on subcontracting" clause?

- Program #7 – Small Disadvantaged Owned Small Business (SDB): This program is not a factor. If you are certified as an 8(a) contractor, you are automatically certified as SDB. However, the SDB is a self-certified program meaning that a firm does not have to be 8(a) certified…can self certify their firm as SDB as long as they meet the small business standards.

It's highly important to distinguish between the differences within each of the programs indicated above. As a reminder, reference to a PWP includes describing _how_ a contractor is going to perform the work associated to a construction effort (15%) or service contract (50%) as a prime contractor. Here are the factors that I feel will have an immediate effect on the survival of the 8(a) Business Development Program both short and long term.

Factor #1: The first factor is any project action procured on a competitive basis does not require a performance work plan. Therefore, those small business set-asides such as HUBZone, SDVOSB, and WOSB set-asides are 100% competitive within each respective category and there is not a mandate that says (as a prime contractor) must meet (as a minimum) the percent of performance for any of the project classifications although there is guidance contained in the "limitation on subcontracting" clause. Again, as required for 8(a) contractors certified in the 8(a) Business Development Program must provide a PWP for negotiated efforts and clearly discuss, show and explain how they are going to meet performance per regulation. Throughout my career, there has been _limited_ pressure on a prime contractor who receives an award on a competitive basis. This specifically means each of the big three firms categorically (HUBZone/SDVOSB/WOSB) may have no intention on developing and growing a firm with integrity and within the rules and regulation established by law. (code red) Let's face the facts, some contractors have no desire to perform at any level. Again, the term Pass-through surfaces. In reality, these firms are not held accountable nor responsible for performance. The absence of a governing oversight body relative to meeting performance requirement is minimal. One may say that this is a part of the job functions performed by the ACO and COR which is to report and ensure performance compliance. The majority of firms (especially who are in the construction field) who are certified in each of these categories, aren't focused on developing and growing a firm for the long term. In essence, any subcontractor can report to the job site and perform as much or as little of the project as desired. A self-check on the validity of this assumption can immediately be verified by asking one simple question to any contract awarded to a contractor under these parameters: "What is your PWP relative to completing this project?" The problem is, there is not a mandate requirement by the government under the rules of competitive actions to provide proof of a PWP. (code red) The clause (limitation on subcontracting) is actually directed toward performance as a prime contractor or is it? Therefore, every time a contractor who is awarded a contract that was a set-aside in any of the three categories is controversial, regarding their <u>intent</u> and long term vested interest in becoming a solid contractor to the government. Ask the question and see the response! A bigger problem is the impression that is given by the 8(a) small business who portrays to be only a "Pass-Through" organization. This stigma haunts any 8(a)-small business who is trying to do the right thing. Again, not all small businesses who are classified/certified in one or several of these categories are bending the rules, but who's holding these firms' "feet to the fire" relative to performance. The same perception exists because those same contractors who are bidding in these respective set-asides may also be <u>*8(a) certified*</u>. Therefore, the same mentality of lack of performance is carried over into those negotiated efforts (if they are lucky enough to obtain an opportunity). This under lies a major problem. If they didn't have to perform under the set-aside effort in their respective category, they are certainly not prepared to meet the performance requirements under the rules applied for negotiated efforts. (code red)

Factor #2: In 1984, the Competition in Contracting Act (CICA) enacted legislation governing contract awards to contractors. It REQUIRES U.S. federal government agencies to arrange "full and open competition through use of competition through the use of competitive procedures" in their procurement activities, unless otherwise authorized by law (code red).[57] By law, each organization is obligated to ensure competitive procedures are used in their procurement process of goods and services. This act is in strict contrast to the intent of the 8(a) Business Development Program for negotiated actions under the authorized dollar threshold. Therefore, how can procurement law (CICA) promote the utilization of "competition" (with certain exclusions) which is in stark contrast to the intent of the 8(a)-program promoting utilization of "negotiations" for sole source actions? Each time a project is awarded under the negotiated process counteracts against federal law and against the performance of that organization relative to competition. (code red) It may not seem to be a crucial factor, but each Chief of Contracting (during my tenue working within the federal sector) is aware of this situation. Do not misunderstand me, there are those organizations led by the Chief of Contracting who supported the negotiated process to the highest level and did not allow this law to interfere with providing an opportunity to those 8(a) firms who were certified and qualified. I can say this with upmost confidence since I worked for an organization for 95% of my career that supported the negotiated process and still tried to follow mandated law required by CICA. It was a known fact, that negotiated efforts reduced overall percent of total competitive actions awarded by an Agency. Despite the negative impact, we were compelled to provide support to the 8(a) negotiated program process. The question is: "Are agencies penalized for engaging in negotiated actions? Are organizations rewarded for ensuring a certain percent of all contract actions done on a competitive basis?" (code red) The fact of this issue should be based on the utilization of the negotiated process when practical, possible and when those firms are fully capable of performing. There should be accolades given within the federal government for those agencies who perform at the highest level on awarding contracts on a negotiated basis. On a national stage, those organizations who are awarding negotiated contracts should be fully recognized throughout the business environment and on an annual basis.

Factor #3: The extenuating correlation between the law supporting the competitive process, verses the negotiation process, has a direct impact on the 8(a) Business Development Program and the development of the big three Set-Aside efforts who just happened to be procured under the competitive umbrella. The original composition of the 8(a) Business Development Program included firms who were a combination of HUBZone, SDVOSB, WOSB, and SDB. Thus, for any action under $4 million could be procured under the negotiated process. But look what has happened. First, the HUB-Zone program was established; e.g., for only certified firms thereof and actions on a competitive basis…these potential opportunities were a part of the 8(a) Business Development Program are now (for the most part) removed (or can be) from the negotiated 8(a) process. The development of the SDVOSB set-aside program which followed the same process as the HUBZone program; e.g., for only certified firms thereof and on a competitive basis. Finally, the same course of action for the WOSB program (set-aside for only woman owned firms and on a competitive basis). Those Set-Aside programs have been great for each of those business categories but has completely weakened the structure and ability in support of actions awarded to 8(a) firms on a negotiated basis. (code red) Therefore, various government agencies can meet/exceed their small business program goals by set-aside projects in each of the competitive small business programs, rather than utilization of the 8(a)-negotiated process. It's completely understandable that it takes different internal resources to negotiate a contract verses those required on actions based on competition. This is an interesting concern but is a fact that more and more government agencies are steering away from the negotiated process (during my career) and even federal law with the latest advent of set-aside for woman-owned firms further support the problems facing the 8(a) Business Development Program from a negotiated standpoint. There are advantages for contracting offices to use the competitive and negotiated process, but at what cost?

Let's take a closer look of how the "dewatering" of the 8(a) Business Development Program will attribute to its own demise. Now that fewer projects are set-aside as negotiated actions, the data and information shown at major conferences are misleading. It's been established that actions can be set-aside for HUBZone, SDVOSB, and WOSB categories, all of which could have been a part of the 8(a)-negotiated process. Information is shown regarding total dollar amounts obligated in each of the categories, as well as dollars awarded to the 8(a) Business Development Program. It must be noted that dollars shown in this category are part of dollars awarded to certified 8(a) firms but are not divided into dollars that were negotiated in comparison to competitive actions. As an example, dollars at a conference may be shown as follows (estimate dollars awarded to small business and associated set-aside categories):

Total Dollars Obligated: $60 million
Large Business (40%): $24 million
Small Business (60%): $36 million
Hub zone (6%): $3.6 million
SDVOSB (4%): $2.4 million
Woman-owned (10%): $6 million
SDB (8%): $4.8 million
8(a) Business Development Program (10%): $6 million

It doesn't matter the amount of dollars shown on the screen. The key factor is contained in the dollars shown in the 8(a) Business Development Program. In the above example, rarely if ever has a question been asked regarding the composition of the dollars awarded in the 8(a) categories (e.g., how much of the $6 million are negotiated or awarded on a competitive basis).

Just imagine if the above numbers represent billions of dollars awarded verses millions of dollars. Normally, an organization within the federal government awards dollars in the millions but collectively result in billions of dollars awarded. What if there were $6 billion awarded to contractors in the 8(a) Business Development Program? Hypothetically, let's assume that 70% of those dollars were awarded on a competitive basis ($4.2 billion) leaving only $1.8 billion awarded on a negotiated basis. Question: "Are contractors who received negotiated opportunities helped by the program or hurt by the process?" The point of this issue is those contractors who are certified as 8(a), WOSB, HUBZone, SDVOSB are now forced to bid on competitive actions as set-asides, therefore opening the door for further misrepresentation and concern. In addition, the majority of the 70 percentiles of those competitive actions probably should be much less, since some fraction thereof (70%) could have been procured as a negotiated action.

A percent of dollars awarded in the HUBZone, SDVOSB and WOSB categories would be of lesser value due to those dollars awarded as a part of the 8(a)-negotiated process. Again, verification of this assumption can be authenticated by asking the question at the next small business conference: "What is the breakdown of those dollars awarded in the 8(a) Business Development Program (e.g., percent competitive verses percent negotiated)?" I have a 100% confidence level that 70% or 80% of all dollars awarded under the 8(a) category are done on a competitive basis thus weakening the original intent and long-term preservation of the program from a negotiated basis. (code red)

Factor #4: Throughout my entire career as Director of the Small Business Program, there was a continuous and on-going strife among groups of individuals relative to negotiated actions awarded to 8(a) firms. (code red) It was a staunch belief that this was the wrong course of action and for those reasons cited throughout this book, the only way to obtain a quality project and best price was through competition. I wasn't the only Small Business Program Manager who was faced with this internal problem. My own peers were faced with the same internal struggles and fight in support of the 8(a) negotiated process in comparison to the competitive process. I discovered towards the end of my career, those who were in control, and decision makers, were winning this war! (Fact #5 will further indicate why I feel that the art of negotiating for 8(a) actions is slowly going away.)

Factor #5: At the end of my career, more and more actions (that were initially part of a negotiated effort) were now being procured under "Waiver Request." (code red) There were known instances when this course of action was becoming a way of life within many organizations. This directly means, actions that supported and provided opportunities to those firms who were performing those job functions on a negotiated basis, were now being procured under a competitive basis as a small business effort, or under one of the other programs for HUBZone, SDVOSB or WOSB set-asides.

As specifically stated in the regulation: "(a) Once a requirement has been accepted into the 8(a) Business Development Programs, any follow-on requirement shall remain in the 8(a) Business Development Program unless there is a mandatory source or SBA agrees to release the requirement from the 8(a) Business Development Programs in accordance with 13 CFR 124.504(d)

(b) To obtain release of a requirement for a non-8(a) procurement (other than a mandatory source), the contracting officer shall make a written request to and receive concurrence from the SBA Associate Administrator for Business Development.

(1) The written request to the SBA Associate Administrator for Business Development shall indicate:

(i) Whether the agency has achieved its Small Disadvantaged Business Goals

(ii) Whether the agency has achieved its HUBZone, SDVOSB, WOSB or Small Business goals and

(iii) Whether the requirement is critical to the Business Development of the 8(a) contractor that is currently performing the requirement

(2) Generally, a requirement that was previously accepted into the 8(a) Business Development Programs will only be released for procurements outside the 8(a) Business Development Programs when the contracting activity agency agrees to set aside the requirement under the small business, HUBZone, SDVOSB, WOSB programs.

(3) The requirement that a follow-on procurement must be released from the 8(a) Business Development Program in order for it to be fulfilled outside the 8(a) Business Development Program does not apply to task or delivery orders offered to and accepted into 8(a) Business Development Program, where the basic contract was not accepted into the 8(a) Business Development Program (code red)."[58]

The above rule is clear for those projects that was a part of the program (staying in the program), only if there are specific and logical rationale to request a waiver.

Regardless of the reasons stated in support of granting a waiver to any contracting agency, the undaunting point was stated in 1(iii) above... "Whether the requirement is critical to the business development of the 8(a) contractor that is currently performing the requirement?" The answer to this question is: "It would have a major impact on the development and sustainment of <u>any 8(a) contractor</u>. (code red) The reason for requesting a waiver by those organizations who have done so is not based on meeting the criteria that allows permission to grant the waiver but is partly based on internal pressure of those who have a multitude of personal reasons why a project should be competed rather than negotiated." (code red)

In attending meeting, after meeting, after meeting, the question would surface: "Why are we negotiating with an 8(a) firm rather than using the competitive process?" Slowly but surely, I believe agencies are requesting more waivers and more waivers are being approved. I have known specific actions who had multiple qualified 8(a) firms who were both certified and qualified to perform those job functions, but a waiver was requested, and approval granted. My own personal viewpoint, there are those individuals who have a personal bias when it comes to 8(a) contractors, even when their ability to perform is at a level that is credible and acceptable. If 8(a) contractors are performing their jobs in accordance to the terms and conditions of the contract have a history of meeting and/or exceeding the minimum performance requirements as a prime contractor; and negotiated a price that was fair and reasonable and within the parameters of the government estimate, then why are waivers being requested? (code red) There were countless numbers of negotiated projects with 8(a) firms that resulted in monumental cost savings to the government, but rarely (if ever) was recognition given as a direct result of the efforts of those who believed in the negotiated process and was done in accordance with procurement law. Again, I'm speaking from my own perspective. If there is an established contractor base that has proven its capability time and time again, then why is there a need to request a waiver regardless of the exceptions noted within regulations? The bottom line is clear, those firms who are certified, qualified, and doing the right things, need every opportunity plausible to obtain a contract on a negotiated basis. The request for waiver only adds "fuel to the fire" both from an internal perspective and for the concerns stated regarding competitive actions within those set-aside efforts for the three categories indicated and discussed above.

Now you have my top five reasons why the longevity and sustainment of the 8(a) Business Development Program is under scrutiny and questionable. Even if there are new firms entering the 8(a) Business Development Program will only suffer from the standpoint of limited opportunities. Clearly and unequivocally, the following issues shall (not maybe) be the detriment of the program:

- No performance work plan for prime contractors participating in the HUBZone, SDVOSB, and WOSB set-aside programs which parallels the limitation on subcontracting clause (require each contractor to provide how they are going to perform in regards to a construction (15%) or service contract (50%). In reality, these are the same percentages required for the 8(a) prime contractors for negotiated actions. 8(a) firms are constantly pressured to uphold this requirement on a continuous basis. Is the same pressure applied to the small business contractors participating in the set-asides efforts for HUBZone, SDVOSB and WOSB categories?

- (2) Competition in Contracting Act (CICA) pressures of competition verses negotiations
- (3) Further expansion of set-aside including woman-owned business (specifically in construction)
- (4) Internal organizational pressures supporting competitive actions verses negotiations
- (5) Waiver Requests (for actions that should not be requested nor approved by the powers to be) (all code red)
- Allowing multiple 8(a) firms to subcontract with the same subcontractor.

Some of the questions that should be asked to every 8(a) firm is simply this: "Is the 8(a)-program working for you (past/presently) in terms of successful opportunities?"; "What are your concerns and why do you feel this way?"; "What would you (as a business owner) recommend to the federal government to improve the situation within the program itself?"

By listening to what contractors say, as well as what they mean, provided me with a clear understanding of the problems associated to the federal government process and 8(a) contractors. This led me to conclude, that both the government and 8(a) firms are directly responsible for the problems, issues, and concerns of creating a situation that does not create a win/win for both entities in the long term. One can easily say that billions and billions of dollars are awarded to small businesses year in and year out. However, under what pretense are these dollars awarded and executed in a fashion that is within the law. It's apparent that data and information can be misleading and subjective. I've always proclaimed that it's better for the government to award $2 million-dollar independent contracts to ten contractors (different contractors) than ever award $10 million-dollar independent contracts to two contractors.

In essence, the answer to my assumption on the critical state and future of the program is one that is going to take a united effort on all accords. If the subdivision of the 8(a) Business Development Program has resulted in competitive Set-Aside efforts for each of the big three categories (HUBZone, SDVOSB, & WOSB), then the following should be required:

- Each of those firms (who are designated as the prime contractor in their respective business designation) should submit and have an approved Performance Work Plan _prior_ to contract award. Even after contract award, hold that firm responsible and accountable for performance. There must be a balance between performing in accordance to an approved PWP and amount of work subcontracted out.

- Modify the premise that agencies should follow rules as stated within CICA, in those instances that involve negotiated efforts, which allow these firms to grow and develop. If you recall, the first four years are development years and the last five years are transition years. How can a firm develop when there are limited opportunities?

- Award agencies who negotiate with responsible, accountable 8(a) firms; don't degrade or penalize an agency who supports negotiated efforts.

- Reduce internal pressures of forcing and manipulating acquisition strategies in support of competition, and support firms who are following rules and regulations as stated within the 8(a) Business Development Program.

- Enforce and support those internal government estimates that indicate a negotiated effort is based on fair and reasonableness and should be rewarded and viewed as a win/win situation for the government and contractor.

- Follow regulatory guidance regarding projects that are initially approved for the 8(a)-program, ensuring they remain in the 8(a) Business Development Program as long as a qualified contractor base is available for those Set-Aside efforts, and negotiations are based on a fair and reasonable basis.

- A waiver request should be based on factors indicated as exceptions, and only those exceptions stated in regulatory guidance, and not assisted by internal bias or undue pressures that are not warranted. There must be a valid reason for waiver approval mainly due to lack of qualified 8(a) firms regardless whether a specific goal has been met or exceeded.

Change the acquisition process set-aside for the big three small business areas (HUBZone, SDVOSB & WOSB), For construction efforts as an example:

(1) A project is advertised (1M) as a HUBZone set-aside (national basis)

(2) Proposals are received...however each company identify on their proposal that they are

(A) local contractor or (B) outside contractor [contractors within a 100-mile radius are considered to be a "local" contractor; contractors exceeding 100-miles are considered non-local (something of that magnitude)

(3) Open/review local contractor's proposals first...if two or more contractors meet the requirements under the stated acquisition method; award the contract to one of those contractors who are within a local vicinity.

(4) If there are no contractors who are qualified in pool (A); go to pool (B) for contract award. By modifying the acquisition process for these set-aside programs ensures:

(a) incentivizes local contractors who desire to work with the federal government to do the right thing and follow the rules

(b) allows local contractors an opportunity to develop their company that's in accordance with regulatory guidance for negotiated and competitive actions for small business and 8(a) Business Development Program

(c) support local contractors in terms of opportunities

(d) reduces fraud relative to performance. Alerts outside contractors that targeted agencies are serious about performance regardless whether you are a local or non-local contractor

Because of identifying problems and recommended solutions to those problems, it is apparent that some alternative course of action must be enforced. There is no simple solution to this situation notwithstanding those alternatives indicated above. Eventually, the only need to utilize contractors in the 8(a) Business Development Program on a negotiated basis, will be based on the acquisition timeline left during the fiscal year. (code red) As discussed in the Business Preparation Module, the only remaining resolution is to utilize the 8(a)-negotiation process, is due to quick turnarounds. Thus, the question must be answered by you – guilty, or not guilty? Is the assumption the long term and future destiny of the 8(a) Business Development Program (as known today) under tremendous pressure for survival? One thing is for sure, whether anyone agrees, or disagrees, the stability of the initial intent of the program has undergone tremendous change and slowly is moving in a direction that does not benefit existing, or new firms entering the program. If the overall intent of the government is to meet and exceed its mandatory small business goals (at any cost), by all means stay the course and continue with the competitive process for all set-aside small business categories, without requiring a perform-ance work plan and enforcing the rules regarding performance. (code red) I can assure everyone this process is not geared toward the development of firms who are creating a business foundation that is based on accountability and being re-sponsible for their actions. The only category of small business firms who must be responsible and accountable are those 8(a) firms who are in an environment where there are limited negotiated opportunities. This is a harsh fact, but it is based on the true reality of how the system was functioning.

Conclusion

I want to personally thank everyone who gave me an opportunity to work with the small business community. Earlier, I asked everyone the question, "How did you get to where you are?" I know how I reached the pinnacle of my dream, and I'm proud to say it's because of my co-workers and those hard-working individuals called small business contractors. The last sixteen years of my career, my organization experienced remarkable success providing negotiated and competitive opportunities to those firms who rightly deserved a chance to make a difference in the business community. There were enormous success stories such as working with an 8(a) firm who specialized in land scaping and through hard work ended up with several construction contract opportunities for my former organization. The greatest achievement was the transformation of a firm who specialized in wood-working, and by the end of the nine-year period in the program, was the agencies number one contractor with the largest 8(a) contract during that period. These are only a couple of examples of the magnificent work that was achieved as a result of everyone's willingness to work hard and follow rules and regulatory guidance.

During my tenure, my agency was constantly among the leaders in dollars awarded (obligated) to 8(a) firms on a negotiated basis. Kudos to the Chief of Contracting, Contracting Officers, and those individuals who believed in the system and were instrumental in achieving our goal to help a firm become a viable contractor. My highest reward came when I was walking through airports, or met someone on the street, and they approached me and said, "Thanks for all your help." This is the highest reward anyone can receive and I'm so happy to say…Thank you for allowing me to be a part of your journey! I must say that working with all of you was not a right, privilege, but an honor, to be a part of your journey!

To all the Small Business Program Managers (in the federal government) stay the course. You are the first stop of the long journey ahead of any 8(a) firm. Take the time to teach and instruct them on the tools they need to be successful. Your job is simple, teach them how to be successful. The Acquisition Strategy Determination (Rules of Engagement, as discussed in the previous modules) dictates 90% of acquisition strategy for both large and small business. I once heard that 85% of your time should be spent in meetings and fighting for projects to be Set-Aside for small businesses, but I beg to differ. By following the rules applicable to small business set-asides and the 8(a) Business Development Program, clearly and distinctly dictate acquisition strategy. Your time must be oriented toward teaching the principles and guidance structures identified in this book. There was once an old statement made by someone much wiser than I: "I can give you a fish and feed you for a day, or I can teach you how to fish, and you can feed yourself for a lifetime." Time has come and gone for me, and I no longer have a voice at the table. It's up to you to speak up and stand up for what is right, for those contractors who deserve and opportunity.

The Small Business Administration must continue to enforce the program by reaching out to those who oversee the organizations, and award contracts. Great work has been done with the certification process, but more work is required to assure those firms are functioning under the rules and regulations. There is much "hoopla" relative to conferences such as HUBZone, WOSB, SDVOSB and annual National Conferences, but what happens next? The plight of the 8(a) Business Development Program must be partly resurrected back to its original intent and that is obtaining opportunities (negotiated) for firms who are indeed certified and qualified. Go and spread the word to those government organizations within your area of responsibility (district or region) that you are concerned with the lack and reduction of 8(a) negotiated opportunities. The 8(a) Business Development Program is a "24/7" effort, and not just for specific periods of time. You are the ones who have the capability, knowledge, and inside connections to ensure opportunities are available for those who warrant such an opportunity. Keep up the great work, and demand even more from that part of the federal government in support of the 8(a) Business Development Program.

The Chiefs of Contracting are the key on the government side of the ledger. You are the ones who make the decision, and ultimately, dictate opportunities whether they are on a negotiated, or competitive basis. I ask you look beyond the past and the current cloudy image of the 8(a) contractor, and work with the Small Business Program Manager to teach, guide, and lead them in the right direction. The Small Business Program Manager should work with you as a team of one for the betterment and opportunities afforded to 8(a) firms. The final decision is yours; the final approval is yours; the power to make or break an 8(a) firm is yours…I only ask you do the right thing for those firms who are trying to follow the rules.

To the 8(a)-small business community, the buck stops with you! For many years, I spent a major part of my career fighting for you! Meeting after meeting, I went there fighting for you! Time has come and passed that I no longer have a voice at the table.

There are those who believe you must be involved (within the system), and with those who are in charge, to affect change. To a great degree, I concur with this assumption. Therefore, I challenge all firms who are in this program for your own personal gain – change your ways! I challenge all those 8(a) firms who have short term goals of making a quick dollar, and have no intention on being a solid, viable contractor to the government – change your ways! If you are only in this business acting as a pass-through contractor – change your ways! There must be a collective effort among each and every one of you, to ensure that everyone is following the rules. It only takes one firm who has a bad reputation, to ruin other opportunities for those who are trying to do the right thing. I once heard a song in reference to a "man in the mirror". To change anyone, change must first start with you…the man or woman in the mirror!

The end is just about here. We've discussed a "little about a lot and a lot about a little."

The time required to interpret this material (information) extends anywhere from six months of training to maybe two years. There are many more things that must be discussed to fully understand all the issues needed in order to work with the federal government. By no means, is this book a panacea for everything that is needed but is certainly a conglomeration of facts. These facts, when utilized properly, are the beginning steps of becoming a successful contractor of working with the federal government. If there was one small thing that you learned from this book, and it resulted in a major change in the success of your company, then, just maybe, that small thing wasn't so small after all. That was my intent and that was my goal!

There were four great individuals mentioned earlier, and each of them had ambitions, desires, and goals. They didn't reach the pinnacle of their objectives, but through their efforts, so changed many lives. I, too, had ambitions, and goals. And like Gandhi, Kennedy, Malcolm, and King, I was not able to reach the pinnacle of all of my objectives either, but I do hope that I had a positive impact upon persons within the small business arena. Sometimes, that's the way the ball bounces! Nevertheless, what if:

- One day, every 8(a) firm who is certified and qualified get that opportunity they deserve.
- One day, this book will become a training tool as a way of teaching 8(a) firms and subcontractors how to correctly reach out to the government.
- One day, this book will become a guide for all new 8(a) contractors to have and review as way of laying a solid foundation toward their goal of working for the government.
- One day, I would like to see this book used as an instructional guide as a way of assisting those in the government see the plight of the 8(a) contractors in a different light.

Well, maybe my dream, too, won't become reality!

The verdict is now up to those who are the decision makers, and those who play a vital role as a potential contractor to the federal government. There are many issues discussed and potential resolutions that are both plausible and achievable. The interrelationships of those involved, hinges upon the degree that trust, honesty, and integrity can be renewed, thus building a solid foundation between the federal government and 8(a) contractors going forward into the future. I'm a firm believer that we as a people will endure the plight of the 8(a) contractors, and together, the longevity of this group of business-men/women will last forever.

Okay, its time! This journey is now over, and complete. As I always state at the beginning of my presentations, "Please don't take anything that I have said negatively or personally." The same premise applies to what has been discussed in this book. I have tried to provide you with something to think about. Again, I want to say that it has been an honor sharing my thoughts with those of you who have a vision, a desire, and dream of working with the federal government. Good luck to those who are climbing the mountain top of opportunity!

One final thought…You can never walk on water, if you never get out of the boat!

Until we meet again to discuss those elements: "Beneath the Surface – those Hidden Facts of 8(a) Firms working with the federal government."

I must reiterate, much have been gained, much have been learned, but there is still "Unfinished Business."

May God Bless You, and May God Keep You!

Testimony from and to My Peers!

I would be remiss if homage wasn't given to several individuals who were instrumental in helping me in ways that are incomprehensible. Throughout one's career, there are many people who come and go for many reasons. In my case, I held several jobs extending a period of over forty years. The true testament lies not only in what you have done to help others, but what others have done to help you! This is the essence of true friendship, which stems not only from a working environment, but from a personal standpoint.

So, with this in mind, I want to pay tribute to a couple of individuals who had tremendous influence on me and my success…Ms. Peggy Straub and Ms. Karen Fountain…thank you for your assistance and support over the years.

This is their story!

Peggy Straub!
One day, during the early part of 2005, I was waiting on a contractor to enter into my office for a meeting. There was nothing special about this meeting… just another contractor seeking a path forward and hoping to receive some type of help and guidance from me. Business as usual!

Entered this individual who was eager, enthusiastic, and full of energy. Introductions were made and thus we exchange thoughts, concerns, and alternative ways for Ms. Straub and her company to move forward working with the Government. There was nothing significant about this meeting…the contractor (Ms. Straub) was somewhat distraught (by the end of the meeting) by my direct manner but through it all she appreciated my candor, directness, and brutal honesty regarding some of the things that needed to be corrected. We met several times later that year. The more I demanded of her the more she responded in a positive manner. One day, Peggy suggested that I write a book. I was bewildered!

Never in my mind would I have thought of doing anything of this magnitude. I thought about this for several days and finally it dawned on me what better way to help the small business community other than to leave them with something that would be used long after my days working in the federal government.

I owe all of this to Ms. Straub for staying the course and providing me with the belief that I could write a book that would be beneficial and worthwhile to those contractors in the future. I want to thank you for all the encouragement; time and time again you would remind and say to me…where's the book – we are waiting! I want to thank you for even today, long after I've retired…again wanted to know where's the book?

Peggy, well here's the book and I owe it all to you! Thank you for your support and you shall always be a special individual who deserves as much of the credit for pushing me and believing in me as in writing this document.

Your friend Glenn!

Karen Fountain!

Throughout the years, I've worked with many individuals from all types of backgrounds with unique skills and abilities. In many cases I was either their subordinate, peer, or even for many years their supervisor or manager.

For the last sixteen years out of a forty-year career, I met this individual whose name was Karen Fountain. Upon accepting this position as Small Business Program Manager, I had the luxury (not like many of my counterparts who held the same position as I) of having a person assigned to me within my office. If you noticed I used the description of "person assigned within my office," rather than refer to this individual as my "subordinate," "my employee," or someone who "reports" to me. From the very beginning of getting to know each other and as each day past, I knew there was something special about Karen.

As a past supervisor of many people, I learned the best way to have a great relationship was to first get to know that (1) individual as a person, then (2) as a co-worker. So, each morning, the first thing we would do is have a cup of coffee and then talk about what happened the previous evening that was family related. For sixteen years, this was my approach. Thereafter, we would discuss the plan of the day and things we first must get accomplished, followed by things that would be nice to finish. This always got the day started on an upbeat and positive way.

I want to say without hesitation and without reservation, that Karen was the best co-worker anyone could want. Anytime a task needed to be completed she ensured it was done on time and in the most efficient manner. Her attitude was always positive and always greeted me with a smile! She referred to me as her "Boss," but I never viewed our relationship in that manner. She was the one who kept me on track relative to meetings, travel arrangements, doctors' appointments, special occasions (birthdays and anniversaries), and all business engagements.

This is my time to pay homage to an individual who was always there for me and always had my back! Thank you for all you did and all that you done for well over sixteen years. See, for the record:

Everyone needs a Karen in their office. Everyone needs a Karen as their friend. Everyone needs a Karen as a part of their life!

For those who are looking for a Karen, just maybe you are looking in the wrong place…Everyone has a Karen; however, you must know how to develop that relationship in the work place!

Thank you for making my job easy and enjoyable. Thank you for always being there for me.

Thank you for just being you!

Your Friend, Glenn!

The Test

(Circle the Correct Ans)

1. The first question related to this book is: "The following is the test; the answers to the test, however:
    A   All answers are based on fiction and non-fiction data
    B   I cannot take the test for you
    C   We can take the test together
    D   None of the above

2. The centerpiece of any successful person, business or organization is the understanding and utilization of:
    A   Mind and Body
    B   Technology
    C   Science
    D   Information

3. Which of the following is the correct usage and definition of the word "information":
    A   Information is knowledge…knowledge is useful…used to make a basic decision
    B   Information is knowledge…knowledge is power…power to make bad decisions
    C   Information is knowledge…knowledge is power…power to make a better-informed decision
    D   Information is data…and data can be useful at some point in time

4. In relative terms, time is something that is constantly moving and can never be gotten back. To put in simplistic terms, use your time in a more positive manner through the following process:

   A   Strategic planning, increased internal communication within the organization, and being prepared in the critical phases of business acumen

   B   Strategic planning, minimal communication, and being prepared in the basic phases of business acumen

   C   Organizational planning, individual self-reliance within the organization and being prepared in the critical phases of business acumen

   D   A and B

5. As a business owner, there are times when you have to change your business model to meet changing demands within the industry. However, which of the following is a true statement regarding working hard and in most cases staying the course of action:

   A   You've got to change your way of doing business, which will result in a better outcome

   B   If you sometimes do what you use to do, then you always will do the same thing in the future

   C   If you always do what you always done…you never get what you never got

   D   If you always do what you always done…you always get what you always got

6. In business and in most cases life, there are a lot of ups and downs. Some individuals handle stress, problems, and issues relative to business and life in different ways. What is the best way to view day to day pressures of being in business when things aren't quite going your way?

   A   Your glass is never full

   B   Your glass is always full

   C   Your glass is empty

   D   Your glass is always half full

7. In many situations, how you view uncertainty dictate the degree of difficulty of being successful or being on the losing end. T or F

8. As a business owner, there are many moving parts that go on from time to time and certainly things are constantly changing. There is one way of ensuring that you and your organization have a clear path forward. I highly recommend that you have:

   A   Plan of the Month

   B   Make up ideas and coordinate those ideas on a collective and continuous basis

   C   A Plan of Action

   D   A Plan is only good for the short term, it's not really necessary

9. Some people are successful in business by doing many different things. The best way to achieve your goal is:

   A   Anything worth having is based on hard work

   B   Anything worth having is based on waiting for opportunities to come your way

   C   Anything worth having is through working as less as possible and waiting for things to come your way

   D   Anything worth having is based on working as little as possible and find ways to beat the system

10. Everything covered and discussed within this book should be taken personally and on a negative basis. T or F

11. What is the true perception regarding the way some individuals or agencies view your company (8(a) firms) relative to image?

    A   Image is not that important, people are going to think and feel a certain way about you regardless of what you do

    B   Image is everything relative to what people see, think, and believe about one's ability or lack thereof

    C   Image is important, but it can be changed within the drop of a pin

    D   Image is overrated

12. Throughout the business community, one's ability to teach as well as learn is a critical factor in overall success of a company. Which of the below axioms is the correct path to take regarding teaching and one's ability of learning?

A "I can give you everything that you need to be successful. All you have to do is follow my direction."

B "I can give you a fish and feed you for a day or I can teach you how to fish and you can feed yourself for a life time."

C "Tell me a little about this subject call business and I'll do the rest."

D "I can give you a fish and you will never go hungry again."

13. Earlier, there was a discussion on image. Image is directly related to the impression and how others view you as a person and as a business owner. The correct definition of "impression" is:

A Your first impression is less important than your last impression

B Impression as to how others view you is not really important

C Your first impression is your least impression is your last impression

D Your first impression is your best impression is your last impression

14. "Always say what you mean and mean what you say when it comes to your capability, which invariably affects your reputation." T or F

15. "You do get a second chance to make a first impression." T or F

16. Which of the following is a true statement regarding imagination and re-lationship with knowledge?

A Knowledge is the most important trait to gain; therefore, it is more important than imagination or anything else.

B Information is more important than acquiring knowledge or having an imagination.

C Imagination is third in the hierarchy behind knowledge and data.

D Imagination is more important than knowledge.

17. In order to be a prime contractor, you must think as a prime contractor and in order to work within the federal sector, you must first understand the federal sector. T or F

18. Prior to setting up a meeting with a potential federal agency, there is a plethora of things that should be done prior to making a phone call to that agency. This process is similar to going on your first interview but

prior to actually going on the interview you were involved in a process called:

A   Studying: (what you are going to say at the interview)

B   Doing your homework: (learning the needs of your target agency)

C   Strategizing: (company meeting to discuss other business opportunities)

D   None of the above

19. What is the most important ELEMENT in our lives?

A   Time, because it is something that we have plenty of

B   Time, because it is based on something that we cannot get back

C   People, because everything is centered around people

D   None of the above

20. There are plenty of mistakes made by contractors during the interview process. What is the biggest problem that most contractors want to portray relative to their capabilities?

A   They are a Jack of all Trades and Masters of None

B   They are good at what they do in limited ways

C   They have limited capabilities

D   Both B & C

21. When entering the agencies room for the interview, you focus on talking about your capabilities in relations to the needs of your target market and not once discussing business opportunities is a part of what strategy?

A   Inverse Psychological Marketing Approach

B   The Direct Marketing Approach

C   The Basic Marketing Approach

D   The Reverse Psychological Marketing Approach

22. All of the below are parts of the Wrong Approach, except which one?

A   Masters of None

B   Discussion of Projects upfront

C   Discussion of capabilities verses needs of your target market

D   Jack of all trades

23. When you clearly and explicitly communicate your company's skills, knowledge and abilities to your target market is basically referred to as:
    A   Telling others story as it relates to your own company's capabilities
    B   Communicating possible attributes of a company you wish to become
    C   Telling your story
    D   A & B

24. All of the parts below of communicating the "Right Approach" are true, with the exception:
    A   Conveying your capabilities verses the needs of your target market
    B   Integrating contractor's strengths and knowledge
    C   Knowledge of target markets needs
    D   All of the above are true

25. What are the four keys to government contracting?
    A   Business Presentation Module, Business Functionality Module, Business Integration Module, & Business Institution Module
    B   Business Theory Module, Business Presentation Module, Business Integration Module, & Business Functionality Module
    C   Business Theory Module, Business Process Module, Business Preparation Module, & Business Functionality Module
    D   Business Theory Module, Business Presentation Module, Business Preparation Module, & Business Functionality Module

26. The amount of time a Small Business Program Manager should spend working with contractors verses internal with the agencies is:
    A   50%/50% (time spent evenly with internal meetings and with contractors)
    B   75%/25% (time spent in internal agency meeting; e.g., 75% versus 25% with contractors)
    C   60% with internal meetings and 40% with contractors
    D   85% with contractors teaching and preaching and 15% with internal personnel

27. Principle #1 (Needs/Capabilities) is to know the needs of your target market through performing due diligence. This is accomplished by researching

and fact finding the desires of your target market. In addition, present your strengths of your company in regards toward meeting the needs of your target market. T or F

28. A careful plan, method, or complex of adaptations toward a goal is an example of:
   A   Strategic goal initiative
   B   Strategic goal overview
   C   Strategic preliminary plan of action
   D   Definition of a Strategic Plan

29. The basic definition of success can be defined as:
   A   Success is based on some sort of failure or setback that occurred somewhere along the way prior to obtaining a certain level of success
   B   Success is based on having success at all levels during your business career
   C   Success is never based on failure at any point in time but is based solely on determination
   D   None of the above

30. Which of the following is a true statement?
   A   The day you are in business (or receive your 8(a) certification) is the beginning of a lifetime of opportunity.
   B   The day you receive your 8(a) certifications is the last day that you have to worry about remaining in business because you are now in the system with a host of opportunities for all.
   C   The day you are in business or have received your 8(a) certifications (nine-year period) is the same day you start preparation to exit the program.
   D   The day you are in business is the beginning of a nine-year period that is full of expectations and opportunities.

31. When you are good in a particular skill or trade, you are considered to have found your way. In some cases, it can be described as an activity or function for which a person is best fitted...or a specialized trade/skill. Better yet, most people in business review this trait as having:

A   The luck of the Irish
B   Been lucky rather than being good or great
C   Found your Niche
D   Both A and C

32. In the review of all business entities, during one period of time they all followed one process that cannot be overlooked or forgotten. What is the common denominator among all large businesses?
A   All business large and small were a part of the 8(a) Business Development Program.
B   All small businesses will become a large business.
C   Every small business will become a large business.
D   Every large business was once a small business.

33. Principle #1 (Niche) is related to determining and develop your Niche in a way that you understand the strengths and weaknesses of your company. T or F

34. Most business owners do not pay attention to the name selected for their firm. Sometimes a name can identify a line of work that is totally 100% related to that type of work although your company may have other areas of expertise. Therefore, when selecting a name, you have to be careful not to:
A   Select a name that will "pigeon hole" your company.
B   Select a name that shows a wide variety of capabilities.
C   Selecting a company name is not important.
D   None of the above

35. Which of the following company names is most suitable for a construction business?
A   J L Williams Construction Company
B   Bird Stone Landscaping LLC
C   John Williams Company, Inc.
D   Williams Construction Company

36. When starting a business, there are several approaches that can be followed. However, there is a new approach introduced that required a

special train of thought that use two distinct business processes. The new approach is called:

A   The Power of Business Intellect

B   The Power of Critical Thinking

C   The Power of Thinking Outside of the Box

D   Both A & B

37. As a follow-up to question 36, the "Inside Out Approach" includes all the following except:

A   Develop your firm based on internal skillset

B   Surround yourself with similar skillset as an owner

C   Identify needs of the business world (success/needs of current businesses)

D   Rely on finding the right market at the right time

38. As a follow-up to question 36, the "Outside In Approach" includes all the following except:

A   Identify needs of the Business World (success/needs of current businesses)

B   Identify Target Market (Public or Private)

C   Marketing company based on a specific identified target market

D   Seek opportunities based on marketing company capabilities to the various undefined target market

39. "Acquisition Strategy Determination" includes four specific areas that predominantly dictates project acquisition strategy. Which of the following include those four areas?

A   Mission Criticality, Complexity, Dollar Value, & Project Location

B   Mission Criticality, Project Location, Complexity, & Project Lead Time

C   Complexity, Mission Criticality, Dollar Value, & Contractor Base

D   Complexity, Mission Criticality, Contractor Base, & Political Interest

40. "Acquisition Strategy Determination" is a great way (on a descriptive basis) to determine acquisition strategy; however, the second element that must be considered is referred to as Rules of Engagement (RoE). There

are two critical RoE that are a part of determining acquisition strategy, which are:

A (1) Rule applicable to projects in the 8(a) Business Development Program and (2) Small Business Rule of Two

B (1) Rule applicable to Large business and (2) Small Business size determination

C (1) Small Business Rule of Two and (2) Unrestricted Business Guidelines

D None of the above

41. In order of priority (which comes first), which of the following is a modified acquisition strategy timeline?

A PDT (Product Delivery Team Meetings), Synopsis, Issuance of RFP, Sources Sought, followed by Contract Award

B PDT (Product Delivery Team Meetings), Sources Sought, Synopsis, Issuance of RFP, Contract Award

C Sources Sought, PDT (Product Delivery Team Meetings, Synopsis, Issuance of RFP, followed by Contract Award

D PDT (Product Delivery Team Meetings), Synopsis, Sources Sought, Issuance of RFP, followed by Contract Award

42. The basic definition of Target Market is an end place or object that is your desired place where your capabilities meet the needs of that agency. However, there is a more in-depth definition or process used to determine whether an agency is indeed a potential target market. That process is based on:

A The analysis that you think an agency needs your skills and capabilities just by what you know about that company

B Determining what type of goods/services the targeted agency need or provide based on an analysis of the percent of four or five of the major services provided by that organization…as it relates to your capabilities

C It's not that important to understand the needs of your target market.

D Both A & B

43. Image is everything for an 8(a) contractor. The overall perception of an 8(a) firm's capability is:

A   8(a) contractors don't perform their required percentage of work; therefore, they are considered to only be a pass-through company.

B   8(a) negotiated contracts are considerably higher than contracts awarded on a competitive basis.

C   Work provided by an 8(a) contractor is of less quality.

D   All of the above

44. As an 8(a) firm there are two basic courses of action to pursue for short-term and long-term survival as a business owner working for the federal government. Those two courses of action for the 8(a) firm are:

A   (1) A Prime contractor and also (2) work as a subcontractor to a prime

B   (1) Work as a Prime contractor and (2) only as a prime contractor

C   (1) A Prime contractor and (2) develop Joint Ventures with other qualified and experience contractors

D   (1) Work only as a subcontractor and (2) only as a subcontractor

45. The true essence of developing and entering in Joint Venture Agreements certainly has benefits to both parties. However, there are red flags that all 8(a) owners must be aware. Those potential red flags are:

A   Lack of interaction between the 8(a) firm and the other company

B   Negative comments made by the other company relative to potential business opportunities

C   Detailed Teaming Agreement

D   All of the above

46. There are approximately ten main areas that should be included within a basic Teaming Agreement. One of the most important problem areas that is a benefit of the 8(a) firm is based on which of the following:

A   Purpose and Scope of the Agreement

B   Limitation of Liability

C   Exclusivity/Non-Competition (working together as one entity)

D   Designation of a Prime Contractor and a Subcontractor

47. The "Presentation Module" is comprised of two main categories, which are: (1) Presentation Format and (2) Pre-presentation Meeting. T or F

48. The composition of a firm is a combination of group/team members and their roles; composition of your company performing such as a prime contractor only; combination of prime and subcontractor; joint venture. The correct title of this group is called:

  A Team Dynamics
  B Team Key Members
  C Subcontractor Team Members
  D None of the above

49. What are the types of Business Presentations to avoid?

  A Individual Presentation (one person/an army of one)
  B Group Presentation (owner doing all the talking)
  C Group Presentation (subcontractor is doing all the talking)
  D All of the above

50. When doing a presentation, the agenda is the first slide that covers the areas of discussion. Every presentation should include four areas that will clearly and distinctly provide the audience a straight path as to your company's capabilities. Every agenda should include which four segments for discussion:

  A Who, What, Roles, and Team Members
  B Who, Why, Roles, and Opportunities
  C Who, What, How, & Why
  D None of the above

51. As a follow-on to question 50, the most important part of any presentation is which of the below?

  A Who (who you and your company are and related capabilities)
  B What (what type of services provided)
  C How (how your company is going to perform the services provided)
  D Why (why does this create a win/win situation for all)

52. A critical part of acceptance as a contractor, professional as well as an indicator of character, demeanor and attitude is:

  A Team Dynamics
  B Appearance

    C   Individual Dynamics

    D   A & C

53. During a presentation, there are questions asked and the answer to the questions are already known. This tactic is commonly used during a grand jury hearing. This process is commonly known as:

    A   The Set Down

    B   The Set Up

    C   The Sting

    D   The Let Up

54. Most 8(a) firms winning contracts (negotiated/competitive) who are located miles and miles away from the job site aren't concerned with performance but are concerned as being construction managers. T or F

55. The following (in most cases) are all true statements about 8(a) firms coming from outside faraway places regarding performance except:

    A   Does not have any intention on performing

    B   In most cases will assign a Quality Control person and/or a Project Manager/Superintendent to the job

    C   Does have a Performance Work Plan relative to performance

    D   Does not have a Performance Work Plan relative to performance

56. What are the top three primary concerns of 8(a) firm's capability of working for the federal sector?

    A   Price, Performance, & Location

    B   Price, Location, & Business Size

    C   Performance, Location, & Bonding Capability

    D   Price, Performance, & Business Size

57. Each contractor who performs work as a Prime contractor receives an evaluation based on certain areas relative to performance and subsequently is entered into a repository for future use. This system is called:

    A   Contractor Performance Assessment Reporting System (CPARS)

    B   Contractor Performance Acquisition Reporting System (CPARS)

    C   Contractor Purchasing Assessment Requiring System (CPARS)

D   None of the above

58. As an 8(a) firm, when you are working in other states, you are required by SBA regulatory guidance to have:
    A   A Post Office box as a place of business
    B   Be collated with your subcontractor using their business address
    C   Have a Bona-Fide Office
    D   You do not have or need a business office there in the project area

59. In some agencies within the federal government, there is a process used (especially for construction projects) to review plans, specifications, drawings, and other areas applicable to the project. These meetings are held prior to releasing the solicitation and normally exclude potential contractors. This process is called:
    A   Biddability, Constructability, Operability, and Contractibility System (BCOCS)
    B   Biddability, Consumption, Operability, and Environmental (BCOE)
    C   Biddability, Constructability, Operational, and Environment (BCOE)
    D   Biddability, Constructability, Operability, Environmental & Sustainability (BCOES)

60. When performing construction services on a negotiated contract basis, there is a percent that must be performed as a prime contractor. When you indicate "how" this work is going to be performed is a process of providing a:
    A   Performance Document Plan (PDP)
    B   Performance Research Plan (PRP)
    C   Performance Work Plan (PWP)
    D   Performance Participation Plan (PPP)

61. A Site Visit is not that important of a meeting between the government and contractor. T or F

62. There is a "Right Way and a Wrong Way involving Site Visits" and how they are conducted. All of the following are considered the Right Way except:

    A   Team members of the prime contractor leading the discussions

    B   Team members of the subcontractor leading the discussions

    C   Team members of the prime contractor making high profile changes and recommendations to government representative

    D   Team members of the prime contractor leading the discussions about the solicitation and job requirements

63. During negotiations, there are four areas that make up the price/cost of your proposal. The term "rate structure" (for a construction effort) is composed of four elements, which are:

    A   Profit, Bond, Direct Cost, & Labor Rates

    B   Profit, Direct Cost, Over Head Cost (field/home), & Bond Cost

    C   Profit, Indirect Cost, Supply Rate, & Labor Rates

    D   Profit, Direct Cost, Over Head Cost (field/home), & Sunk Cost

64. There are a lot of moving parts working with and within the government system. As a business owner, the two most important areas in the execution of a government contract are:

    A   Performance and Execution

    B   Execution and Integration

    C   Performance and Work Delays

    D   Performance and Administration

65. The number one priority to the government and to you as a contractor (working) at the job site is:

    A   Speed in Project Completion

    B   Quality of work performed

    C   Security

    D   Safety

66. You start preparation of exiting the 8(a) Business Development Program the same day you receive your certification. T or F

67. What document is considered the Bible of Government Contracting?

    A   Federal Acquisition Regulation (FAR)

    B   Federal Registration Document (FRD)

    C   Start Acquisition Regulation (SAR)

    D   Federal Procurement Booklet (FPB)

68. There is a distinct difference between private sector contracting and public sector contracting when it comes to profit. Which of the following is a true statement regarding working in the private sector verses the public sector?

    A   Private sector contracting is based on fair and reasonable.

    B   Pubic sector contracting is based on being profit driven.

    C   Public sector contracting is based on being fair and reasonable and Private Sector contracting is based on being profit driven.

    D   Private and Public-sector contracting is based on getting as much profit as possible.

69. There is a contracting term/phase that implies "a contract is solely between the government and prime contractor," therefore excluding any type of contractual agreement with the government and subcontractor. By definition, the correct term that describes this relationship between government and subcontractor is:

    A   Contract Supplement

    B   Private Relationship

    C   Privity of Contract

    D   Both A & B

70. The key to and art of negotiations is:

    A   Knowledge

    B   Preparation

    C   Documentation

    D   None of the above

71. There are many rules for bargaining during negotiations. Which of the following are true regarding rules for bargaining?

    A   Be prepared

    B   Give yourself room to compromise

    C   Use concessions wisely

    D   All of the above

72. Normal acquisition lead-time for negotiated contracts are ___ days and for competitive acquisition are ___ days.
    A   45 days: 70 days
    B   30 days: 65 days
    C   45 days: 75/90 days
    D   20 days: 75/90 days

73. As a follow-up to question 72, the fiscal year for the federal government ends 30 September. The latest time frame that a competitive action can be released is approximately:
    A   July 15 of that fiscal year
    B   July 20 of that fiscal year
    C   July 25 of that fiscal year
    D   None of the above

74. As a follow-up to question 73: The only way to (in effect) award a contract after the 75-time frame has elapsed is through what process?
    A   Competitive process on an unrestricted basis
    B   Competitive process using one of the small business set-asides
    C   Competitive process restricted to only small businesses
    D   Negotiation process using an 8(a) contractor

75. Once a contract has been awarded for construction, which of the following is true?
    A   You can start work at any time thereafter.
    B   You can start work only after Notice to Proceed (NTP) has been issued.
    C   You can start work prior to the submission of bonds and submittals.
    D   Both A & C

76. The two most important government representatives while working in the field at the project site are:
    A   Administrative Contracting Officer (ACO) and Quality Assurance Representative
    B   Administrative Contracting Officer (ACO) and Contracting Officer Representative (COR)

  C Contracting Officer Representative (COR) and Safety Officer (SO)

  D Both A & B

77. A "Contracting Officer" receives his/her authority from:

  A Secretary of State

  B Head of Contracting Activity

  C Small Business Administration

  D Warrant

78. The "Contracting Officer" is the only official who can legally bind the government to a contract. T or F

79. "Code Red" as defined in this book is a term that is describing:

  A This phrase is used to identify minor areas of concern relative problems, issues, or concerns within the organizational framework of a small business

  B This phrase is used within the federal government to indicate that a contractor is fully performing in an exceptional manner, no problems or concerns

  C This phrase is used about life and death situations

  D This phrase is used to indicate a difficult or dangerous situation has deteriorated drastically so as to constitute an emergency or a need for change

Answers to the Test!

1.	B	25.	D	49.	D	73.	A
2.	D	26.	D	50.	C	74.	D
3.	C	27.	T	51.	C	75.	B
4.	A	28.	D	52.	B	76.	B
5.	D	29.	A	53.	B	77.	D
6.	D	30.	C	54.	T	78.	T
7.	T	31.	C	55.	C	79.	D
8.	C	32.	D	56.	A		
9.	A	33.	T	57.	A		
10.	F	34.	A	58.	C		
11.	B	35.	D	59.	D		
12.	B	36.	B	60.	C		
13.	D	37.	C	61.	F		
14.	T	38.	D	62.	B		
15.	F	39.	C	63.	B		
16.	D	40.	A	64.	D		
17.	T	41.	B	65.	D		
18.	B	42.	B	66.	T		
19.	B	43.	D	67.	A		
20.	A	44.	C	68.	C		
21.	D	45.	D	69.	C		
22.	C	46.	C	70.	B		
23.	C	47.	T	71.	D		
24.	D	48.	A	72.	C		

List of Abbreviations

SBA:	Small Business Administration
FBDP:	Federal Business Development Program (BD)
SBPM:	Small Business Program Manager
DE:	District Engineer
DoD:	Department of Defense
POA:	Plan of Action
KO/CO:	Contracting Officer
PDT:	Product Delivery Team
PDT:	Project Delivery Team
APTAC:	Association of Procurement Technical Assistance Center
LPTA:	Lowest Price Technical Acceptable
IFB:	Invitation for Bid
POC:	Point of Contact
SB:	Small Business
SDB:	Small Disadvantaged Business
WOSB:	Woman Owned Small Business
HUBZone:	Historically Underutilized Business Zone
SDVOSB:	Service Disadvantaged Veteran Owned Small Business
MOU:	Memorandum of Understanding
FAR:	Federal Acquisition Regulation
RoE:	Rules of Engagement
PDTM:	Product Delivery Team Meeting
S/Sought:	Sources Sought
FPDS-NG:	Federal Procurement Data System - Next Generation
HBCU/MI:	Historically Black College University/Minority Interest
JV:	Joint Venture
PWP:	Performance Work Plan
BCOES:	Biddability, Constructability, Operability, Environmental & Sustainability
VE:	Value Engineering
BFO:	Bona-Fide Office
DCAA:	Defense Contract Audit Agency

CPARS:	Contractor Performance Assessment Reporting System
RFQ:	Request for Quotation
IFB:	Invitation for Bid
BV:	Best Value
RFP:	Request for Proposal
FEDBIZOPPS:	Federal Business Opportunity System
COC:	Certificate of Competency
IDIQ:	Indefinite Delivery Indefinite Quantity
TO:	Task Order
G&A:	General and Administration
IGCE:	In-house Government Cost Estimate
PCR:	Procurement Center Representative
QCP:	Quality Control Plan
APP:	Accident Prevention Plan
EPP:	Environmental Protection Plan
NTP:	Notice to Proceed
WCM:	Weekly Construction Meeting
ACO:	Administrative Contracting Officer
COR:	Contracting Officer's Representative
NAICS:	North America Industrial Classification System
CICA:	Competition in Contracting Act
SBRC:	Small Business Review Committee
PM:	Project Manager
HTRW:	Hazardous Toxic Radioactive Waste
MILCON:	Military Construction
SOW:	Statement of Work
POP:	Period of Performance
DFARS:	Defense Federal Acquisition Regulation Supplement
DoDAAC:	Department of Defense Activity Address Code
FUSRAP:	Formerly Utilized Sites Remedial Action Program

Author's Favorite Quotes

"The following is the test; the answers to the test; however, I cannot take the test for you!"

"The centerpiece of any successful person, business and/or organization is the understanding and utilization of information."

"Information is knowledge…knowledge is power…power to make a better-informed decision."

"Use your time in a positive manner through strategic planning, increased internal communication within the organization, and most of all, being prepared in the critical phases of business acumen."

"If you always do what you always done…you always get what you always got."

"The glass is always half full."

"How you view uncertainty dictates the degree of difficulty of being successful or being on the losing end."

"Always have a Plan of Action."

"Anything worth having is worth working hard to achieve your goal."

"Do not take anything I say personally nor negatively."

"Image is everything relative to what people see, think and believe about one's abilities or lack thereof."

"I can give you a fish and feed you for a day, or I can teach you how to fish and you can feed yourself for a lifetime."

"Your first impression is your best impression is your last impression."

"Always say what you mean and mean what you say when it comes to your capability, which invariably affects your reputation."

"You do not get a second chance to make a first impression."

"If I knew then what I know now, then where would I be?"

"A little bit of effort now is worth a lifetime of success and reward later."

"In order to be a prime contractor, you must think and act as a prime contractor, and in order to work within the federal sector, you must understand the federal sector."

"Doing your homework"

"One cannot be held accountable for things not known but for things known every attempt must be made to ensure full advantage is taken to increase the level of success going forward as a business entity."

"Think before you act."

"Jack of all trades but a master of none"

"Telling your story"

"The power of critical thinking"

"The same day you are in business or have received your 8(a) certifications is the same day you start preparation to exit the program."

"Success is always based on some sort of failure or setback that occurred somewhere along the way prior to obtaining a certain level of success."

"Every large business was once a small business and a small business was only a "thought" someone had in the back of their mind."

"It only takes one bad apple to ruin the entire barrel."

"In reality you are only as good as others perceive you to be."

"Somebody, someplace, somewhere gave you an opportunity."

"Surround yourself with people who are knowledgeable/experts in areas you are less knowledgeable."

"Apples to apples and oranges to oranges"

"All contract opportunities are not good opportunities and all money is not good money."

"Thus, be conscious of good/bad opportunities."

"It is virtually impossible to have a great ending without having a great beginning."

"How did you get to where you are today?"

"To change anyone, change must first start with you…the man/woman in the mirror."

"You can never walk on water if you never get out of the boat."

"Whatever you do, give it your all; leave nothing on the table; whether it is in sports, business, or life; just don't cheat yourself out of anything and with that life is good!"

Bibliography

Introduction
1. Federal Acquisition Regulation. "Small Business Programs." Accessed January 30, 2019. Acquisition.gov. https://www.acquisition.gov/content/part-19-small-business-programs.

1. U.S. Small Business Administration. "8 (a) Business Development Program." Accessed January 30, 2019. https://www.sba.gov/federal-contracting/contracting-assistance-programs/8(a)-business-development-program.

2. Bible, New International Version (NIV), Ecclesiastes 1:18 Accessed January 30, 2019

Chapter #1 – Business Theory Module
3. U.S. Small Business Administration. "Federal Contracting." Accessed January 30, 2019. https://www.sba.gov/federal-contracting.

4. Webster Universal College Dictionary, 1997 Edition Published by Gramercy Books – New York, "Time", page 823

5. U.S. Small Business Administration. "SBA Performance." Accessed January 30, 2019. https://www.sba.gov/about-sba/sba-performance/ .

6. Federal Acquisition Regulation. "Small Disadvantaged Business, General Policy." Accessed January 1, 2013. https://www.acquisition.gov/.

7. Federal Acquisition Regulation. "Woman-Owned Small Business (WOSB) Program." Accessed January 30, 2019. https://www.acquisition.gov/.

8. Federal Acquisition Regulation. "Historically Underutilized Business Zone Program." Accessed January 30, 2019. https://www.acquisition.gov/.

9. Federal Acquisition Regulation. "Service-Disabled Veteran-Owned Small Business Program." Accessed January 30, 2019. https://www.acquisition.gov/.

10. Webster Universal College Dictionary, 1997 Edition Published by Gramercy Books – New York, "Strategy", page 778

11. Federal Acquisition Regulation. "Total Small Business Set-Aside." Accessed January 30, 2019. https://www.acquisition.gov/.

12. Webster Universal College Dictionary, 1997 Edition Published by Gramercy Books – New York, "Complexity", page 167

13. Federal Acquisition Regulation. "Release for Non-8(a) Procurement." Accessed January 30, 2019. https://www.acquisition.gov/.

14. Federal Acquisition Regulation. "Total Small Business Set-Aside." Accessed January 30, 2019. https://www.acquisition.gov/.

15. Association of Procurement Technical Assistance Center. "Sources Sought Notices – An Opportunity." Accessed January 30, 2019. www.aptac-us.org/sources-sought/.

16. Federal Procurement Data System-Next Generation. Accessed January 30, 2019. https://www.fpds.gov/.

17. U.S. Small Business Administration. "8(a) Mentee/Mentor Protégé Program." Accessed January 30, 2019. https://www.sba.gov/federal-contracting/.

18. IBID

19. IBID

20. IBID

21. Federal Acquisition Regulation. "The Small Business Program."

Accessed January 30, 2019. https://www.acquisition.gov/.

22. Federal Acquisition Regulation. "Contracting Teaming Arrangement." Accessed January 30, 2019. https://www.acquisition.gov/.

23. U.S. Small Business Administration. "8(a) Mentee/Mentor Protégé Program." Accessed January 30, 2019. https://www.sba.gov/federal-contracting/.

Chapter #2 – Business Presentation Module
24. Federal Acquisition Regulation. "Historically Underutilized Business Zone Program." Accessed January 30, 2019. https://www.acquisition.gov/.

25. U.S. Army Corps of Engineers. "Regulation No. 414-1-11." Accessed January 1, 2013. https://www.publications.usace.army.mil/.

26. Defense Contract Audit Agency (DCAA), DCAA Manual No. 7641.90; Enclosure 6, page 71, https://www.dcaa.mil/ &
Federal Acquisition Regulation. "Indirect Cost." Accessed January 30, 2019. https://www.acquisition.gov/.

27. Federal Acquisition Regulation. "Contractor Performance." Accessed January 30, 2019. https://www.acquisition.gov/.

Chapter #3 – Business Preparation Module
28. Federal Acquisition Regulation. "Parts/Subparts." Accessed January 30, 2019. https://www.acquisition.gov/.

29. IBID

30. Federal Acquisition Regulation. "Synopsis of Proposed Contract Actions." Accessed January 30, 2019. https://www.acquisition.gov/.
Federal Business Opportunities. Accessed January 30, 2019. https://www.fbo.gov/.

31. Federal Acquisition Regulation. Part 13 - "Simplified Acquisition Procedure." Accessed January 30, 2019. https://www.acquisition.gov/.

32. Federal Acquisition Regulation. Part 14 - "Sealed Bidding." Accessed January 30, 2019. https://www.acquisition.gov/.

33. Federal Acquisition Regulation. Part 15 - "Contracting by Negotiations." Accessed January 30, 2019. https://www.acquisition.gov/.

34. Federal Acquisition Regulation. Part 15 - "Lowest Price Technically Acceptable Source Selection Process." Accessed January 30, 2019. https://www.acquisition.gov/.

35. Federal Acquisition Regulation. Part 15 - "Requests for Proposals." Accessed January 30, 2019. https://www.acquisition.gov/.

36. Federal Acquisition Regulation. Part 16 - "Types of Contracts." Accessed January 30, 2019. https://www.acquisition.gov/.

37. Federal Acquisition Regulation. Part 16 - "Fixed Price Contracts." Accessed January 30, 2019. https://www.acquisition.gov/.

38. Federal Acquisition Regulation. Part 16 - "Cost Reimbursement Contracts." Accessed January 30, 2019. https://www.acquisition.gov/.

39. Webster Universal College Dictionary, 1997 Edition Published by Gramercy Books – New York, "Negotiations", page 534

40. Federal Acquisition Regulation. "Uniform Contract Format." Accessed January 30, 2019. https://www.acquisition.gov/.

41. Federal Acquisition Regulation. "Part I – The Schedule." Accessed January 30, 2019. https://www.acquisition.gov/.

42. Federal Acquisition Regulation. "Selection, Appointment, and Termination of Appointment for Contracting Officers." Accessed January 30, 2019. https://www.acquisition.gov/.

43. Federal Acquisition Regulation Site (FARSite), Defense Federal Acquisition Regulation Supplement (DFARS), Part 215, Subpart 215.404-71, Weighted Guidelines Method, Accessed January 30, 2019.
Accessed January 30, 2019.
http://farsite.hill.af.mil

44. Federal Acquisition Regulation. "Indefinite Delivery Contracts." Accessed January 30, 2019. https://www.acquisition.gov/.

45. Federal Acquisition Regulation. "Differing Site Conditions." Accessed January 30, 2019. https://www.acquisition.gov/.

46. Federal Acquisition Regulation. "Bid Guarantees." Accessed January 30, 2019. https://www.acquisition.gov/.

47. Federal Acquisition Regulation. "Performance Bonds." Accessed January 30, 2019. https://www.acquisition.gov/.

48. Federal Acquisition Regulation. "Payment Bonds." Accessed January 30, 2019. https://www.acquisition.gov/.

49. Federal Acquisition Regulation. "Government Estimate of Construction Cost." Accessed January 30, 2019. https://www.acquisition.gov/.

50. U.S. Department of the Interior. "IGCE Accuracy and Completeness." Accessed January 30, 2019. https://www.doi.gov/.

51. Federal Acquisition Regulation. "FAR 28 Bonds and Insurance." Accessed January 30, 2019. https://www.acquisition.gov/.

Chapter #4 – Business Functionality Module
52. Federal Acquisition Regulation. "Default (Fixed-Price Supply and Service)" and "Delinquent Notices." Accessed January 30, 2019. https://www.acquisition.gov.

53. IBID.

54. Association of Procurement Technical Assistance Centers. Accessed January 30, 2019. www.aptac-us.org/.

55. History. "The Star-Spangled Banner." Accessed January 30, 2019. https://www.history.com/topics/19th-century/the-star-spangled-banner.

56. Federal Acquisition Regulation. "Limitation on Subcontracting." Accessed January 30, 2019. https://www.acquisition.gov/.

57. Federal Acquisition Regulation. "Full and Open Competition." Accessed January 30, 2019. https://www.acquisition.gov/.

58. Federal Acquisition Regulation. "Release for Non-8(a) Procurement." Accessed January 30, 2019. https://www.acquisition.gov/.